HINDU

MONASTIC

LIFE

Frontispiece. The Car Festival (Ashokashtami Yatra). The ''car'' (*ratha*), carrying bronze images of Shiva, Parvati, Durga, and Vishnu and loaded with temple priests, is pulled by devotees through the streets of the Old Town during a major festival at Bhubaneswar. In the background are two of the oldest monasteries, founded in the medieval period, which had provided the car with food offerings as it passed by their porches.

HINDU

MONASTIC

LIFE

by David M. Miller **the**

and **Monks**

Dorothy C. Wertz **and**

McGill-Queen's University Press **Monasteries**

Montreal & London 1976 **of**

Bhubaneswar

ISBN 0-7735-0190-8 cloth; 0-7735-0247-5 paper

Bibliothèque nationale du Québec
Legal Deposit first quarter 1976

This work has been published with the help
of a grant from the Humanities Research
Council of Canada, using funds provided
by the Canada Council.

Printed in the United States of America by
Vail-Ballou Press, Inc.

To

Cora,

Molly,

and

Dick

Contents

Tables

Illustrations

Figures

Preface

The following study of Hindu monastic life was part of the Harvard–Bhubaneswar Project directed by Professor Cora Du Bois of the Department of Anthropology of Harvard University under the sponsorship of the National Science Foundation. The field research on ascetics was conducted in Bhubaneswar by Dr. David M. Miller, then a graduate student at Harvard University, from July 1963 until December 1964, and was supported by grants from Harvard University, the Hattie M. Strong Foundation, and the American Institute of Indian Studies to whom we wish to express our appreciation. With the help of two interpreters, Dr. Miller was able to interview the head ascetics of Bhubaneswar's twenty-two monastic establishments and to enrich his studies through a series of informal contacts with other ascetics. The traditional Hindu receptiveness and courtesy offered to all sympathetic observers meant that Dr. Miller was able to observe and to participate in the daily routine of monastic life.

The original intent of the research was to ascertain what changes, if any, were occurring in ancient religious institutions, such as "holy men" and monasteries, as India comes under the influence of Westernization. Such changes as could be observed seemed to have little direct connection with currents of modernization. In India what appears to be a new emphasis may actually be a revival of an ancient practice or belief. Instead of moving toward secularization, people may be simply shifting their religious values and re-organizing their institutions. Thus traditional monasteries and ascetics may continue to exist alongside modern institutions. The words "traditional" and "modern" appear in this book only because no other terminology exists to sort out the complexity of the situation for Western minds. "Traditional" is applied to institutions, roles, and values that in their ideal conceptions pre-date urbanization and industrialization. "Modern" is used either to describe newer kinds of institutions, roles, and values that coincide with the appearance of urbanization, or to describe changed conceptions of older structures. Because types and directions of change did not emerge clearly from Dr. Miller's observations, the intent of this study was revised, and the material was restructured and totally rewritten jointly with Dr. Dorothy C. Wertz, who brought her training in the sociology of religion to bear upon Dr. Miller's field notes. Unfortunately, neither author was able to return to Bhubaneswar to up-date the findings; but a reasonable guess is that life in Old Town Bhubaneswar exists today much as it did in 1964.

The basic objective of the present book is to provide for the undergraduate teacher and student a thorough description of the practice of Hindu monasticism in a medium-sized pilgrimage centre as it existed in 1964. We do not pretend to offer an exhaustive description of the origins and history of Indian asceticism. Such a study would be another book altogether. G. S. Ghurye's *Indian Sadhus* is a step in that direction, and the reader may find listed in our bibliography principal material in English dealing with Hindu monasticism.

We also do not provide a complete history of monastic institutions at Bhubaneswar because of the insufficiency of historical materials. K. C. Panigrahi's *Archaeological Remains at Bhubaneswar* contains a good history of cultural developments in ancient and medieval Bhubaneswar.

We have unfortunately had to omit the role of women in Hindu monastic life because the five female ascetics who resided in the Bhubaneswar monasteries could not be approached by a Western male observer.

Although our book has been written for the undergraduate student, we have presupposed a basic knowledge of Hinduism and have not attempted detailed discussions of Hindu doctrine, symbolism, art, or architecture. The principal Vedantic schools of thought, so important for the history of Hinduism, are mentioned only briefly.

We would like to thank those whose help made this work possible. Our deepest debt is to Professor Cora Du Bois, who first suggested the project and whose continued care and attention have seen the work through many rewritings to completion. Her clarity of thought and attention to detail have been invaluable, as has her support in obtaining research grants. She has been all that one could ask of a teacher; at times she was a stern taskmaster, and at times a concerned friend. Professor Du Bois also made available to us the files of the Harvard–Bhubaneswar Project, in particular her field notes, and those of Richard P. Taub, Manamohan Mahapatra, and Richard Shweder. We are indebted to them for the materials we have used in this manuscript.

During the final stages prior to publication the manuscript was read by Robert H. L. Slater, Professor Emeritus, Harvard University and Professors H. Daniel Smith and Agehananda Bharati of Syracuse University, and Professor Shiela McDonough, of Sir George Williams University, to whom we are grateful for their detailed criticisms and suggestions for revision. We wish also to thank the typist, Mrs. A. H. Benade, who was also responsible for the glossary, Hymie Blutchitz and Shalvah d'Apollonia who proofread the text prior to submission to the Press, and Sylvia Haugo of McGill-Queen's for her editorial work. Publication costs have been partially supported by a grant from the Humanities Research Council, to whom we are most thankful.

Finally, we shall always be indebted to our Hindu informants, whose names appear throughout the text and to Nityananda Pati and Sadananda Patnaik, our faithful interpreters and close friends. Our colleague, Dr. Manamohan Mahapatra, a resident of the Old Town, was instrumental in offering directions to eighteen of the monasteries. Throughout this project Dr. Mahapatra remained a vital link with the monasteries and with the officials of the Lingaraja Mahaprabhu Temple where he and his father were hereditary priests.

Mr. B. Venkatraman, I.A.S., former Home Secretary for the State of Orissa, and Mr. L. Panda, then Commissioner of Hindu Religious Endowments, both provided formal letters of introduction to the three monasteries under control of the Endowments Commission.

The Hindus whom the reader will encounter vary greatly in many respects; yet, they all welcomed an interested Westerner into their own monasteries and homes as a friend. To know Hindus as people, possessing as much variety and complexity as human beings anywhere, is, we believe, to come to some small understanding of Hinduism.

A Note on Transliteration

In India, transliteration into English from Sanskrit or vernacular languages takes many forms. One only need look at the Calcutta telephone directory to confirm this fact. For simplicity and uniformity names of deities, historical personages, and well-known religious works are given without diacritical marks, as are the names of contemporary people and places. The principal substitutions in transliteration are: r=ri; c=ch; ch=chh; s=sh; $ś$=sh. The technical words that appear throughout the text and in the Glossary conform to standard transliteration procedures.

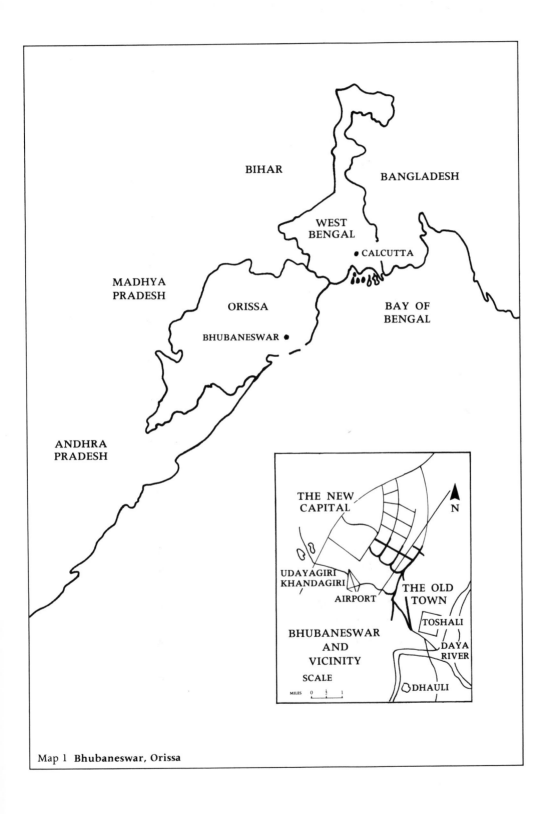

BIHAR

BANGLADESH

WEST
BENGAL

• CALCUTTA

MADHYA
PRADESH

ORISSA

BAY OF
BENGAL

BHUBANESWAR •

ANDHRA
PRADESH

THE NEW
CAPITAL

N

UDAYAGIRI
KHANDAGIRI

AIRPORT

THE OLD
TOWN

TOSHALI

DAYA
RIVER

BHUBANESWAR
AND
VICINITY

SCALE

MILES   0   ½   1

DHAULI

Map 1 **Bhubaneswar, Orissa**

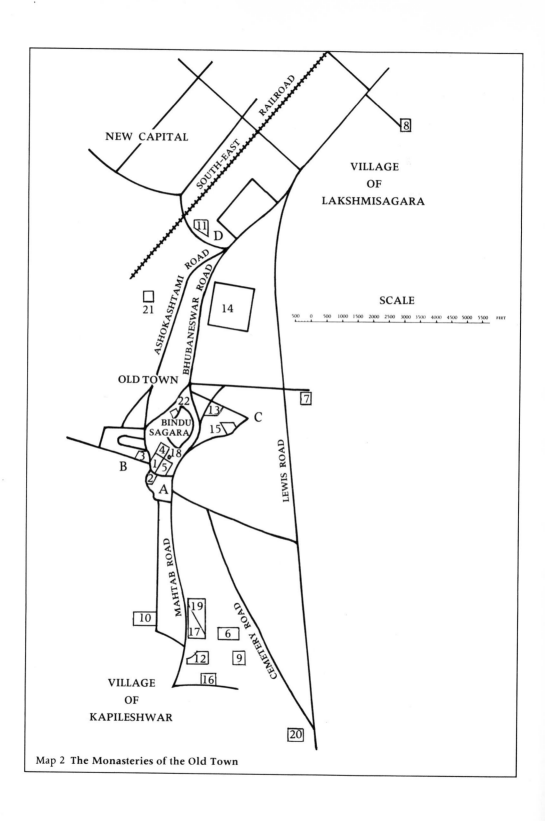

NEW CAPITAL

RAILROAD

SOUTH-EAST

VILLAGE
OF
LAKSHMISAGARA

8

11

D

ASHOKASHTAMI ROAD

BHUBANESWAR ROAD

21

14

SCALE

500 0 500 1000 1500 2000 2500 3000 3500 4000 4500 5000 5500 FEET

OLD TOWN

22

13

C

BINDU
SAGARA

15

7

LEWIS ROAD

4 18

3

1 5

B

2

A

MAHTAB ROAD

CEMETERY ROAD

19

10

17

6

12

9

16

VILLAGE
OF
KAPILESHWAR

20

Map 2 The Monasteries of the Old Town

Key: Monasteries

Endowed
1. Gopala Tirtha Matha
2. Kapali Matha
3. Sadavrata Pitha
4. Shankarananda Matha
5. Shiva Tirtha Matha

Patronized
6. Arya Rishikula Bhuvaneshvari Ashrama
7. Arya Rishikula Vasishtha Yogashrama
8. Chintamanishvara Mandira
9. Harihara Satsangha Ashrama
10. Jagannatha Deva Mandira
11. Nigamananda Ashrama
12. Nimbarka Ashrama
13. Radhakrishna Sevashrama
14. Ramakrishna Matha
15. Sadguru Nivasa Ashrama
16. Shadbhuja Chaitanya Mandira
17. Tridandi Gaudiya Matha

Non-corporate
18. Bhavani Shankara Matha
19. Someshvara Mahadeva Pitha
20. Pashupatinatha Gita Ashrama
21. Trinatha Gosvami Matha
22. Vishrama Ghatta Matha

Temple complexes
A. Lingaraja Mahaprabhu
B. Yameshvara
C. Kedara–Gauri
D. Rameshvara

Introduction

Backgrounds in Tradition and History

Hindu Asceticism and Monasticism

One of the oldest roles in India is that of the "ascetic" or the "holy man," and one of the oldest existing Hindu religious institutions is the monastery. The heads of monasteries have been, for many Hindus, the bearers of a cultural tradition that goes back to Vedic times. The holy man and the monastery provide a centre of sacredness and learning, available to anyone who wishes to approach it. Despite the influence of modernization, which is occurring in all parts of India, the lives of such holy men as Shankara, Ramanuja, and Chaitanya still represent ideals that are relevant to contemporary men, whether they live in the village or in the city. These holy men, and others, are also the "gurus," whose disciples are having a dynamic impact upon the youth of North America and Europe. Unfortunately, there is little literature in the English language that attempts a scholarly presentation of Hindu asceticism and monasticism.[1] The basic objective of this study is to meet this scholarly need, if only partially, by providing a thorough, analytic description of the practice of Hindu monasticism at Bhubaneswar, Orissa, a medium-sized pilgrimage centre, as it existed in 1964. Before we turn our attention to Bhubaneswar, we must provide a brief outline of Hindu asceticism and monasticism.

According to Hindu tradition, the word "ascetic," used here as an all-inclusive translation

1. Perhaps the best study is: G. S. Ghurye, *Indian Sadhus*.

for *sādhu* (holy man), has a variety of meanings. An ascetic may be the highly respected teacher of a Sanskrit school or a wandering beggar. In practice, most ascetics fulfil roles somewhere between these two extremes.

Basically an ascetic is one who depends upon gifts from the laity for his food, clothing, and shelter. He lives in a religious sphere set apart from the secular world and has renounced economic gain as his primary goal, but he does not necessarily practise self-mortification. A Hindu *sādhu* does not fulfil all connotations of the English word "ascetic," for he may enjoy a modicum of physical comfort. The word "ascetic" may refer to:

1. A resident ascetic who belongs to a monastic order and who lives in a monastery which is supported by the laity or by endowments of land. Hindus of the Brahman and Kshatriya socio-religious groups are more likely to become resident ascetics because members of the lower castes are refused entrance to many monastic orders and are unlikely to obtain patronage from the higher castes.

2. A wandering ascetic who travels from place to place begging for sustenance and who may or may not belong to a monastic order. Wandering ascetics are often from low or "scheduled" castes. They may also be mentally or physically handicapped and unable to make a living in any other way. A wanderer with unusual musical talents, for example, may ultimately receive patronage and settle down, often as a solitary ascetic.

3. A holy man who is not a member of a monastic order, but is believed by laymen to possess "holiness." He may be closely associated with a monastery without actually residing in it.

Ideally, the ultimate goal of an ascetic is salvation or release (*mokṣa*) from the cycle of rebirth (*saṁsāra*). Meditation, self-control, austerities, selfless actions, and devotional practices may all be methods of attaining one's goal. Religious striving is individualized; each man must work out his own salvation without help from others, although normally he is guided by a guru. The certainty of salvation comes either through a decisive vision of the deity (*darśana*) or through a state of concentrated absorption (*samādhi*) so deep that one's entire being becomes one with the deity.

According to Hindu tradition, which accords with modern sophisticated lay expectations, a *sādhu* should have the following capabilities: "charismatic qualities," rather loosely described as a holiness or saintliness, that the layman can worship or revere; knowledge of Hindu religious thought, including both ancient Sanskrit texts and the teachings of more recent religious leaders; devotional knowledge of ritual performances (*pūjā*) or of religious songs (*kīrtana*); a distinctive style of life, accompanied either by austerities or by ordering one's entire life around a schedule of devotions and recitations of the name of his chosen deity; the observance of vows of celibacy, poverty, vegetarianism, and abstinence from intoxicating beverages.

Asceticism goes back to the four stages (āśrama) of life described in the Vedas. The young novice or pupil (brahmacārin) must be ruled by obedience to his spiritual teacher (guru), to whom he owes the loyalty of a son. The sacred thread given by the guru to boys of the three upper or "twice-born" varṇas at their initiation ceremonies becomes a spiritual umbilical cord linking the student to his teacher. Brahmacārins have to observe strict chastity and certain other rules of routine Brahman asceticism.

The stage of pupilship is only temporary, because the young man soon enters upon the life of a householder (gṛhastha). He marries, begets sons and grandsons, and carries on his paternal craft or business. In the second half of life, as physical energy wanes, the former delights of householdership become a burden. The aging man regards worldly pleasures as transitory and remembers the guru of his youth as a man possessed of supernatural wisdom and holy power. He leaves his occupation and possessions in the hands of his grown sons and departs with his wife to enter upon the third stage, that of forest hermit (vānaprastha). Vedic society urges those who have outlived their economic usefulness to leave the sphere of their former activities and to concentrate on spiritual goals. The second half of life has a purpose of its own: the search for one's true self and for release from birth and death.

The third or vānaprastha stage is only a preparation for the fourth and last stage, that of the wandering holy beggar (sannyāsin), who has made a final renunciation of all worldly ties and limitations. He sacrifices all the fruits of his actions and is utterly devoted to union with a theistic deity (īśvara) or absorption into the absolute state of brahman.

In practice a man or woman may become an ascetic at any age, without going through the intervening stages of life. A man may style himself as a novice ascetic (brahmacārin) or a retired hermit ascetic (vānaprastha) rather than as one who has taken final vows of renunciation (sannyāsin). In recent centuries some ascetics have even been householders (gṛhasthas) who maintain customary marital relations, though this represents a departure from the earliest tradition.

In general, laity seek out ascetics of their choice, often of their own caste, as spiritual advisors who can also on occasion impart worldly wisdom. The educational and medical services performed by some monasteries today represent a more modern form of the social functions traditionally associated with some ascetics and with some orders. The forms have changed, but the basic content of the services remains the same.

The source of the earliest trend toward formal monasticism can be found among the pre-Buddhist teachers and court debaters who gathered disciples about them and who developed the beginnings of mystical thought as recorded in the Upanishads. Their loosely organized schools represent the earliest types of quasi-monastic institutions, predating even Buddhist and Jain orders. The latter two religions established the first monastic orders with definite hierarchies, dress, rules of conduct, and residences. Medieval Hinduism adopted the Buddhist conception of settled monastic orders, but some ascetics remained wandering mendicants, reflecting the origins of asceticism among individual practitioners. Even today among the settled ascetics, discipline and regulations remain loosely defined, and an ascetic is usually free to resign from the monastery at any time.

Hindu monastic orders are organized around the concept of a teaching tradition (*sampradāya*) related to a famous teacher (*ācārya*) who first enunciated the philosophical–religious system of the order. Although monastic orders no doubt existed prior to the time of Shankara (788–820 A.D.), the systematizer of Advaita Vedanta (non-dualism), tradition regards him as the first major organizer of Hindu monasticism. Legendary accounts claim that Shankara established four monasteries, one in the north at Badrinath; one in the south at Sringeri, another in the east at Puri, and one in the west at Dwaraka. In addition he is said to have created ten sub-orders (*daśanāmī*) of ascetics or Sannyasins. Hence members of his monastic order are called Dashanami Sannyasins (see table 1). His followers established other Dashanami Sannyasin monasteries throughout India, causing the Dashanami Sannyasins to become one of the largest and most influential orders in India today. Yet each branch monastery, unlike those in Christian monasticism, is autonomous in matters of discipline, polity, and economics. At the folk level Shankara is thought to be an incarnation or manifestation of the god Shiva, and often the principal deity or chosen deity (*iṣṭadevatā*) of a Dashanami Sannyasin monastery will be a representation of Shiva or his phallus (*liṅgam*). This has led G. S. Ghurye to classify Dashanami Sannyasins as Shiva ascetics.[2] The actual situation is, however, much more complex and we shall call Ghurye's classification into question.

Tradition claims that after Shankara, four other Acharyas appeared; each formulated a different philosophical system and established a monastic order to carry on his teaching tradition. The four Acharyas were Ramanuja (ca. 1017), Nimbarka (ca. 1162), Madhva (1199–1278), and Vallabha (ca. 1500).[3]

2. Ghurye, *Indian Sadhus*, pp. 70 ff.
3. The Vallabha monastic order was the only major order not represented at Bhubaneswar.

Table 1
A Comparison of Traditional Monastic Orders

Monastic order	SHANKARA DASHANAMI SANNYASIN; TEN SUB-ORDERS (DASHANAMI)	RAMANANDA VAIRAGIN	NIMBARKA VAIRAGIN	MADHVA GAUDIYA VAIRAGIN	TANTRIC YOGI SANNYASIN
Founder and date	Gaudapada (700?) Shankara (788–820)	Ramanuja (ca. 1017) Ramananda (ca. 1300)	Nimbarka (ca. 1162)	Madhva (1199–1278) *Chaitanya (1485–1533)	The Tantras (700–1200)
System of religious thought (darśana)	Advaita Vedanta (non-dualism)	Vishishtadvaita Vedanta (non-dualism qualified by theism)	Dvaita–Advaita Vedanta (dualistic non-dualism)	Dvaita Vedanta (dualism)*	Shakti Tantra (doctrine of power)
Chosen deity (iṣṭadevatā)	Shiva; sometimes syncretistic	Sita and Rama	Radha and Krishna	Radha and Krishna	Shakti (the wife of Shiva)
Appearance	Ochre loincloth; (*langoti*) necklace of 54 *rudrākṣa* beads; 3 horizontal white forehead markings; single-pronged staff (*ekadaṇḍa*)	White *dhoti* of heavy cloth; necklace of 108 *tulasi* beads; 2 white and 1 red vertical forehead markings; three-pronged wooden staff (*tridaṇḍa*)	White *dhoti*; single ¾ inch *tulasi* bead; U-shaped white or black forehead marking	White *dhoti*; 3 strands of small *tulasi* beads; V-shaped white forehead marking	Ochre loincloth (*langoti*) necklace of *rudrākṣa* beads; three-pronged iron staff (*triśūla*)

* The specific *darśana* of the Chaitanya school is known as *Acintyabhedabheda,* "incomprehensible monism."

The four Acharyas appealed to a wider audience by preaching that devotional practices and mystical knowledge were equally valuable ways to salvation. Ghurye classifies the monastic orders founded by these men as Vaishnava orders, since the deity chosen by each group is often Vishnu or a deity or an incarnation associated with Vishnu.[4] In addition, each of the four founders is believed to be the embodiment of a particular aspect of Vishnu or a Vaishnava deity. Members of the four orders prefer the ascetic title Vairagin (one who is freed from worldly passions) to that of Sannyasin (see table 1). Thus, an ascetic follower of Nimbarka is known as a Nimbarka Vairagin. The orders founded by Ramanuja and Madhva eventually produced sub-orders that, in time, have overshadowed the maternal organizations. Ramananda (ca. 1300), a follower of the Ramanuja teaching tradition, formed a sub-order that, according to Ghurye, today has more members than any other Vairagin order.[5] The Madhva Gaudiya sub-order, founded by the Bengali saint, Chaitanya (1485–1533), has become the largest Madhva sub-order on the north-east coast. The connection of Chaitanya with the Madhva teaching tradition is not clear, and it appears that the followers of Chaitanya joined the Madhva Vairagins in order to gain the sanction of authority.

The last monastic order of importance is that of the Tantric Yogi Sannyasins, whose teaching tradition was begun by no one historical founder. It might be argued that the Tantric Yogi order is older than the Dashanami Sannyasin order established by Shankara; at least this is the case at Bhubaneswar. However, the teaching tradition of the Tantric Yogi Sannyasins was systematized in the Tantras at a date later than Shankara. The chosen deity of the Tantric Yogis is often a manifestation of Shakti.

The monastic tradition to which an individual ascetic belongs is immediately obvious from the distinctive symbols that he wears on his forehead, the colour of his clothes, and such additional accoutrements as rosary beads, waterpot, and staff (see table 1, and also photographs).

Lest the Sanskrit names of the various monasteries become confusing, we add the following explanation of terminology. "Monastery" is the most useful translation for three different Sanskrit terms: āśrama, matha, and maṅdira. Āśrama, the negative of the Sanskrit verbal root śram (to exert oneself), means "a place of peace." Specifically, it designates a forest hermitage, surrounded by gardens. Matha, from the root math (to dwell), may mean the residence of one or several ascetics, a school, or a temple, but usually indicates a monastery

4. Ghurye, *Indian Sadhus*, pp. 150 ff.
5. Ghurye, *Indian Sadhus*, p. 170.

located in a town and associated with a temple dedicated to a major deity. Monasteries of the Shankara Dashanami Sannyasin order founded in the medieval period were called *matha*, because in Shankara's time a *matha* represented a more complex establishment than an *āśrama*.

In the nineteenth century, some Hindu revivalists looked back to the Vedic period for inspiration and used the term *āśrama*. The term *maṅdira* is today the popular word for a temple and connotes a royal palace where the deity reigns as king. If a *maṅdira* houses an ascetic, it becomes a monastery in the minds of the laity. Villagers refer to all monastic establishments as *matha*, regardless of their official titles. Finally, the head ascetic of a monastery may be known as *mahānta* (superior), *svāmi* (master), *mahārāja* (great king), or *thākur* (chief); choice of title generally reflects individual preference.

The Setting: Bhubaneswar, Orissa

Bhubaneswar, capital of the state of Orissa, is a double-town of a type common throughout India. Each town has its own nucleus. The Old Town clusters around the spires of the Lingaraja Mahaprabhu Temple, visible for several miles across the surrounding plains, while the New Capital founded in 1947 centres around the massive concrete structure of the Secretariat Building, which rivals the temple in size (see maps 1 and 2). The New Capital has numerous other large government buildings, all constructed in the same post-Independence style, a new state university, and an agricultural college.

The Old Town has enjoyed prominence as a religious centre for over two thousand years. As Toshali, the town was capital of the Kalinga kingdom in the fourth and third centuries B.C. King Ashoka made the town his provincial capital after conquering Kalinga and carving his edicts into rock at Dhauli, five miles to the south. Jain monastic caves, found in the nearby Khandagiri Hills, date from the third century B.C. Under the Oria kings from the sixth to the twelfth centuries the town underwent a period of Hindu revival. It became the cultural centre of Utkal, the great Oria-speaking Hindu kingdom of that period.

During this time, several important temples were built by the Oria kings, including the Lingaraja Mahaprabhu Temple and its complex of large religious establishments. The temple houses a rough-hewn block of stone eight feet in diameter reputed in legend to have been found in a mango forest south of the Old Town. This stone is believed to possess particularly sacred powers as the *liṅgam* of the god Shiva and attracts many pilgrims from other parts of India. The temple was originally called Tribhuvaneshvara (Lord of the Three Worlds) Temple, the epithet of Shiva from which Bhubaneswar takes its name.

Between the eleventh and fifteenth centuries, Vaishnava influences became so strong that the temple was renamed the Lingaraja Mahaprabhu Temple. Lingaraja (king of the Lingam) is an epithet of Shiva; Mahaprabhu (Most Powerful One) is an epithet of Vishnu-Krishna. The stone *lingam* itself is today called Harihara, a combination of Vishnu (Hari) and Shiva (Hara). A natural cleavage in the *lingam* is said to manifest its dual Shaiva–Vaishnava character.

According to Mitra, who records the legendary account found in the *Kapila Samhita*, a local Sanskrit manuscript, "Bhubanesvara was established as a rival of Benares, and with a view to divert to it a part at least of the halo of religion which surrounded that holy city; and from accounts elsewhere given, it appears that nothing was omitted in the way of details to make it the exact counterpart of its prototype."[6] The legend which Mitra cites indicates, however, that Vasudeva (Vishnu) resided first in the mango grove at Bhubaneswar. Vishnu granted Shiva the boon of living beside him in the mango grove because Shiva wished to leave Benares which had become "greatly over-crowded and injurious to devotion." When Shiva hesitated because his sacred rivers and pools were in Benares, Vishnu pointed out waters at Bhubaneswar that were the equivalent of those in Benares, including a stream that was believed to be the Ganges River flowing from underground. Shiva thereupon settled beside Vishnu in the form of the *lingam* of the Lord of Three Worlds.

In the last book of the *Śiva Purana*, a Shaiva sectarian work, Shiva names Bhubaneswar as his "secret retreat like unto Benares."

> It (Bhubaneswar) is resplendent with grandeur of every kind, and the wealth of all the six seasons are ever present there. O Parvati, it is as gorgeous as Kailasa (Shiva's heaven), and adorned with trees and creepers, all bearing blossoms of the six different seasons. It is resonant with the sweet notes of birds of various kinds and beautified by rivers of clean water that are covered with expanded lotus flowers and lilies, having fine steps leading to them. It grants final liberation to all. I have, my darling, described this secret sanctuary to you for your amusement; it is as excellent as Varanasi (Benares), and is adorned with one crore (ten million) of Lingams.[7]

According to this legend, which is still a popular one in Old Town today, Parvati left Benares for Bhubaneswar where she created a sacred lake, named the Bindu Sagara, by collecting droplets (*bindu*) from every sacred body of

6. Rajendra Lala Mitra, *The Antiquities of Orissa*, vol. 2, p. 113.
7. Mitra, *The Antiquities of Orissa*, vol. 2, pp. 115–16.

water in India and placing them in the centre of the town. Thereafter, she was joined by her husband, Shiva. No mention is made of Vishnu.

In medieval times over seven thousand small shrines are said to have surrounded the sacred lake of Bindu Sagara. Here the waters of an underground river, famous for healing physical and spiritual illness, well to the surface and are captured in twelve large pools or tanks for drinking and bathing. Pilgrims visiting the temple and the tanks were from medieval times lodged in guesthouses provided by the various monastic establishments clustered around the main temple. Most pilgrims halted only for a few hours or overnight on the road to the major pilgrimage centre of Puri. During the British period the Old Town became a centre for Bengali "vacationers" from Calcutta, who came to enjoy the cool off-shore breezes.

Mitra estimates that in 1872 one-sixth of the population were professional temple priests and that one-quarter of the population were temple servants.[8] Together the priests and servants must have equalled nearly half the community. The other half of the residents existed by serving those who served the temples. Today service to the Lingaraja Mahaprabhu Temple and to the thousands of pilgrims who arrive annually, as well as to the well-to-do vacationers, remains the Old Town's major source of livelihood. The majority of the residents live in one-story mud or laterite stone houses densely packed around the temple. Some more substantial stone houses, several stories high, belong to wealthy merchants and civil servants, most of whom are immigrants from Bengal. On the whole, however, the Old Town is an area inhabited by groups at the lower end of the economic scale. A housing shortage produced by the rapid expansion of population has caused some formerly single-caste wards to become heterogeneous.

Two miles away, on the other side of the main trunk railway from Madras to Calcutta, stands the New Capital. The total Notified Area of Bhubaneswar (which includes the Old Town, the New Capital, several nearby villages, and some open land) comprises 13.9 square miles, with the Old Town clustered in the quarter to the south and east of the railway, an area of about 4.4 square miles. The disproportion in both area and population between the old and new towns will continue to increase as more people from Orissa and other states immigrate to the New Capital.

The New Capital accounts for about two-thirds of Bhubaneswar's total population, which was about 40,000 in the 1960 census. Because the New

---

8. Mitra, *The Antiquities of Orissa*, vol. 2, pp. 100–1.

Capital continues to grow, a rough guess would place the figure for Bhubaneswar as a whole at about 48,000 in 1964. Construction of the New Capital was begun in 1947 when the capital was moved twenty miles from the congested city of Cuttack, which offered no room for expansion. The decision to build a new capital city at Bhubaneswar was based on a combination of historical, religious, and practical considerations. Bhubaneswar was the ancient religious and cultural centre of Orissa. It was also located on the major railway trunk lines, had an airport, a good road, some temporarily usable buildings left by the British, and a ready availability of government-owned waste land. Its cool climate compared to that of Calcutta, presented an added attraction. Like the Old Town, the New Capital had no major industry or natural resources. Just as the Old Town existed to serve the great temple complexes, so the New Capital was founded for the single purpose of serving the Orissa State Government. About three-quarters of its residents in 1964 were government employees.[9]

The Orissa civil service has brought in a large variety of government workers from other parts of Orissa and also from Bengal. Since the beginning of the British period, Bengalis have tended to predominate in the higher posts of the Orissa government, although Orias are now beginning to regain some power. In any case, the new workers belong mostly to higher economic groups than do the residents of the Old Town. The government- and privately built residences of the New Capital are generously spaced along broad, landscaped streets and have electricity and modern plumbing, luxuries generally absent from the Old Town. The dwellings range in size from eight rooms for a government minister down to one room for a sweeper, and are allotted according to the resident's official status in the civil service. Until very recently construction has not kept pace with the influx of population. Therefore some young men who have arrived to work as junior administrators or technicians in the New Capital have been forced to find lodgings in the Old Town. Often they have taken advantage of the relatively inexpensive rooms rented out by some monasteries. The New Capital has produced a minor building boom in the Old Town, as landowners have suddenly found it profitable to construct rows of houses and shops to rent to new arrivals. Conveniently situated monasteries have to some extent shared in this construction boom.

Double-towns like Bhubaneswar inadvertently provide opportunities for perpetuating a traditional social pattern already found in many Indian villages that are divided into two main districts, an "upper" and a "lower" ward. At

9. For information on the New Capital and its bureaucratic elite see the excellent study: Richard P. Taub, *Bureaucrats Under Stress.*

first, there appeared to be an almost total lack of interaction between the two towns. The Old Town seemed like a survival of the past encysted by the growing New Capital. Eventually a certain pattern of very ambiguous and complex interaction did become apparent. Civil servants, including some engineers, scientists, and university professors living in the New Capital, provide a major source of financial support for some monasteries in the Old Town and also attend ceremonies held within them. A few leading ascetics give advice to some government officials who are their patrons. The officials may use their contact with those ascetics who are considered religious leaders to gather information about the political climate in the Old Town. In 1964, the monasteries' patrons represented the most important and perhaps the only connection between the New Capital and the traditional religious establishments of the Old Town.

From now on we shall concern ourselves primarily with the Old Town, though the reader should keep in mind the existence of the New Capital.

A Tentative History of Monasticism at Bhubaneswar

An accurate history of monasticism at Bhubaneswar cannot be written because the materials that exist are wholly inadequate. The only sources of information are: four local Sanskrit mythological texts, only one of which mentions a monastery founded in the medieval period; inscriptions bearing the dynastic names of the Oria kings that appear on the cornerstones of two other medieval monasteries; a piece of sculpture dated in the sixth century A.D. and located in the wall of the oldest monastery that was extant in 1964; lists of gurus (*guruparamparā*) for several monasteries; records of the Orissa Hindu Religious Endowments Commission relating to income and expenditures for the three monasteries under its control; the memories of living individuals, many of whom came to Bhubaneswar after 1945.

However, it is possible to outline a tentative history of monasticism based upon the monasteries that were extant in 1963–64. The reader should keep in mind that the actual history of monastic establishments can never be reconstructed, principally because of the fluid character of Hindu monasticism.

In 1963–64 there were twenty-two monastic establishments, all located in the Old Town. A total of forty-one ascetics resided in the monasteries. Table 2 lists by date of founding the twenty-two monasteries, which are divided into three categories for purposes of historic comparisons: the five founded in the medieval period between the seventh and fifteenth centuries A.D., the ten founded between 1918 and Independence in 1947, and the seven founded after 1947. Other monastic institutions must have been established at Bhubaneswar

Table 2
Monastic Establishments Listed by Date of Founding

DATE	NAME	MONASTIC ORDER	CHOSEN DEITY (*iṣṭadevatā*)
Monasteries Established in Medieval Times			
600s	Sadavrata Pitha	Dashanami Bharati	Kamakhya
700–1500	Kapali Matha	Tantric Yogi	Kapali
1000–1500	Gopala Tirtha Matha	Dashanami Tirtha	Radha–Krishna
1000–1500	Shiva Tirtha Matha	Dashanami Tirtha	Shiva Lingam
1400s	Shankarananda Matha	Dashanami Sarasvati	Lakshmi–Narayana
Monasteries Established between 1918 and 1947			
1918	Radhakrishna Sevashrama	Dashanami Sarasvati	Radha–Krishna
1919	Ramakrishna Matha	Non-sectarian	Worship of gurus
1921	Someshvara Mahadeva Pitha	Shankara	Shiva Lingam
1933	Tridandi Gaudiya Matha	Madhva Gaudiya	Chaitanya and Radha–Krishna
1934	Nimbarka Ashrama	Nimbarka	Radha–Krishna
1938	Jagannatha Deva Mandira	Madhva Gaudiya	Jagannatha
1938	Vishrama Ghatta Matha	Ramananda	Jagannatha

during the nearly fourteen centuries that represent the range of founding dates of the monasteries extant in 1964, but no evidence remains to document the existence of those institutions.

The five monasteries founded by Oria kings in the medieval period illustrate a process of synthesizing or blending diverse traditions, a characteristic of Hindu tradition throughout India which is also found at Bhubaneswar. Upon the basis of archaeological evidence, Panigrahi claims that the Sadavrata Pitha is "the oldest *matha* of the place" and that the monastery belonged to the Pashupata group of ascetics, whose principal deity was Shiva.[10] In 1964, however, the chosen deity of the monastery was Kamakhya (Durga), a Shakta deity,

10. Krishna Chandra Panigrahi, *Archaeological Remains at Bhubaneswar*, p. 226.

Table 2
Monastic Establishments Listed by Date of Founding (continued)

DATE	NAME	MONASTIC ORDER	CHOSEN DEITY (*iṣṭadevatā*)
1940	Sadguru Nivasa Ashrama	Madhva Gaudiya	Worship of gurus
1941	Shadbhuja Chaitanya Mandira	Madhva Gaudiya	Shadbhuja Rama–Krishna–Chaitanya
1945	Arya Rishikula Bhuvaneshvari Ashrama	Dashanami Tirtha	Worship of gurus
Monasteries Established between 1947 and 1964			
1950	Chintamanishvara Mandira	Non-sectarian	Shiva Linga, Hanuman, gurus
1954	Trinatha Gosvami Matha	Non-sectarian	Trinatha (Brahma–Vishnu–Shiva)
1955	Arya Rishikula Vasishtha Yogashrama	Dashanami Tirtha	Worship of gurus
1958	Pashupatinatha Gita Ashrama	Ramananda	Sita–Rama
1959	Bhavani Shankara Matha	Shankara	Durga
1962	Harihara Satsangha Ashrama	Non-sectarian	Jagannatha
1964	Nigamananda Ashrama	Dashanami Sarasvati	Worship of gurus

and the institution belonged to the Bharati sub-order of the Dashanami Sannyasins. The second monastery founded in the medieval period worships Durga in her classical form as Mahishasuramardini (the destroyer of the buffalo demon, Mahishasura), who is known in Old Town as Kapali, the patron deity of the Kapalikas, an austere order of medieval ascetics. Ghurye asserts that Kapalikas should be classified as the forerunners of the Tantric Yogi Sannyasins.[11] The monastic order to which Kapali Matha belongs is the Tantric Yogis, which appears to verify Ghurye's conclusion. The history of the two earliest monasteries indicates that Bhubaneswar was first inhabited by austere Shaiva and Shakta–Tantric ascetics, who were, at least in the case of the

11. Ghurye, *Indian Sadhus*, p. 128.

Sadavrata Pitha, later brought under the influence of Shankara's Dashanami Sannyasins.

The picture of medieval monasticism becomes even more complex when we look at the three other monasteries founded in the Middle Ages. In the eleventh century two important events took place that were to contribute significantly to the development of monasticism at Bhubaneswar. The first was the completion of the temple at Bhubaneswar during the reign of the Somavamsha kings (950–1065). The official faith of the Somavamsha dynasty was Shaivism, and the temple was initially dedicated to Shiva as Tribhuvaneshvara, the Lord of the Three Worlds.

The Ganga kings (1078–1435), who were Vaishnava, seized control of Orissa after the Somavamshas, and toward the end of the eleventh century, Ananta-varman Chodagangadeva, the founder of the Ganga dynasty, completed the temple at Puri dedicated to Jagannatha (Krishna). During the Ganga period Vaishnavism became influential in Bhubaneswar, resulting in a synthesis of the Shaiva and Vaishnava cults that markedly altered the course of religious development in that area. From this time onward, the temple dedicated to Tribhuvaneshvara became known as the Temple of Lingaraja Mahaprabhu.

The three monasteries established at Bhubaneswar during the Ganga period reflect the syncretism of the times. All three belong to Dashanami Sannyasin sub-orders, which normally select Shiva as their chosen deity; yet two of the three monasteries worship Vaishnava images, Radha-Krishna and Lakshmi-Narayana.

Vaishnavism was reinforced in the early years of the sixteenth century, when the Bengali saint, Chaitanya (1485–1533), came into Orissa. After paying his respects to Lingaraja Mahaprabhu at Bhubaneswar, he remained at Puri until his death. Chaitanya brought with him the devotional (*bhakti*) type of religion associated with the worship of Krishna and his consort Radha. The Chaitanya movement has continued to play an important part in the formation of the monasticism characteristic of Bhubaneswar in the twentieth century.

In 1568 Afghan Muslims subdued Orissa and ruled until the mid-eighteenth century. During the period of Mughal rule, the Muslim king Aurangzeb (1618–1707) issued the following decree: "Every idol-house built during the last ten or twelve years, whether brick or clay, should be demolished without delay. Also do not allow the infidels to repair their old temples."[12]

The massive building of temples and monasteries at Bhubaneswar came to a close. When the Hindu Marathas from western India repeatedly raided Orissa

---

12. R. D. Banerji, *History of Orissa*, vol. 2, p. 57

in the mid-eighteenth century, they drained off most of the revenue that might otherwise have built monasteries. By the late nineteenth century, Bhubaneswar, then under British control, had lost much of its population and had shrunk to the area immediately surrounding the temple. Writing in 1872, Mitra said, "The whole place has a cheerless, woe-begone, lifeless look about it, which loudly proclaims that the sun of its glory has long since set."[13] Lord Curzon, however, was apparently impressed with the remains of ancient Oria culture and helped the passage of the Ancient Monuments Preservation Act of 1904. Areas of jungle were cleared around some of the temples and more pilgrims ventured to visit them.

This situation changed between 1918 and 1948, during which period at least ten new monasteries are known to have been established in the Old Town area. Two were Oria and eight were Bengali. To account for the influx of Bengali institutions we will summarize the modern relationships between Orissa and Bengal.

In 1803 the British gained control over Orissa, placing the territory in the Presidency of Bengal. In 1912 the territories of Bihar and Orissa were united into one province, and in 1936 Orissa became a separate province. Throughout the nineteenth and early twentieth centuries Bengalis occupied practically every civil service post available to Indians in the province of Orissa. After 1805 increased interaction between Bengali and Oria peoples resulted from a series of land revenue acts that enabled the government to foreclose the properties of landlords unable to pay the land tax. In 1806 the estates of default-ing Oria landlords were put up for sale in Calcutta, and many Bengali specu-lators and administrators bought valuable properties at low prices. Although the immigration of other peoples to Orissa declined in the early years of the twentieth century, Bengalis continued to own considerable tracts of land. The entrenched interests of Bengalis formed a channel for the introduction of Bengali religious movements into Orissa.

The influx of Bengali monastic institutions further strengthened the in-fluence of Vaishnavism, especially the Chaitanya cult, upon Bhubaneswar. Of the eight Bengali monasteries, half belong to the Madhva Gaudiya order estab-lished by the followers of Chaitanya. However, prior to 1947 almost no social interaction occurred between the Bengali and the Oria communities, each of which preferred monasteries founded by members of its own linguistic group. In general, the Oria monasteries remained clustered about the temple, whereas the Bengali monasteries were located on the fringes of the Old Town where

13. Mitra, *The Antiquities of Orissa*, vol. 2, p. 102.

large numbers of Bengali immigrants lived. Many of the Bengali monasteries, especially those established in the 1930s, are large institutions rivalling the medieval monasteries in size.

Since Independence in 1947, seven monastic establishments have appeared. Three of these were established by Bengali ascetics. Compared to the monasteries founded at Bhubaneswar in the 1920s and 1930s, those founded after 1947 are more modest in physical appearance, although two are branches of fairly large Bengali institutions. The most striking fact about the monasteries established since Independence is that three are non-sectarian in the sense that the ascetics adhere to no one teaching tradition. The chosen deities of these three institutions represent a continuation of the process of syncretism characteristic of medieval monasticism. Another trend is toward a reassertion of Oria patronage as Orias move into influential positions in business, politics, and civil service. Four of the seven monasteries attract both Orias and Bengalis, which indicates a lessening of the ethnic barriers previously separating the two linguistic groups.

We shall conclude our history of monasticism at Bhubaneswar with a brief look at the range in size and income of the monasteries. The twenty-two monastic establishments varied greatly in physical dimensions, income, number of ascetics in residence, and number of servants. By far the largest compound belonged to the Ramakrishna Matha, which covered a larger area of ground than the Lingaraja Mahaprabhu Temple complex. The monastery compound included, in 1964, a three-story main residence and an equally large guest-house for special dignitaries, a library of 2,232 books, a charitable dispensary that treated 23,000 cases a year, a primary school for 250 students, and a high school under construction. By contrast, the smallest establishment was an abandoned temple into which a solitary ascetic had moved his bed and blanket roll and where he had set up an altar with a popular eight-by-ten inch print of the goddess Durga.

The wealthiest institution, the Gopala Tirtha Matha, one of the five oldest monasteries located in the centre of town, had an annual cash income of over Rs. 35,000, of which Rs. 22,000 derived from landholdings. A total of six institutions owned substantial amounts of land; four of these were endowed by medieval kings and two were founded in the twentieth century. The Ramakrishna Matha, which had the largest expenditures for welfare activities, ranked below four of the older institutions in income. The poorest monasteries were the residences of solitary ascetics whose hand-to-mouth existence depended on daily donations of food from clients.

In this introductory chapter we have tried to set the scene for the reader by describing the physical surroundings in which the ascetics and monastics continue their daily lives. We have listed the distinctive characteristics of several types of holy men. The histories and characteristics of ascetic orders or teaching traditions are, however, far more complex than we have been able to indicate in the simplified outline presented here.

The following chapters build upon these introductory materials in an attempt to present a comprehensive description of monastic life in Bhubaneswar in 1964. The role of the ascetic in India predates the existence of settled monasteries and even today, many ascetics are not dependent upon monasteries. Hindu asceticism, with its emphasis upon the individual search for salvation, allows for almost as many lifestyles as there are persons searching for salvation. Indeed, the diversity and individualistic character of Hindu asceticism continues to predominate and to restrict the scope of development of monasteries as institutions. The most interesting aspects of Hindu monasticism therefore are found in the varied types of individual ascetics rather than in the social structures of the monasteries they inhabit. In Part One we have chosen first to present nine life-histories of the forty-one ascetics we encountered, in order to give the reader an idea of the great variety of lifestyles possible in Hindu asceticism. These life-histories include some that typify traditional views about *sādhus* and some that are distinctly atypical as evidence that not all ascetics are bound by tradition. The life-histories are followed by a synopsis of stages of the monastic career. In the last chapter of Part One, we have utilized Professor Cora Du Bois's "Study of Values" (Harvard–Bhubaneswar Project) in order to present the laity's perception of ascetics.[14]

14. Cora Du Bois, "Study of Values, 1965" (interview guides in the files of the Harvard–Bhubaneswar Project, Cambridge, Massachusetts).

Part One

The

Ascetics

Chapter 1

Religious Leaders: The Ascetic as Guru and Preacher

The two ascetics described in this chapter, Saccidananda (the "Guru") and Jagadananda (the "Preacher"), are the religious leaders of the Old Town Oria and Bengali communities respectively. Both men are Brahman intellectuals with considerable knowledge of Sanskrit who meditate and perform austerities and devotional practices in the pattern of the tradition established by Shankara. Both follow the Dashanami Sannyasin path of other-worldly searching for salvation, yet both are concerned with social welfare activities. They can amply substantiate their claims to wealthy and influential patrons.

The Guru (Jagadguru 1108 Dandi Saccidananda Sarasvati, Svami of the Shankarananda Matha)

Saccidananda, the head ascetic of the Shankarananda Matha, was the one ascetic in Bhubaneswar in 1964 who fulfilled all of the community's expectations of an ideal ascetic. Saccidananda's name is encumbered with titles: "Jagadguru" means "teacher of the universe," a title given to both Shiva and Shankara; 1108 is the superlative of the sacred number 108, indicating something roughly comparable to "his holiness"; "Dandi" means that the bearer of this name has the right to carry the Brahman *sannyāsin*'s bamboo staff (*daṇḍa*); "Saccidananda," his chosen name, means "being–consciousness–bliss"; "Sarasvati" indicates his sub-order of the Dashanamis; and finally, "Svami," meaning "master," is the title of a head ascetic. Most people address him as "Maharaja."

Of all the ascetics whom we interviewed at length, Saccidananda was the most reticent about his life before entering orders. It was as if his vows had obliterated his former life completely; at initiation, he had died to the secular world of personal relationships and personal feelings and had been reborn as an ascetic intent upon things eternal. He saw his role in the traditional terms of one who practises meditation and austerities to attain his own release from the cycle of birth and death. Such an authentic and sincere *sādhu* could not afford to be distracted by his personal feelings and considered it improper to waste time talking about himself as a distinct individual at all, because individuality belongs to the world of illusion (*māyā*). He insisted upon answering any questions about himself by giving us written pamphlets about his school or his monastery, because these were examples of his life-work. Thus the "Guru" emerged as the most distant of our informants, possibly for the very reason that he most nearly approximated the traditional ideal of the ascetic.

We gleaned the following outlines of Saccidananda's life. He was born in 1904 of a Yajur-veda Brahman family in an Oria village not far from the Jagannatha Temple at Puri. He attended a Sanskrit school in Puri that instructed young Brahmans in the performance of Vedic ritual (*karma-kāṇḍa*) and there he attained the title of Acharya, or spiritual preceptor. At the age of twenty-one, with the approval of his parents, he gave his property to the village elders to be used for the benefit of the poor and entered the Shankarananda Sarasvati order at Puri. After making two pilgrimages to "the four corners of India," he came to Bhubaneswar in 1932 and built himself a thatched cottage on the grounds of the Shankarananda Matha. Here he had a series of religious experiences.

One morning before sunrise he found a lady in a white sari walking around his garden. He thought she might be a prostitute come to steal flowers, but she suddenly vanished. An old man from a neighbouring village told Saccidananda that he had seen the Mohini goddess (a form of the consort of Shiva) from a neighbouring temple, and that this vision had freed him from most of his sins. Later in his life the goddess appeared once again, emerging from her temple as a blue-and-white light.

The turning point in Saccidananda's life was an overwhelmingly powerful vision of Vishnu that he experienced as the result of his austerities. At the age of twenty-five, four years after he had entered monastic orders, Saccidananda began a fast based on the phases of the moon (*cāndrāyaṇa vrata*). On the full-moon night (*pūrṇimā*) of Phalguna (February–March) he ate thirteen handfuls of rice. He diminished the amount of his food by one handful of rice for each night of the waning half of the lunar month. On the evening of the new moon he abstained from all food. The next evening he ate one handful of rice and increased this amount by one handful for each night of the waxing half of the lunar month until the full moon. Saccidananda was so weakened by the fast that he was unable to walk. On the night of the full moon of Chaitra (March–April), as he lay on his bed, Saccidananda saw "a circle of radiant blue light" that encompassed the whole room. At the centre of the light stood life-sized figures of Narayana, the aspect of Vishnu as the Cosmic Man, and Lakshmi his wife. Later that night he again experienced the radiant light and the images of Narayana and Lakshmi. Saccidananda said that during this mystical experience, "I felt as if I had no contact with the physical world. I was the Supreme Being (Vishnu) and belonged to the Supreme Soul (Atman). I had realized *samādhi*, absorption into God (Ishvara)." The intensity of this experience was so great that Saccidananda has had no desire to repeat it, but he did hope that he would have a similar experience at the hour of his death. Thus he would attain final release (*mokṣa*) and would be absorbed into Ishvara for all eternity.

Saccidananda later had a third vision of the deity in the Temple of Jagannatha at Puri. While meditating before the figures of Jagannatha, Balarama, and Subhadra (Krishna and his brother and sister), he saw only Narayana. Instead of seeing the deity in a multiplicity of forms, he preferred to envision the deity as a cosmic unity.

The dignity of his bearing and the extreme intensity of Saccidananda's face give the impression that he is one who has indeed seen the deity. Today, however, he no longer strives for visions; he is more concerned about preserving the national culture and the traditions of Orissa, and halting "the cancer of Westernization." Thus we had to be very careful when approaching him, lest he think that we were irreligious modern Westerners, or worse still, Christian missionaries.

At our first meeting, Saccidananda began the conversation immediately by lecturing our interpreter in Oria:

If the American had not worn a *dhoti* or similar Indian dress, I would not have permitted him to enter the monastery. When the Congress Party under the leadership of Nehru came into power, the uniqueness of Indian culture was uprooted and truth was no longer present within the subcontinent. Nowadays, the wife is disloyal to her husband, the son is disloyal to his father, and the friend is disloyal to his friend. The cinema focuses upon nakedness and all morality is being destroyed. Co-education is another factor that makes all the students interested in members of the opposite sex, but uninterested in their studies. They are not attentive when reading [studying]. All this is due to the influence of Western civilization. The Government of India has forgotten its ancient culture and religion.

This attack upon the "Westernization" of Indian culture and the plea to return to Hindu tradition have been Saccidananda's primary concerns since he entered monastic orders.

In 1926, at the death of his guru, Saccidananda became head of the Shankarananda Matha, and in 1927 he was appointed president of the managing committee for his former Sanskrit school at Puri. Eight years later, in 1935, Saccidananda attended a conference of Oria Sanskrit school instructors (*paṇḍitas*) held at the Nilakantha Temple in Berhampur, Orissa. At the meeting Saccidananda proposed that a Sanskrit school similar to that located at Hardwar, Uttar Pradesh, be established at Bhubaneswar. His suggestion gained the approval of the scholars present, and upon returning to Bhubaneswar he began to plan the founding of the school.

Two of his goals were the preservation of traditional caste distinctions and the restoration of Orissa to its former glory, particularly to the cultural leadership of India. In a booklet describing the Sanskrit school, Saccidananda wrote:

India began as a nation with the ancient Aryan scholars. These Aryan *ṛṣis* [sages] developed the *varṇāśrama dharma* [division of society according to socio-religious groups] for the benefit of mankind. These sages were influenced by the climate and geography of the country and by the wisdom of the ages, and they wished to advance the civilization, culture, knowledge, customs, and conventions of India by establishing a religious basis for society.

Now, under the influence of the prevalent Westernized education, the *varṇāśrama dharma* is becoming extinct, and our ancient learning and civilization are coming to an end. Because of the sacrilegious treatment of caste rules, there is no unity in India. Because of the elimination of distinctions between "high" and "low" and because of the eradication of caste distinctions, revolutions and conflicts have appeared. This state of affairs creates disbelief and distrust of caste, creed, religious profession, conventional practices, and culture, and culminates in the deterioration of our civilization.

History confirms, and the scriptures proclaim with a resonant voice, that Orissa is a "Land of Lords." By means of their spiritual power the inhabitants of Orissa once occupied the pinnacle of the world. If the present-day Oria thinks about the glorious past of Orissa, its literature, music, sculpture, art, valour, bravery, and wealth, he suddenly becomes overcome with awe.

Our motherland, Orissa, should be restored once more to her former glory and wealth. The spiritual life should be revived in every Oria village and the *varṇāśrama dharma* should be proclaimed once again. The delicate, yet fibrous bonds that exist among caste, society, and religion will again become strong and sturdy.[1]

The key to social reform was to be individual reform. In these words Saccidananda described both his own role and the life of the ideal Oria layman:

Of utter importance are various personal restraints that lead to a simple and austere life, for such discipline is at the root of all spiritual development. The progress of society is dependent upon the development of each individual.

Saccidananda's answer to the encroachment of Westernization was to found the Sanskrit school.

The Guru himself spoke Oria, Bengali, and Hindi, wrote English, and claimed "to use Sanskrit daily like my mother-tongue." He spoke in lengthy sentences with a rich vocabulary, and our interpreter, a graduate student at the Orissa state university and a high caste Brahman, was thoroughly impressed with the Guru as a genuinely learned man. Saccidananda also claimed knowledge of astrology, Ayur-vedic medicine, Tantric philosophy, the four Vedas, the Upanishads, the Bhagavad Gita, and the Puranas.

The main function of his institution, according to Saccidananda, was to give religious teaching and moral advice to others, "so that they might become honest, peace-loving, independent, moral, and well-behaved." Other functions of the monastery were "to provide education in Sanskrit, to feed guests, to give money to the poor, shelter to the helpless, and burial to the dead who have no family." He placed great emphasis on the virtues of celibacy and self-control in one's personal life, and gave us the following outline for "obtaining liberation (*mokṣa*) through self-realization."

One should be pure and clean, completely detached from desires, firm-minded, self-confident, should possess unswerving faith in the words of his guru and deity, should maintain control over his body and senses, be liberated from all dilemmas, and be free from sorrows and sufferings. He should be knowledgeable in the principal philosophical schools and should remain unattached to any and all dogmas.

He then enumerated ten elementary steps to liberation:

1. Saccidananda Sarasvati, *Report of the Utkalmani Gurukula Brahmacaryashrama of Bhubaneswar,* pp. 5–6.

1. Leave bed before sunrise.
2. Pay homage to the Sun God Savitri every morning and evening [i.e., recite the Gayatri].
3. Recite other sacred verses [*mantras*] and the name of one's chosen deity while bathing.
4. Offer sacrificial fire [*homa*] and perform yogic postures.
5. Serve all guests.
6. Perform *śrāddha* [funeral offerings] for one's forefathers at noon.
7. Take sacred food [*prasāda*] after noon and before evening.
8. Worship one's chosen deity in the evening.
9. Meditate upon the welfare of humanity before going to sleep.
10. Sleep from 11:00 P.M. to 4:00 A.M.

Practice precedes knowledge in importance. A list of "Secondary Steps toward Liberation" was really a list of austerities, mostly different kinds of fasts. Saccidananda insisted, however, that the help of a guru is absolutely essential to reach enlightenment.

Philosophically, Saccidananda classified himself as an Advaita Vedantist. What he meant by the term *advaita*, following the tradition of the Shankarananda Matha, was not what Shankara meant. To illustrate this point we shall quote from the *guruparamparā* (list of gurus) for the Shankarananda Matha, which provided the following sketch of the life of Shankara:

> Shri Shankaracharya who is God Shiva incarnate, much learned, a yogi and poet and who is all-knowing and kindhearted, was born to protect religion. This Shankaracharya was well-versed in the culture of Veda and Vedanta and was well-acquainted with the *pūjā* functions of Shiva . . . he wrote a commentary on the Vedanta Sutras compiled by Vyasa and made the opinions of the Buddhists, the Charvakas, and the Jains [three groups considered heretical] fall to the ground. Thus beating down the worshippers of other deities and the atheists he upheld the Advaita theory, theory of One God, as being the gift of Vedanta philosophy.[2]

The term *advaita* means "non-duality." For Shankara an intuitive experience of a state of non-duality was at the same time the attainment of Absolute Knowledge (*parāvidyā*); therefore, *advaita* alone was real. Everything that denoted a duality of subject and object, God and creation, was an experience grounded in ignorance or illusion (*avidyā*). Shankara concluded that God (Ishvara) and

---

2. *Guruparampara of the Samkarananda Math*, trans. K. J. M. Rayguru and J. M. S. Tirtha, pp. 1–2.

the whole phenomenal world of duality were illusory from the standpoint of absolute knowledge.

Neither the compiler of the *guruparamparā* nor Saccidananda made a distinction between absolute knowledge (*parāvidyā*) and illusion (*avidyā*). Both men held that *advaita* meant "the theory of One God (*eka deva*)." From the One God evolved the material universe including all the various creatures locked within it. Saccidananda, therefore, held that the elements of the universe were real and not illusory, since they had evolved from God: "Because Advaita philosophy says that God [Ishvara] is omnipresent, the sun, moon, stars, planets, and the five elements [space, air, fire, water, and earth] are all parts of God . . . the Creator God is one in all."

Saccidananda, however, is not a "pantheist," one who holds that "All (the cosmos) is God and God is the All." Rather, Saccidananda is better described as panentheist, one who believes that "All (creation) is in God, but God is not identical with the All." God does not exhaust himself in his creation. A spiritual portion of God stands behind or transcends his material creation as its soul, or, in the words of the Brihadaranyaka Upanishad 3.7, as the Inner Controller (*antaryāmin*) who directs the All from within. Therefore, Saccidananda's philosophical position was closer to the theistic interpretation of Ramanuja (Vishishtadvaita Vedanta) than it was to the absolutistic interpretation of Shankara, even though Saccidananda considered himself to be a follower of Shankara. Saccidananda lived within the folk tradition; in describing his world view he used theistic terminology although he felt it was a matter of preference whether Ishvara was called Vishnu or Shiva. The relative ease with which the Hindu changes his emphasis when referring to his deity will always be a problem for the Western observer.

In order to realize the spiritual identification of man's soul (the microcosmic spiritual principle) with God (Ishvara, the macrocosmic spiritual principle), Saccidananda advocated *ātmā darśana*, or "the realization of the soul," that is, union of the soul with God. His explanation of *ātmā darśana* stressed adherence to body-control exercises, vows of austerity, and the like, rather than philosophical inquiry into the nature of the *ātmā* or the soul. Elaborating upon this point, he said:

At first he who seeks to realize the truth of Shankaracharya's philosophy should be sacred and pure in heart. In order to be a pure man, he should adhere to certain practices. These practices are nothing but different kinds of austerities [*tapas*]. . . . In order to obtain purity and sacredness of thought, he should perform difficult vows like *chāndrāyaṇa vrata* [fasting regulated by the course of the moon, described earlier in this chapter]. By so doing he can destroy the evil effects of his past action [*karma*]. . . . Furthermore, by perfecting these vows, he will be able to subdue evil attitudes known as *rajas* [passion] and *tamas* [apathy]. These are the devils that stand as a barrier to the attainment of *ātmā darśana*. By subduing *rajas* and *tamas* he will develop *sattva* [purity], which is characteristic of a sacred, serene, and truthful mind. The sattvic mentality enables man to realize God.

Saccidananda exerted his influence in revitalizing Hindu tradition while accepting certain changes as inevitable. In 1958 he was elected president of the Muktimandapa Sabha at Puri. A literal translation of *mukti maṇḍapa* is "the temple or hall (*maṇḍapa*) of release (*mukti*)." In the present context, *mukti* means "legal release," rather than "spiritual release"; *sabhā* means "assembly or council." The Muktimandapa Sabha is composed of learned Hindus, both ascetic and lay, who meet at the Jagannatha Temple, Puri, twice a month to decide upon cases involving infractions of interpretations of Hindu law.

Shortly after Saccidananda was appointed president, the Muktimandapa Sabha handled a case that required an interpretation of the admissions policy for the Jagannatha Temple. Entrance into the Jagannatha Temple was restricted to Hindus of Indian ethnic stock. The temple policy thus barred non-Indians who claimed to be Hindus. The case at issue involved four American women who, according to Saccidananda, had been converted to Hinduism at a Ramakrishna Vedanta Society in the United States. The four women while visiting Puri wanted to enter the Jagannatha Temple. To gain permission they approached the Raja of Puri, who in turn placed the decision before the Muktimandapa Sabha. Saccidananda said that in order to decide the case he would have to talk to the Americans. He was profoundly impressed by the American women, who wore Indian dress and who expressed a familiarity with Hindu manners and customs. Saccidananda's "test of a true Hindu" is worth quoting:

> The American ladies had put on saris and veils and they bowed their heads before their superiors just as Indian ladies do. They were reserved and respected their husbands as embodiments of the deity. They were not short-tempered. They did not eat fish, mutton, beef, or any other meat. They were fully knowledgeable of Hindu principles of life. They took a morning and evening bath and prayed for the welfare of humanity. They were honest and very sympathetic towards the poor and the sick. . . . They had become truly Hindu.

In other words, to Saccidananda, "conversion to Hinduism" meant acculturation to a pious version of a certain Hindu life-style. Saccidananda decided that the Americans should be allowed entrance into the temple and a majority of the other members of the Muktimandapa Sabha backed his decision. According to Saccidananda, this was the first time that the Muktimandapa Sabha had granted permission for Americans to enter the Jagannatha Temple.

Throughout his life Saccidananda remained a strict, orthodox Dashanami Sannyasin, but one who successfully combined the roles of educator, administrator, religious reformer, and mystic.

In the thirty-eight years that he had been head ascetic, Saccidananda broadened his attitude toward societal change. In the 1930s he had advocated a return to the *varṇāśrama dharma* of the past. Even then his interpretation of the *varṇāśrama dharma* had evidenced a concern for social reform; in theory at least, he had been willing to admit members of all four socio-religious groups into his Sanskrit school. In 1958, as president of the Muktimandapa Sabha, Saccidananda was instrumental in changing the admissions policy of the Jagannatha Temple in allowing non-Indians to enter. Saccidananda's attempt at social reform, however, ended in 1964 when the Muktimandapa Sabha reversed its previous decision and denied temple entrance to several American members of the Ramakrishna Vedanta Society.

Saccidananda balanced his this-worldly concerns with a spiritual quest for self-realization (*ātmā darśana*). He was the last of his kind. None of the other ascetics at the medieval-founded monasteries commanded as much respect from the laity. In January, 1965, Saccidananda died at the age of 61, holding the hope of final absorption into the deity (*samādhi*). His successor, a much younger man, does not appear to possess the charismatic qualities of his mentor.

The Preacher (Jagadananda Bhakti Shastri Tirtha, Maharaja of the Arya Rishikula Bhuvaneshvari Ashrama)

An important role of the guru at monasteries which are dependent upon lay financial support, is that of a preacher. Jagadananda, the head ascetic of the Arya Rishikula Bhuvaneshvari Ashrama, was considered the most eloquent preacher in the Old Town.

Like the Guru, the Preacher's name is encumbered with titles: "Jagadananda" means "universe of bliss"; "Bhakti" represents the path of devotional practices; "Shastri" indicates that the Preacher is learned in Sanskrit; "Tirtha" designates his Dashanami sub-order; and like Saccidananda "Maharaja" is the title he assumed as head ascetic of his monastery.

Between 1928, when he was initiated into monastic orders, and 1945, when he settled at Bhubaneswar, Jagadananda had been an itinerant preacher, or, as he described himself, "a missionary." During his years of wandering his principal aim was to renew the spirit of Hindu tradition and win back to the Hindu fold converts to Islam and Christianity. For a short period of time in 1940 he worked in conjunction with the Hindu Mahasabha, a political party whose aim was an undivided India under the control of the Hindu majority. In recent years he had broadened his judgement of other religions to the extent that in 1964 he adhered to Ramakrishna's statement that different creeds are but different paths to reach God.

Jagadananda was less concerned with austerities and with the restoration of tradition than was Saccidananda. He enjoyed interaction with groups of laymen and thought of himself primarily as a preacher before public audiences rather than as an advisor or guru for individuals. In general, he was far more talkative and outgoing than was Saccidananda and provided more information about his personal background. He was a master of homiletic techniques and was gifted with a deep, resonant voice. He delighted in telling mythological and legendary stories both to entertain his listeners and to communicate in metaphoric terms his religious beliefs. His vivid imagination tended to blend myth and fact in his own life-history. No witnesses were available to substantiate his legendary accounts; hence it was impossible to separate his actual experiences from his exaggerations.

Jagadananda was born in 1901 in West Bengal and studied in a Sanskrit school for ten years, eventually attaining the degree of Acharya, which entitled him to become a Sanskrit teacher. While in Sanskrit school, he learned yogic practices from his principal, played the musical instruments used in worship, and acted the role of Krishna in religious plays. At first he practised *hatha yoga* (bodily control exercises) only to increase "the beauty of his appearance," but at the age of fifteen he was introduced by the principal of his school to a guru with whom he participated in the chanting of religious songs (*bhajanas*). While chanting, Jagadananda closed his eyes and saw a blue ray of light. He lost consciousness for two hours, during which his body was "as soft as butter," and he "shed tears like rain." At that time he knew nothing of the nature of *samādhi*, the state of supreme consciousness or absorption into *brahman*. The people around him thought he had been attacked by witchcraft and gave him Ayur-vedic medicines.

When he was sixteen or seventeen, Jagadananda attended a religious conference where he saw his guru in a state of meditational trance (*samādhi*). Jagadananda was astonished to see that his guru was encircled by a bright light; the guru, whose eyelids were half closed and whose body remained rigid, appeared not to be breathing at all and remained in this state for many hours. When the guru returned to consciousness, his body began to shake violently and Jagadananda heard "a weird sound like the sound of thunder come from his mouth." The ground shook. Then the guru chanted what Jagadananda described as "a highly philosophical and thoughtful verse." The guru sang: "O, Absolute Spirit [Vishnu], I want to remain with you forever in that *samādhi* state."

Jagadananda requested to be initiated (that is, be given ascetic *dīkṣā*) by the guru, who felt that Jagadananda was too young to leave his parental family. After much discussion the guru finally agreed to accept Jagadananda as a lay pupil and teach him how to realize *samādhi*. The following is a translation of Jagadananda's description of his first instruction:

> I arrived at 5:00 A.M. after a sleepless night spent thinking about questions I wanted to ask Guruji. He told me to sit in the lotus posture and to look into his eyes without blinking. He put his hand on my chest and told me to concentrate there. As soon as he touched me I felt as if an electrical current were passing through me. I lost consciousness. When I regained consciousness, I found that I had my head on the lap of Guruji and that he had kept his hand on my chest. Guruji told me to remember this experience but not to tell these things publicly to anybody.

Thus at the age of seventeen Jagadananda received lay *dīkṣā* by touch, which is an integral part of most lay initiatory rites. Jagadananda was now torn between worldly life and his desire to experience *samādhi*. Finally after reading a number of religious books suggested by his guru, including the writings of the Buddha and Shankara, he decided to become an ascetic. However, in his account a lapse of ten years took place between his lay initiation and his decision to take the final vows of ascetic initiation.

At the age of twenty-seven Jagadananda underwent the formal ascetic *dīkṣā* ceremony into Dashanami Sannyasin orders at the hands of Nityananda Chaitanyaghana Sadhu Maharaja, the head ascetic at the Arya Rishikula Matha at Hardwar in Uttar Pradesh. (Nityananda was not the same teacher under whom he had taken lay initiation.)

At the completion of the initiation ceremony Jagadananda vowed that he would wander about preaching to the masses of rural Indians in the hope of reviving Hinduism by winning converts back into Hinduism from Christianity and Islam. He returned to West Bengal, where, with the financial assistance of a wealthy Bengali, he established a monastery at Sarangabad, fifteen miles southwest of Calcutta. From 1928 until 1933 Jagadananda travelled throughout India, visiting all the sacred pilgrimage centres. He then began an extensive missionary tour of West Bengal and Orissa.

In 1936 Jagadananda travelled to Dariapur, Nadia District, West Bengal, which he described as "a well-educated village." He preached to the residents of Dariapur and the surrounding area for a period of fourteen days and led his listeners in songs and dances (*kīrtanas*) popularized by Chaitanya. On the fourteenth day, several residents who belonged to the Madhva Gaudiya teaching tradition submitted to Jagadananda a list of seventy-four questions related to the life of Krishna. He gave the following answer to the last ten questions:

> Krishna at Dvaraka preached disciplined action [*karma yoga*]; Krishna at Kurukshetra in the Mahabharata War taught mystical knowledge [*jñāna yoga*]; Krishna at Vrindavana was the essence of love [*prema* or *bhakti yoga*].

This answer satisfied all but a few. Jagadananda felt as if a supernatural power helped him. Finally a Dashanami Sannyasin resident who was head of the lecture committee declared that Jagadananda had answered all seventy-four questions adequately, and the conference ended. As a result of his success, Jagadananda gained approximately twenty lay disciples and numerous other sympathizers.

As he and several of his ascetic disciples left the town and prepared to enter a river boat, they were arrested by the local police on the charge of "issuing books that had created a rebellious attitude among the public against the government." The ascetics were jailed awaiting a court decision. On the next day they were released when it was determined that the officer in charge had arrested Jagadananda and his party on false charges provoked by those whom Jagadananda had defeated in debate. Jagadananda claims that the police officer who arrested him was later arrested on the same day for fathering an illegitimate child. In Jagadananda's stories his opponents are always punished by the deity for their evil-doings.

Jagadananda and his followers then travelled to Calcutta where their Hindu friends encouraged them to pursue their missionary efforts in the heavily Christian area of Diamond Harbor, thirty miles to the south. There, Jagadananda and his disciples went from village to village preaching, singing devotional songs, and dancing. According to Jagadananda his mission was highly successful: "Hundreds of villagers returned to Hinduism."

During his missionary journeys he underwent many hardships, sometimes being forced to take open boats by night or to walk forty miles in a day. Often the villagers refused to feed or lodge him, and he had difficulties finding shelter for the night. A tiger or some other ferocious animal was always roaring somewhere in the background in these stories. Within about three-and-one-half months he had covered forty villages.

On another journey Jagadananda and a young *brahmacārin* disciple went to Cuttack, Orissa, where they were guests of the Excise Police Commissioner. For five days Jagadananda preached in the bazaar. On the sixth day he was invited to speak at the home of the Chief Engineer, Electrical Division. His companion did not attend the meeting, and when Jagadananda returned to his host's residence, he discovered that the young *brahmacārin* had stolen all his money. This temporarily ended Jagadananda's activity in Orissa and he returned to Calcutta on the night express. Toward the end of 1941 he travelled in north-central India. He reached Benares in 1942 when Hindu nationalists were becoming restless. He advised non-violence.

In 1944 he re-entered Orissa and toured Balasore District on the north-east coast of Orissa, where he was bedridden for some time with malaria. Later in the year he developed a stomach ailment and came to Bhubaneswar to take its medicinal waters. He had been a wandering ascetic–missionary for seventeen years, and the hardships endured during that period were now beginning to affect his health. A Bhubaneswar lawyer encouraged him to build a monastery and to settle down permanently.

Philosophically, Jagadananda was a syncretist and an eclectic. He believed that *karma yoga* (disciplined action), *bhakti yoga* (devotional practices), and *jñāna yoga* (mystical knowledge) were equally important paths to the same goal. He had been influenced by the nineteenth-century Hindu reformist-revivalists, in particular Ramakrishna Paramahansa, who tried to universalize Hinduism by eliminating its divisive aspects, such as caste, and by proclaiming its ancient teachings as the essence of all true religion. Jagadananda claimed to reject the caste system, although his views on the subject were often inconsistent:

When I was on a missionary journey to revive Hinduism, some Indians who had converted to Christianity or Islam said that they had done so because in Hinduism there is a great difference between higher and lower castes, and the higher caste people disrespect the lower castes, who then convert to Christianity. I said that disrespect to the lower castes is not written in any Hindu code of religion; it is nothing but a prejudice of the higher castes. The higher-caste people dislike the lower-caste people because they are not neat and clean and eat bad foods that are not permitted in the Hindu code of religion. If the lower-caste people will be as neat and clean as the upper castes they will be accepted by the upper castes.

There was no evidence of Jagadananda's ever having admitted members of the lower castes as guests in the monastery, though some did come to the dispensary. The audience at monastery festivals was exclusively upper-caste.

When asked who was a true *sādhu*, living or dead, Jagadananda gave a very inclusive list: "Those who are now dead, but have lived their lives according to my philosophical principles: Ramakrishna Paramahansa, Vivekananda, Shankara, Ramanuja, Buddha (to some extent), Gandhi, Tagore, Nehru (to some extent, with a technical mind), the kings of Orissa, especially at Puri, Chaitanya, and the seven Great Rishis of the Vedic Age, who are stars of the Big Dipper." He also listed sixteen living people, who included all his ascetic disciples, a number of the patrons of his monastery (including a Member of Parliament who had provided considerable financial support), Vinoba Bhave, his guru's wife, some Muslim families of Kotalpur, and Bertrand Russell. This eclecticism showed appreciation for non-Hindus. He felt that the essential matters about human brotherhood could be learned from the Koran as well as from Hindu philosophy, reflecting his deep sympathy for the non-sectarianism of the Ramakrishna movement.

Jagadananda stressed non-violence (*ahiṃsā*) as essential to all right behaviour. He summed up his ethical philosophy as follows:

A man should realize the heart of a man, otherwise he is a brute. The main aim of philosophy is to bring forth love, affection, and kindness from the heart of a man who is living in ignorance. . . . A man should observe the daily duties of praying to the deity in the morning and evening for the well-being of humanity, should utilize his whole life for the benefit of his fellow men, should offer *ārati* [waving-of-light ceremony] and perform *āsana* [meditation] to control his passions and evil emotions, should restrict his diet and should not violate *ahiṃsā* by eating beef, mutton, eggs, fish, and excess *ghī*. [We notice the stress on vegetarianism, which seems to be an important test of right behaviour.]

He then listed ten precepts of ethical behaviour:

1. Be kindly toward a cruel man and you will change him.
2. Do not dislike others even though they may dislike you, because the wicked must someday repent and submit when their power and policy fail. This is a universal truth.

3. Control the manner of your speech; this is one of the main factors that makes a man a friend or enemy.

4. Respect the right of others to speak as they must because each was created by God.

5. Do not disrespect a man of low caste because you may be like him in your next rebirth.

6. Realize that caste and colour are nothing but foolish prejudice in an ignorant man's mind.

7. Consider superiors as well-wishers and inferiors as blessed.

8. Be independent, but at the same time try to take care of your parents who have made you a man on this earth by sacrificing their money, matter, and life.

9. Pray to the deity for the happiness of mankind, not for yourself. The deity only listens to the man who prays for others.

10. Do not grasp after things [i.e., be a materialist]; *brahman*, the Supreme Spirit, is everywhere and pervades this universe.

These ten maxims, somewhat reminiscent of the biblical sayings of Jesus, sum up Jagadananda's practical if somewhat incoherent ethic. Its application to world affairs he stated in approximately the following fashion:

Only sacrifice can bring peace and serenity into this world; the motive for sacrifice should be the desire to serve all humanity, and it should not have the slightest touch of selfishness. Here is an example: suppose China is aggressive. If we take up arms against China, that act will destroy international peace. Many lives will be lost. There can be no doubt that a person, however aggressive or inhuman he may be, will repent in the long run. He who can change the heart of a man before anything is destroyed will be regarded as the noblest and the most ideal man. So we all should try to change the evil-doers of society into ideal and noble men before destruction happens. From the very beginning of Indian history, India has faced horrible wars, depicted in the Ramayana and the Mahabharata. But spiritually minded men have always wanted peace; therefore let the ideological differences of the nations of the world be solved by negotiations and not by mass murder.

In addition to preaching humanitarianism and world peace through non-violence, Jagadananda, as we said earlier, loved to tell legendary stories about his guru and even about his own life. The following is a charming example of a myth Jagadananda related about his guru, Nityananda Chaitanyaghana.

Sadhu Nityananda wandered over most of India to find a good and noble guru who could teach him the philosophy of mankind. Finally he went to meditate on Vishnu in the snow-capped Himalayan ranges. He promised to die in meditation, because it is written that that which a man desires during the moment of his death he will obtain in the next life. As the moment of death came nearer he uttered the words, "Oh Vishnu, give me a noble and learned guru." Suddenly he saw a man with a white beard and long white hair. The stranger inquired if Nityananda had a family. Nityananda said that he was not married. The stranger then held up his left palm and asked, "Who is this?" Nityananda was astonished to see an image of his wife in the stranger's hand, and fell down at the stranger's feet and begged to be excused for his falsehood. Then the stranger said, "Do not worry. I know why you lied to me. You thought that if you told me you had a wife I would have asked you to return home. You were wrong. But if you really want to find a noble guru, you must eat only one cooked banana every day and meditate on Vishnu." Then the stranger vanished. Nityananda felt absolutely helpless, for he could not imagine how he might find a banana in the snowy rocks of the Himalayas, much less how to cook it. But the next day he did find a banana, and so also each day for twelve years. He spent his days alone, without talking to anyone. When twelve years were over, the same stranger appeared and said, "I am highly pleased with your hard meditation and your strict penance. Close your eyes until I tell you to open them." Nityananda did as he was instructed. The stranger then asked him to open his eyes and describe what he saw in front of him. Nityananda said that he could see only four snow-covered pillars. The stranger said that these were not pillars, but four sages [*ṛiṣis*] who in the course of their meditation had been covered by snow.

Then the stranger said, "I am highly pleased with you. I will give you *dīkṣā* today. After taking *dīkṣā* you must remain in *samādhi* for three years. Then you will be able to preach the real truth and to understand the philosophy of mankind." The stranger initiated Nityananda and then vanished. The stranger was none other than the Rishi Vasishtha, one of the seven Vedic sages whose position is sixth in the stars of the Great Bear. The little star next to Vasishtha is his wife Arundhati. [Vasishtha is one of the seven Great Sages who according to legend founded Jagadananda's order and who is worshipped in his monastery.]

Jagadananda described similar experiences in his own life. The following

"Tale of the Three Sadhus" serves as a good example of the preacher's penchant for story-telling.

Once I was travelling near the Darjeeling Hill Station with a friend named Banarji who did not believe in the existence of deities and who was a hedonist. While we were walking along the road, we came across a *sādhu* who was wearing a round iron rod around his waist with an undercloth attached to it from front to back to hide his nakedness. The glare of divinity emanated from him. He was accompanied by two *brahmacārins*. I was very anxious to talk with them, but Mr. Banarji said, "They are nothing but beggars. Why are you interested in them?" Banarji convinced me to ignore the *sādhus*.

I then went to a lonely place to meditate, but was unable to concentrate. Suddenly I saw my guru [Nityananda] standing before me and he said, "My son, I am greatly shocked by your disbelief in that *sādhu*. Whoever he may be, you should not be persuaded by your friend to think evil of him. This is the age of disbelief and egoism. Before you jump to any conclusions about anyone you should talk with him first."

I begged pardon from Guruji, but he said, "Don't ask forgiveness from me. You can be pardoned only if you repent your grave mistake before that *sādhu*." So I promised to find that *sādhu* even in the dense forest, and if I failed to find him, I vowed to fast until death. As I began my search, I could see the images of the *sādhu*'s two *brahmacārins*, who looked like Krishna and Balarama, dancing before my eyes. Then I encountered a man in the forest who told me that the *brahmacārin* who looked like Krishna was the son of a king. The woodsman also told me that the king had, many years before, asked the *sādhu* to grant him a boon of twin sons in order to insure an heir to the throne. The *sādhu* promised to grant the boon if the king would give him in return the first-born twin. Thus, the twin grew up under the *sādhu*'s care.

Finally I found a betel shopkeeper who told me to cross the river and follow the sound of a Darjeeling horn. I did as he suggested and found the *sādhu* and *brahmacārins* sitting in a garden. The *sādhu* said, "I know why you have come. I also know that at first you disbelieved me, but you have heard a divine voice saying that Vishnu may come in the form of a *sādhu* to live on earth. I am not Vishnu, only a poor *sādhu*. What do you want from me?" I said, "I do not want anything except your forgiveness for my grave offence, because this is the age of disbelief, corruption, and egoism." The *sādhu* said, "It is not entirely your fault. An honest man can be affected by the atmosphere of dishonesty and disbelief that surrounds him." The *sādhu* asked whether I had any questions, and I asked him how I might realize the deity.

The *sādhu* gave me a sacred object [a small stone] that had the power of granting me two wishes. My two wishes were to attain *samādhi* and to perceive Rishi Vasishtha, who had revealed himself to my guru. The *sādhu* said that in time my wishes would be fulfilled, but I had to be patient.

One day I was invited to lunch by a friend. When we were about to eat, a thin and impoverished *sādhu* came to the door of the house and asked for food. My friend grumbled but I said, "I will give you my meal." So I invited the *sādhu* into the house, offered him a place to sit, and arranged all the prepared foods before him. We were amazed to see the *sādhu* eat not only my food but all the food prepared by my friend. After finishing his meal, the *sādhu* did not dispose of his plantain leaf as is the custom, but immediately went out to wash his hands and face. I picked up the plantain leaf and threw it into the cows' trough but at that moment the *sādhu* vanished before our eyes.

Later I went to the *sādhu* who had given me the wishing stone to ask him about this strange event. As I approached, the *sādhu* said, "My boy, all your desires are fulfilled, so why have you come?" I said, "I have come to learn how to perceive Rishi Vasishtha." The *sādhu* said, "You have already perceived him and served him as a guest."

In 1964 Jagadananda was critically ill and under the constant care of a doctor who lived near the monastery. Yet, in our conversations Jagadananda's reminiscences seemed to transport him back into the days when he was a wandering preacher–ascetic. Sitting behind a large wooden desk, the Preacher emotionally dramatized and relived for us the events of his missionary journeys. Whether or not his stories were factually based or mere fantasies made little difference to us; we were convinced that Jagadananda was one of the most dynamic preachers we had ever heard. Unfortunately, much of the emotional intensity with which Jagadananda told his stories was lost as the tale was transcribed in this text. We have, however, attempted to reproduce these tales as they were actually told to us.

Ill as he was, Jagadananda drew a crowd of nearly a hundred people on the Dola Purnima celebration in which he was honoured as the guru. The audience, which included several influential Bhubaneswar residents, listened attentively for an hour as the Preacher addressed them, constantly illustrating his major points with mythological tales. As a preacher, he was without a rival in Bhubaneswar.

Many of the Preacher's illustrative stories were derived from his experiences as a wandering missionary; he talked about the period of his residence in Bhubaneswar only when questioned. This was understandable. Most of his dreams for his monastery remained unfulfilled: he needed medicines for his dispensary, and the religio-cultural hall, in which the Dola Purnima celebration took place, remained a mere shell without a roof. Furthermore, he wanted to establish a Sanskrit school, but had no funds with which to make a beginning. Even if the Preacher had had the funds available to the Guru, we doubt that Jagadananda would have made an able administrator. Rather, he was a dreamer, a visionary whose humanitarian, syncretistic ideals could not be easily, if ever, realized. He was not the realistic, practical administrator that the Guru was. The Preacher beautifully articulated religious ideals while the Guru realized certain goals that required compromise with the society within which he lived.

Summary

In our estimation the Guru and the Preacher were the religious leaders of the Old Town. Both had influential patrons, many of whom lived in the New Capital, Puri, or Cuttack. The Guru listed over three hundred patrons, among them the former Minister of Revenue of the State of Orissa, now editor-in-chief of the widely read Orissa newspaper, the *Samaj* (published in Cuttack), who served as President of the Managing Committee of Saccidananda's Sanskrit school. Although we never saw him visit the monastery, he sent his assistant editor from time to time to keep abreast of developments. Notices of festivals held at the monastery would usually appear in the *Samaj*. It also printed a short article describing the founding of the Harihara Satsangha Ashrama in which Saccidananda, the Guru, had played a part. There was never any editorial comment in these articles.

Some of the Guru's other patrons included the Speaker of the Orissa Legislative Assembly, the Curator of the State Museum at Bhubaneswar, two Lecturers in Oria at Ravenshaw College in Cuttack, an Assistant Secretary of the Department of Works and Transport for the City of Bhubaneswar, and the owner of a bookstore in Cuttack.

Jagadananda, the Preacher, as leader of the Bengali religious community in Bhubaneswar, also listed some impressive patrons, including a Member of Parliament. In 1958 the Member of Parliament had laid the foundation for the religio-cultural hall still unfinished in 1964. This patron was the most popular politician from the Old Town area and was careful to keep himself informed on the religious climate among his constituents. When he was in New Delhi on business, his secretary kept in touch with Jagadananda.

Unlike the Guru, the Preacher could claim both Bengali and Oria patrons of note, including the Home Minister of Orissa, the former Minister of Health, the former and present Ministers of Education, the Speaker of the Legislative Assembly, and the editor of the *Samaj*. Several of these were also Saccidananda's patrons. Thus the two leading ascetics in the Old Town were both in a position to influence city and state politics. The exact nature of the matters about which they were consulted, the advice they transmitted to government officials, and the importance these officials attached to such advice were not revealed.

Jagadananda also differed from Saccidananda in that he was openly opposed to the current administration of Orissa and hoped for the election of his patron to the post of Chief Minister. Yet, Jagadananda was strongly opposed not only to any and all kinds of government control, including the Orissa Hindu Religious Endowments Commission, but even to government support for schools or medical dispensaries connected with monasteries. He said:

> It is better that the government not support any of the *mathas*, even if the *mathas* are working for the improvement of the people. Rather, the government should help the people directly, and should provide improved medical and educational facilities for them. Then if the people are properly cared for, they may decide that monasteries are important for religious growth. Then they will help those organizations without any reservations. So the first duty of the government is not to interfere with the operation of *mathas* or *āśramas* but to work for the progress of the people.

The Guru represented the traditional concept of the head ascetic at an endowed institution. He was a charismatic figure, learned in Sanskrit and a master of austere practices, who held a strict, orthodox point of view. At the same time he was an able administrator and educator. He managed his monastery's endowment so efficiently that his institution was not under the control of the Orissa Hindu Religious Endowments Commission. During the Guru Purnima at his monastery, his disciples revered him as a symbol of sacredness by washing his feet, throwing flowers upon him, and kneeling before him in an act of humility. The atmosphere that surrounded the Guru was highly formal and impersonal. He remained apart from the laity, who held him in awe.

The Preacher was also a charismatic figure and learned in Sanskrit. But instead of providing his disciples with a model of austerity, he instructed them through sermons concluding with moral comments on the state of affairs in contemporary India. At Dola Purnima he actively participated with his ascetics and lay disciples in the performance of the *kīrtana*, and although his sermon was the major event, he was only one speaker among others.

Administratively, the Preacher as head of a patronized institution cooperated with a managing committee in maintaining the institution. Whereas the Guru remained apart from the laity, the Preacher worked actively among them. The Preacher's definition of a true saint (*sādhu*) was "one who is dedicated to the concept of international brotherhood, who serves for the benefit of humanity as a whole." Furthermore, in his denouncement of Hindu sectarianism, he illustrated the difference between a strict, orthodox sectarian position, such as that advocated by men like the Guru, and a tolerant, non-sectarian attitude characteristic of the Ramakrishna movement.

Chapter 2

Common Lifestyles: Non-Intellectual Devotion and Solitary Withdrawal

The four men described in this chapter represent very different lifestyles from the Guru and the Preacher. Whereas both the Guru and the Preacher were highly respected religious leaders in the Old Town, had attained the degree of Sanskrit scholar (Acharya), had had visions of the deity, and were followers of Shankara, the men of this chapter could not be considered religious leaders and are not learned. All four are basically oriented toward daily devotions (*bhakti*) and reflect the impact of the Chaitanya movement with its emphasis on music and ecstasy. All have a few clients and all are considered genuine ascetics by the lay community. Two, a father and son, are former cloth merchants who have built a temple to Chaitanya and who order their lives around forms of daily worship that generate intense feelings. One, the Troubadour, is a Shudra who was encouraged to settle in a non-sectarian, religious park because of his beautiful voice and his talent as a leader of devotional singing. The fourth, the Solitary Ascetic, is a typical resident of a small establishment. He is a sincere but not highly educated man. The first three ascetics are Vairagins, and the last is a self-styled Shankara Brahmacharin. None has had a traditional Sanskrit education, and two have had only a few years of schooling. The conversation that takes place in the Solitary Ascetic's cell over *gañjā* (*Cannabis sativa*) typifies the level of discourse in a monastery whose residents are of village background.

These four ascetics are probably more representative of the ''average'' ascetic in Bhubaneswar than are either the Guru or the Preacher.

The Bhaktas, Father and Son (Nibaran Mukharji and his son, Gaura Dasa Mukharji, of the Shadbhuja Chaitanya Mandira)

Nibaran Mukharji was a successful Brahman cloth merchant whose heart lay in religious devotions, *kīrtanas*, and pilgrimages, and who finally left secular life to found a temple to Chaitanya at Bhubaneswar. His son, Gaura Dasa, after economic failures, turned his heart to religion, taking refuge as an officiant in his father's temple. Nibaran and Gaura Dasa belonged to a Madhva Gaudiya sub-order that existed exclusively for householders (*gṛhasthas*).

Nibaran was born in 1894 in East Bengal (Bangladesh). He completed Class 11 in grammar school. He says that his parents worshipped Shakti (Durga). As a child he participated in many *kīrtanas* and acquired a distaste for caste distinctions. In his youth he was poor. As a schoolboy he lived for some time in a monastery where his only food was the *prasāda* of the deity at noon and bread at night. After a time, he suffered from dysentery and malaria and was taken in by his elder brother. Nibaran started working as a Brahman cook for a government official. Subsequently he worked his way into a clerkship at the Radhakrishna Cotton Mill in Calcutta on the basis of his good handwriting, finally becoming head clerk. He seemed to have been a winning, enterprising youth who rose from poverty to comparative affluence. Meanwhile, he remained a devotee of Durga and participated in as many religious ceremonies as his work allowed. Sometimes *kīrtanas* kept him away all night. The leader of one of these *kīrtanas*, a Chaitanya ascetic, so impressed Nibaran that he transferred his devotions from Durga to Chaitanya. His participation was punctuated by religious dreams, and he became renowned for his devotion.

The people of a distant village once sent for him because their image of Durga had lost a finger, and they were afraid the goddess would leave them unless Nibaran, who had been revealed to them in a villager's dream as the reincarnation of a former ascetic of their village, sent a token of his good will. Nibaran, who did not believe their story, nevertheless sent them a piece of fruit as a token. According to Nibaran, the image of the goddess was miraculously repaired.

Once Nibaran spent the entire night at a *kīrtana*. His wife became quite worried when he did not return. A *sannyāsin* appeared to her in a dream and told her not to be afraid; the figure in the dream turned out to be the very *sannyāsin* who was leading the *kīrtana*.

Finally Nibaran began spending so much time at *kīrtanas* that his boss suggested that he resign his job and attend *kīrtanas* full-time. Nibaran was so furious at this suggestion that he immediately resigned and used his separation pay to go on an extended pilgrimage, leaving his wife and children with a disciple. At this time Nibaran was thirty-five. He walked about five hundred miles, reaching the Himalayas begging for his food. He said, "The food obtained by begging tastes sweet at a particular stage in one's life. The food obtained by begging would not taste sweet to one who is still attached to worldly pleasures." Nibaran, who has since passed through the *vānaprastha* or hermit stage of life, said that the food obtained by begging would no longer taste sweet to him now.

After his Himalayan pilgrimage, Nibaran returned to the Radhakrishna Cotton Mill once more as head clerk. He accompanied one of his superiors on yet another pilgrimage. Finally, at the age of forty-seven, he gave up the secular life altogether and emigrated to Bhubaneswar in 1940 where one year later he founded the Shadbhuja Chaitanya Mandira.

Since Nibaran had a reputation as a leader of *kīrtanas* and player of the cylindrical drum (*khol*) he was asked by a former Calcutta disciple who had moved to Bhubaneswar to organize a twenty-four hour *kīrtana*. Having only ten rupees to buy food for the four hundred participants whom he had invited, he wrote to a disciple in Calcutta for more money. This disciple meanwhile had heard a voice telling him to go to Bhubaneswar, which he did, bringing five hundred rupees to celebrate the *kīrtana* in grand style. Nibaran, carrying a picture of Shri Chaitanya, led the procession to the temple of Lingaraja Maha-prabhu, where the priests at first refused him entrance but later relented. In disgust at the temple priesthood, Nibaran promised to build his own temple dedicated to Shri Chaitanya. Half the money to build this temple was donated by the assistant surgeon of the Old Town hospital; the rest came from Nibaran's personal savings, supplemented unwillingly by his eldest son who was forced to donate twelve thousand rupees that he had won in the Calcutta Rangers' Club Lottery. Nibaran claims that this son later became truly devout after he had had a dream of Chaitanya.

From time to time in his life, Nibaran has had dreams of the goddess Durga or of Krishna, as well as other religious experiences. According to him, a stone image of the baby Krishna, which he was visiting on one of his many pil-grimages, leaped onto his neck, and on another occasion he heard a mysterious sound emanating from a nearby Shiva temple.

The building of his temple at Bhubaneswar was the culmination of his religious life. The image of Shri Shadbhuja Krishna Chaitanya Mahaprabhu, more popularly known as Rama–Krishna–Chaitanya, is the central deity of the temple, which stands as a monument to Nibaran's quest for spiritual fulfilment.

In 1964, Nibaran felt that his present goal in life was preparation for death. In the words of Chaitanya, Nibaran would say, "Oh, Death, you are my Krishna, and I want to be taken by your nocturnal blessing."

The story of Gaura Dasa, Nibaran's son, presents a somewhat different picture of motivation for entrance into the ascetic life. Gaura Dasa was born in 1926 and married at the age of twenty-five. His wife died three months after the wedding, and three months after her death he married again. In thirteen years of marriage, his second wife, Prema Devi, has given birth to five children, only one of whom lived beyond infancy. This child, called Shanti Rani, was six years old in 1964.

Gaura Dasa typified the religious devotee (*bhakta*) whose experience of the deity Rama–Krishna–Chaitanya was so intense that he was concerned with little else, much like Chaitanya himself. His acts of devotion were performed as he was taught by his father. He had no interest in either the act or its theological implications. It was in the emotional involvements of ritual acts that he received his satisfaction.

Between 1943, when he completed the eleventh class, and 1948, when he became a resident of Bhubaneswar, Gaura Dasa had changed his place of employment seven times and had declared bankruptcy as an independent businessman five times. Gaura Dasa stated that during those five years he had been employed in Calcutta as timekeeper and night-shift foreman at the Hanuman Glass Factory, salesman at the State of Bengal Ration Food Store, salesman at the Durga Glass Works, bill collector for the Durga Rolling Mill, salesman at the Dhara Glass Company, dispatch manager of the Ranuka Glass Works, and bill clerk at the Radhakrishna Cotton Mill. This list of positions sounded very impressive, but Gaura Dasa admitted that he had held each position for only a few months before he "gave it up for one reason or another." Between jobs he went into business for himself with repeated failures. At various times Gaura Dasa borrowed money, in amounts ranging from Rs. 200 to Rs. 500, to establish himself as a glassware salesman. Each attempt ended in the loss of the capital invested. Gaura Dasa would thereupon seek employment in order to pay off his debts. In his last venture he borrowed Rs. 200 from a Bengali businessman. After failing once again, he used his wife's jewelry to pay the debt. Like most Indian men Gaura Dasa was ashamed that he could no longer discharge his debts in any other way.

Consequently, late in 1958 Gaura Dasa and his family left Calcutta for Bhubaneswar and joined his father and mother at the Shadbhuja Chaitanya

Mandira. His father, Nibaran Mukharji, had employed two men to assist in the management of the monastery. One of the assistants served as an officiant (*pujārī*); the other managed financial matters. After the arrival of Gaura Dasa, Nibaran dismissed the Brahman officiant and assigned those duties to his son. In October of 1959, the financial manager was implicated in a theft, as a result of which Nibaran discharged him, assuming the management of the finances himself.

Later in the year Nibaran went to Calcutta and remained there for several months. In his father's absence, Gaura Dasa used some of the temple funds to open a fruit and vegetable stand in the Old Town. He placed his younger brother, who was staying at the monastery, in charge of the stand. Within a short time Gaura Dasa was once again in debt. His father returned to Bhubaneswar, angered that his son "had squandered temple funds."

Gaura Dasa failed not because he was engrossed in religious devotions but because he lacked the ability to be a successful entrepreneur. His father's anger forced him to give up all hope of financial success. Nibaran commanded his son to concentrate his energies upon the worship of Chaitanya and the maintenance of the temple.

One year after his last failure in business, Gaura Dasa had a mystical experience that intensified his religious devotion. At noon one day in July 1960, Gaura Dasa was performing the midday offering before the six-armed image of Rama-Krishna-Chaitanya. He decorated the image with flowers and placed two platefuls of rice at the base of the altar. Next he performed the waving-of-light ceremony (*ārati*) and left the inner sanctum, drawing the curtain at the doorway so that "Chaitanya might have his privacy." Gaura Dasa sat upon the floor of the audience hall in front of the sanctum chanting devotional songs (*bhajanas*). After several minutes had passed, he arose and re-entered the sanctum. As he knelt to pick up the plates of food he noticed the outlines of two footprints clearly stamped upon the pillow-covered bench known as the seat or *āsana* of the deity. Gaura Dasa called his father and the other residents of the *mandira* and showed them the imprints. All present were convinced that the footprints were made by Rama-Krishna-Chaitanya. Gaura Dasa's younger brother verified this conclusion by comparing the measurements of the imprints on the bench cushion with the feet of the image. The impressions in the pillow, which by 1964 were hardly recognizable as "footprints," were exactly the same length as the feet of the image. Nibaran Mukharji marveled that "such a manifestation of God could have occurred." He reasoned, "Surely God dwells within this temple, and if he wants to be properly worshipped, then he will

somehow provide the financial resources for the maintenance of the temple."
For Gaura Dasa this event was a decisive conversion experience.

Since then he has concentrated a large portion of his waking hours on the
worship of Chaitanya. In 1964 he had no intention of returning to the secular
world. He was content to spend his life in religious devotions. His ultimate goal
was no longer to make money but rather to see the deity face to face; that is, to
have the personal experience (*darśana*) of the deity that every Hindu *bhakta*
seeks.

The following is a detailed description of a typical day in Gaura Dasa's life in
1964. It is presented here in order to emphasize the informant's concern with
religious feeling rather than religious knowledge or action for the benefit of
mankind.

At 5:30 A.M. Gaura Dasa arises, draws water from the well, and feeds the
cow. He goes to the temple, changes the cloth draped around the six-armed
image of Rama-Krishna-Chaitanya, and cleans the floor.

At 6:00 A.M., Gaura Dasa begins the Mangala (morning) Arati. His six-year-
old daughter, Shanti Rani, stands in the audience hall and bangs a gong
(*ghanta*). Gaura Dasa then leaves the sanctum, kneels before the sacred *tulasī*
plant, and chants the following hymn to Lakshmi, Vishnu's wife, whose
presence it symbolizes:

> Salutations, O Tulasi, great queen, queen of all;
> Salutations, Mother, salutations, Narayani.
> Shine forth in compassion, absorbing sin with your touch;
> Your glory is rooted in the Vedas and the Puranas.
> Salutations, salutations.

After touching their heads to the ground, the father and daughter re-enter the
audience hall. Gaura Dasa beats a cylinder-shaped drum (*khol*), accompanied
by his daughter on the gong; both sing a *mahāmantra* (great verse):

> Shri Krishna-Chaitanya, Prabhu Nityananda,
> Hari Krishna, Hari Rama, Shri Radha Govinda.

This is a Madhva Gaudiya form of the salutation of Vishnu, literally a list of
names of various incarnations of Vishnu (Rama, Krishna, and Chaitanya). It also
lists Nityananda, the foremost disciple of Chaitanya, and Radha, the lover of
Krishna.

The two circumambulate clockwise around the verandah. They chant two
more *mantras*:

Hari Krishna, Hari Krishna, Krishna, Krishna, Hari, Hari;
Hari Rama, Hari Rama, Rama, Rama, Hari, Hari.

Jai Radha, Radha Govinda,
Jai Jai Nimai, Gaura Haribol.[1]

Finally they face the six-armed image, kneel before it, and touch their foreheads to the floor. Upon rising, Gaura Dasa murmurs , "Jai Mahaprabhu" (Hail to the Great Lord Vishnu).

From 6:30 until 7:15 A.M. Gaura Dasa drinks a cup of tea and collects flowers for the altar. At 7:15 A.M. he begins the morning ritual known as Bala Bhoga, the first offering of food. He decorates the altar with flower petals and places two saucers of sliced cucumbers and sliced bananas at its base. He assumes a cross-legged position and begins to mumble sacred verses (*mantras*), occasionally clapping his hands, ringing a small bell, and sprinkling the food with water, as prescribed in the traditional liturgy. He distributes the food to any devotees who may be present and places a wooden flute, symbolic of Krishna, in the blue-coloured pair of hands of the image.

From 8:00 A.M. to 12:00 noon Gaura Dasa shapes cow-dung patties to be dried for fuel, purchases food and supplies at the Old Town market, and waters the trees and plants on the monastery grounds. At noon he returns to the sanctum to conduct the Madhya (midday) Arati. The rice to be eaten by the residents of the monastery as a midday meal is offered to the deity. At the end of the ceremony Gaura Dasa recites a long devotional song (*bhajana*). Then he retires to the main residence where all eat the rice and several vegetable curries.

From 1:45 to 2:00 P.M. Gaura Dasa sits on the floor of the audience hall silently reciting his own sacred *mantra* while counting the *tulasī* beads of a rosary (*japa mālā*). From 2:00 to 4:00 P.M. he rests. At 4:00 P.M. he and his family have tea and cookies. Until 6:00 P.M. he chats with whoever may visit. At 6:00 P.M. Gaura Dasa celebrates the Sandhya (dusk) Arati.

Gaura Dasa then talks with friends or reads newspapers. At 7:00 P.M. he goes once again to the sanctum and performs the Saya (night-time) Arati, the last ritual of the evening. Gaura Dasa removes the flute from the hands of the image, closes the doors to the sanctum, and sings several short devotional songs such as the following "to put Mahaprabhu to sleep":

---

1. The word "jai" means "hail" or "victory"; "Nimai," according to one tradition, was a name given to Chaitanya at birth; "Gaura," "the yellow-limbed" or "fair-skinned," is another name for Chaitanya; "Haribol" loosely translated means "say the name of Hari."

> Victory of Shri Guru, full of love, desired as a sweet-smelling flower, symbol of bliss, remove ignorance from my heart with your knowledge, as the radiance of the moon penetrates through the deep darkness. O, world of happiness, by whose grace the name of Hari was given to such a low and fallen man like me, I bow down before you. I had never hoped to obtain your love and blessing because of my wicked mind and evil motives. O, feet divine, splendour of devotional prayers, guide me. Sprinkle the world with your pure and heavenly nectar and fulfil the deepest desire of your devotee.

Whatever his loud voice lacks in musical quality, he more than makes up in enthusiasm.

After the ceremony is over, Gaura Dasa spends a half hour helping his daughter with her schoolwork. At 9:30 P.M. he and his family eat the food offered earlier at the Sandhya Arati. From 10:00 until 10:45 P.M. Gaura Dasa is again at leisure. Then he spends fifteen minutes reciting his *mantra* by counting *tulasī* prayer beads. At 11:00 P.M. he retires to his bedroom along with his wife and daughter.

No verbal description can fully convey the intensity of feeling that Gaura Dasa experiences performing these ritual acts taught him by his father. Whenever asked about the significance of his actions, Gaura Dasa turns to his father, Nibaran Mukharji. Nibaran has had considerable training in Sanskrit and can speak English fluently. He supplies the answers that his son cannot give. The point is that Gaura Dasa is not interested in the meaning of the acts that he performs. The ritualistic procedures, the devotional songs, and the prayers that he has been taught are satisfying in themselves. These acts create within Gaura Dasa feeling-states that lift him into the sacred sphere where he can experience the presence of the deity.

Nibaran seems to have mixed feelings about his son's vocation. On the one hand, he feels such a strong emotional attachment to his son that he will probably leave Gaura Dasa all his property, disinheriting his other two sons. On the other hand, he is somewhat reluctant to let Gaura Dasa take charge of the temple, for he fears that after his death his present patrons will stop their donations abruptly, leaving the temple and its residents to fend for themselves. He fears that cessation of patronage may lead his son to "religious beggary." In 1964, however, it appeared that the present Bengali patronage from Calcutta might be replaced by the support of several young Bengali families who had come to work in the New Capital and who were enthusiastic about devotions at the *maṅdira*.

The Troubadour (Virendra Natha Sadhukhan of the Chintamanishvara Mandira)

The Guru, the Preacher, and the two Bhaktas all followed different paths toward the goal of final release. The first two were men of learning and action; the last two were almost exclusively oriented toward devotional acts. Yet all four had one factor in common: they were Brahmans, who, though they may have known poverty, never had to face socio-religious discrimination from other castes.

It is rare for a Shudra to become a resident ascetic, since most orders refuse them entrance. In any case, it is difficult for a Shudra to obtain patronage from the higher castes. The following sketch presents the only Shudra ascetic resident in the Old Town. This man claimed that the family into which he was born had once been wealthy but had lost all its lands and money through a seemingly endless series of disasters. The informant took the vows of an ascetic upon reaching maturity and began to wander through northeastern India. His unusual musical talent enabled him to obtain patronage from some Bhubaneswar merchants and he settled in the Chintamanishvara Mandira, a "religious park" that had been established by a group of prominent Oria citizens.

This young Shudra ascetic, whose name was Virendra Natha Sadhukhan, heard that we were collecting life-histories of ascetics. In March 1964 he came to our house accompanied by a young Bengali who was employed as a clerk in the Secretariat. Virendra Natha said that he would dictate his life-history to the clerk, who would translate it from Bengali into English. Eight days later Virendra Natha handed us a "blue book" in which the clerk had transcribed the autobiography. This autobiography is typical of the man who has failed in the business world but who has gained fame in the religious sphere. The following is a slightly condensed version of the original statement as translated by the clerk who spoke and wrote English relatively well. In the interests of faithful reproduction of the Troubadour's self-told story, we have included the inconsistencies found in his manuscript.

Sachindra Natha Sadhukhan had two sons named Virendra Natha Sadhukhan (hereafter referred to in the first person) and Rabindra Natha Sadhukhan, and also a daughter named Larul Kala.

I was an enjoyable child. I played a lot, but I did not like to study. When my teacher forced me to study, I pretended not to hear her. So my teacher complained to my father about my disinterest in my studies. So my affectionate father persuaded me and also advised me to study. He explained the bright side of learning. In spite of it I did not study. One day my father beat me severely to correct me. A refugee from Pakistan who was renting from us observed this pathetic sight. He came forward and told my father, "After all he is a child, do not beat him." For a few days I began to study. I studied under the guidance of a teacher. Now I am repenting for my lack of interest. I was a naughty boy during my school career. I got into mischief with my classmates. I put pins under their seats during the time of roll call. When they took their seats, the pins penetrated into their bodies. I did not like a particular friend of mine. In order to take revenge on him I placed a pin on his seat. So he told the teacher. The teacher made me stand upon a bench for one half hour. After some days that boy passed by our roadside. I threw a small stone at his head. Alas, the stone struck his head and he began to bleed. No one was near to help, so he went home sobbing.

We owned about five hundred acres of land and two mud houses. We owned such a vast amount of land. So my father cultivated some of the land and some of the remainder he rented to others who paid in kind: paddy, wheat, jute, etc. My father took all the responsibilities of supervising the land. It was very difficult on the part of one man to supervise such a huge amount of land. So he fell ill. In addition to these possessions, we had six buildings in Krishnanagar. We rented out four of these buildings. The tenants did not pay us regularly on account of illness of my father. We sold fifty acres of land to pay for his treatment. My father gradually became well.

Also we owned thirteen granaries at Subaran, Bihar. A competitor to my father set fire to all of our granaries. They were reduced to ashes. The fire continued for four days. As the villagers were also against us, they did nothing to extinguish the fire. We were informed about this after the destruction of all our granaries. We sold one hundred acres of land in order to maintain such a huge family.

On another occasion my father went into partnership with another businessman. Actually my father was in need of money at that time. He was concerned about his previous position and respect. He wanted to regain his previous status. But he had no money. Again he sold two hundred acres of land, but the business later failed. He also sold another building in the town. In order to maintain daily expenses, he sold one hundred acres of land. He invested in a mustard oil company. He was paid Rs. 40 per month. It was an attractive salary in those days. He worked for a considerable time.

Again disorder in our family life occurred due to the Hindu–Muslim riots. It was started in the year 1946. As a result of this, all companies were closed. The mills stopped work. So my father returned home bankrupt. He left all his earnings and prospects. Because of his absence from the village, the villagers took over his last fifty acres of land. He also sold one of the buildings to a lawyer.

My mother became ill. She was admitted into the Gowari hospital for treatment. She suffered for eighteen days. All of a sudden her condition became serious and she died. My father was deeply saddened. After two months he sold his other buildings. He started a business in Dignagar. Again he received a pain in his stomach. He went to a doctor in Krishnanagar. The pain gradually increased. The village doctors advised him to go to Berhampur, Orissa, for better treatment. My father went there immediately, but he died after twenty-two days. The doctor informed my paternal uncle about his death.

We (Virendra Natha, his brother, and his sister) stayed in our uncle's house for a few days. Then I told my paternal aunt that I did not want my inheritance. I gave our former home as a gift to a poor man in need of a house. I was twenty-one years old. I looked for a job at Nabadwip. I worked for a business man. I sent a little money to my paternal aunt in order to arrange a marriage for my younger sister. They arranged a marriage for my sister.

At times I went to hear the Mahamantra "Hari Krishna, Hari Krishna, Krishna, Krishna, Hari, Hari. Hari Rama, Hari Rama, Rama, Rama, Hari, Hari." I practised this Mahamantra very often. The Mahamantra was recited by a group of men for a whole week. I participated with them. I sang the Mahamantra with all of the joy of my melodious voice. They became pleased with my musical abilities. They sang the Mahamantra throughout the town.

A fair was held every year in honour of the god Gopinatha at Ayardip, a few miles off from our residence. A group of men sang the Mahamantra with great enthusiasm. A son of a mill owner and I took the lead in the group. Sages from different parts of India came to that place to hear the Nama Sankirtana [chanting the names of God, that is, the Mahamantra]. Without any break I continued the chanting for five hours. One of my half brothers took an interest in the Mahamantra. We both fed the saints who gathered there. Once at 3 o'clock I proceeded to the temple of Gopala. I sang the Mahamantra very loudly until 7 o'clock. Many sages and saints also joined me. I lost consciousness. The others asked one of my friends to take me home. That friend stayed with me and tried to make me eat my meal. I did not want to eat anything. I do not know why such an incident took place.

We came back from the fair to Krishnanagar. I could not concentrate. I tried to work, but I could not. I had no interest in work. I went to my paternal uncle's house. When they saw me, they thought I was sick. They asked, "Are you suffering?" I said, "No, I am not suffering." I returned to Krishnanagar. I thought there would be no end to the tragedies and miseries in my life. I prayed to God to lessen the tragedies in my life. I thought about my younger brother. "Oh God descend down from heaven to help my younger brother." My relatives felt a change of situation would help me. They came to me and talked to me about my future. They advised me not to become a *sādhu* at such a young age. I told them I did not like to work for anyone. I took a small amount of money from them and returned to Krishnanagar.

I took religious instructions from a guru. I requested my younger brother to go to our paternal uncle's house. I advised him also to be obedient to them and to continue to study attentively. I remained in Nabadwip for four days. I met my sister before my departure to Puri.

I liked Puri very much. For a few days I lived near the Jagannatha Temple. I also liked to go to the sea shore. I found that in the back of the Jagannatha Temple the disciples of Omkarnathababa were singing the Mahamantra. I made friends with them. I led a very happy life there. They advised me to go to Bhubaneswar. I came to Bhubaneswar without taking any money from them. Bhubaneswar was about forty miles away. I had been advised to chant the Mahamantra as loud as possible. I was very glad to sing the Mahamantra. The inhabitants of the Capital derived pleasure out of my singing.

I liked Bhubaneswar very much because the architecture of the temples is excellent and the stone images are very beautiful. A man is sculptured just like a man; a horse just like a horse. Varieties of sinful social customs have been engraved on the temple walls. So I thought how beautiful will be my God. By His direction people engraved these monuments of stone. I occasionally was worried. I went to these temples and the impressions of the temple completely changed my mind. I forgot everything when I looked at them.

I travelled from place to place. I did not like to give my address to my relatives, but they kept a detailed account of me. They wrote many letters requesting me to return home. I mailed a letter that said: "Actually we have no relationship with each other. The former relationships are not real relationships. Everybody pretends to have a relationship. As long as one lives in this world, he is attached to a relationship. When he leaves this world for good, this attachment will be no more. I am waiting for those days when there will be an end to my life."

I derive pleasure by singing the name of God. I have a strong faith in Him. I have not seen Him. I am waiting for the days when I shall *see* Him.

Virendra Natha Sadhukhan found a temporary home at the Chintamanish-vara Mandira, where his "melodious voice" has attracted many others to join in the singing and chanting of the Mahamantra. The fact that he was a Shudra did not limit his popularity. Those who gathered about him were mostly Brahmans, although all castes were, at one time or another, represented. On one evening students at the Depressed League School, located one quarter mile north of the temple, participated in the singing.

In December 1964 Virendra Natha and his friend came again to my house. The clerk said that he was soliciting funds with which to purchase a portable harmonium for Virendra Natha. His plan was to have Virendra Natha walk about the New Capital playing the harmonium and chanting the Mahamantra. His hope was that through the beauty of Virendra Natha's voice the Mahamantra would be heard in all areas of the New Capital.

The other resident of the Chintamanishvara Mandira was a Shankara Brahmacharin named Mauna (silent) Babaji, a Gujarati Brahman of forty, who, after wandering across southern India, had settled in a small storehouse in one corner of the compound. Although he had taken a vow of silence, he had a marvellous talent for expressing himself with grunts, groans, and gestures, and had a wonderful sense of humour which made him one of the most popular ascetics in town. He spent much of his time outside the monastery, circulating among the laity at tea stalls or smoking *gañjā* and joking and pantomiming. He was also capable of serious endeavours. In spite of his vow of silence, he had supervised the construction of a small Hanuman Temple and a large bathing tank on the monastery grounds.

Virendra Natha, the Troubadour, was fiercely jealous of his fellow resident's popularity. He told the interpreter:

My guru has told me that it is not desirable to speak against others, but if somebody asks me I have to tell them. Mauna Babaji claims to be silent, but he is not silent. He sounds much when he needs to. He is silent so far as talking is concerned but he can express everything by gesture and posture. He is not doing any ritualistic duties now in the monastery and is performing neither meditations nor devotions. He spends most of his time outside the monastery and is now strongly addicted to smoking *gañjā* and to sitting in the tea stalls drinking tea. He is most fickle-minded and cannot sit in one place for a long time; this is not proper for a man who has renounced worldly life. Renunciation of worldly life does not mean mixing with all kinds of people and giving them noble advice, or taking ten cups of tea in the tea stall or engaging in cheap talk with shopkeepers or having jocular fights with friends by the roadside. When he came to this *mandira* he was as serious as possible, but every day he is becoming more light-headed.

Shortly after this, Virendra Sadhukhan took a vow of silence for two months, so that he could not be asked any further questions on the subject of his fellow resident.

The Solitary Ascetic (Bhavani Shankara Babaji of the Bhavani Shankara Matha)

Bhavani Shankara Babaji lived in a small temple adjacent to the Parvati Temple in the centre of the Old Town. He was typical of the solitary ascetic at a monastery, who must depend upon his clients for his food and clothing. Because he was client supported he did not beg for his food, but on a socio-religious scale of ascetics Bhavani Shankara Babaji would be at the bottom. At the Bhavani Shankara Matha the atmosphere was highly informal and personal. A sketch of the interior is included.

Bhavani Shankara had lost most of his paternal property in East Pakistan at the time of the Partition. In 1959, during a period of further Hindu–Muslim disturbances, he left his job in East Pakistan and became a self-styled Shankara Brahmacharin who neither took ascetic *dīkṣā* nor formally joined an order. He simply donned a pinkish cloth and a necklace of *rudrākṣa* beads and left his remaining property and his family of procreation in the hands of his brothers. He did not say whether or not he had a guru. He travelled to Bhubaneswar on a pilgrimage and came upon a small semi-abandoned temple with a reclining image of Parvati, an aspect of the consort of Shiva. Here he had a dream in which Durga, another aspect of Shiva's consort, promised to supply all his needs. For five years he used this small Parvati temple as his dwelling, at first depending upon donations from pilgrims, later upon two Old Town shop-keepers who became his clients. In 1964, annoyed by an increasing flow of pilgrims, he moved into the diagrammed building (see figure 1). This was an abandoned, imageless temple overgrown with brush which concealed an entrance about four feet below the present land level. Bhavani Shankara cut down the undergrowth, excavated the entrance, and installed a small shrine to Durga. This consisted of a wooden box with an eight-by-ten-inch print of Durga and prints of Shiva and Parvati.

The former audience hall of the temple served as his living room, where he talked with guests and at times smoked *gañjā*. The stone floor was clean and bare, except for three straw mats and an earthenware lamp that provided the only light. Bhavani Shankara had plastered the walls with mud, insulating the interior from the heat. He once remarked that his monastery was the only air-conditioned *maṭha* in the Old Town. The wooden box to the left of the entrance

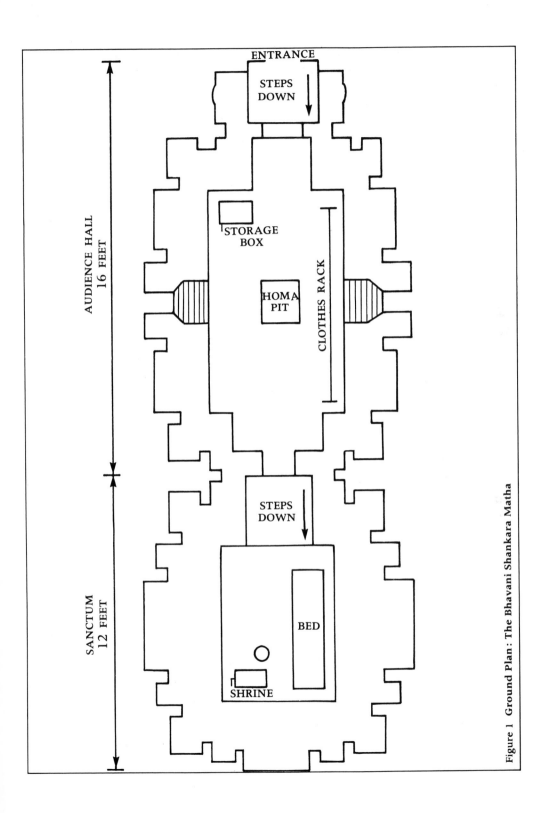

ENTRANCE

STEPS
DOWN

STORAGE
BOX

HOMA
PIT

CLOTHES RACK

AUDIENCE HALL
16 FEET

STEPS
DOWN

BED

SHRINE

SANCTUM
12 FEET

Figure 1 Ground Plan: The Bhavani Shankara Matha

contained the few items that Bhavani Shankara owned: a Bengali translation of the Upanishads, Bengali magazines, a brass plate and cup, a box of wooden matches, and several coconut husks. He burned cow dung in the temple's *homa* pit during the cold weather from November through January.

Bhavani Shankara had converted the former sanctum of the temple into his bedroom. Wooden crates formed the base of his bed, which had a thin mattress, a blanket, and a blanket-roll for a pillow. Bhavani Shankara said that he did not perform daily worship, but that he lit the *ghī* lamp in front of the shrine during the evening. Bhavani Shankara often played host to university students, who wandered in casually to eat, drink, smoke *gañjā*, and gossip, perhaps gaining some religious advice in the course of a rambling afternoon's talk. Sometimes he would give counsel and spread gossip, not at his "monastery," but at the local tea stalls, which gladly provided him free tea in exchange for his talk and the occasional business he attracted. Many solitary ascetics, having no large institution to administer, had nothing else to do but to go from tea stall to tea stall, perhaps imparting some bits of religious knowledge here and there in the course of an afternoon.

When we visited Bhavani Shankara's monastery, often accompanied by Kamakara Brahmacharin, the Fun-Lover, we would usually smoke *gañjā*, using what Bhavani Shankara called an "Indian pipe," made of clay.

Typical of our conversations while smoking *gañjā* was the following, which occurred during the second pipeful. Pointing to his pipe, Bhavani Shankara said: "This is my father, my mother, my guru." A pause occurred as he inhaled. Then he said, "I want to go to America—Chicago, like Vivekananda." As we took the pipe and inhaled, Kamakara Brahmacharin said, "If you take *gañjā* for three days then you go to Ganga [the Ganges]." He laughed. We passed the pipe to Kamakara Brahmacharin and asked, "What is the test of a true *sādhu*, like Vivekananda?" Kamakara answered, "When you are not excited when you see a nude woman, when a female reaches into your pants and holds your penis, there will be nothing. Then you will see the deity; then you will become a true *sādhu*. If you spend semen by lady or hand, then you will not get concentration." This "test of a true *sādhu*" represents an ancient folk tradition still popular among the less sophisticated ascetics.

At this point a short stocky man, dressed in the ochre cloth of a *sannyāsin*, appeared in the entrance-way. Bhavani Shankara asked him to enter and introduced him as Naga Tapasya Kalasa Giri. The first element of his name indicated that he belonged to the militant section of the Dashanamis. The Naga Sannyasins traditionally wear little clothing except a band of cloth covering their genitals.

Kalasa was completely robed, and his face, hands, and feet were swollen. Later Bhavani Shankara explained that his acquaintance was a leper.[2]

Before the onset of his infection, Kalasa had been a cook at the Kapileshwar Temple. After he contracted leprosy, he was forced to abandon his profession and entered monastic orders as an alternative. He lived in Tapas Cave near the village of Kapileshwar.

Kalasa sat down and took his turn puffing the pipe. He used his own rag for a filter. No one seemed to be alarmed that he was a leper. Utilizing Kamakara as an interpreter, we interviewed Kalasa. He frequently addressed us as "Sahib," a term of respect that none of our other informants had used. At the conclusion of the interview Kalasa said something to Bhavani Shankara, who immediately exploded in anger. Kalasa arose and departed. Kamakara then told us: "The *sannyāsin* was a tourist *sannyāsin* [wandering ascetic], a beggar. He demanded that you buy [him] a new cloth; the *bābājī* [Bhavani Shankara] was angered at the rudeness of the *sannyāsin*'s request. The *bābājī* does not beg for money."

This situation revealed a major difference between a resident solitary ascetic and a religious beggar. Although Bhavani Shankara might be near the bottom of the scale if all our informants were ranked according to social status, he never asked for money. As an expression of our appreciation for his cooperation, we gave him a Bengali translation of the Bhagavad Gita, which he treasured. Because he possessed the kind of engaging personality that attracted lay support, Bhavani Shankara did not have to beg for a living.

Kalasa, on the other hand, was typical of the religious beggar who actively plays upon the sympathies of the pious in order to gain food and clothing. Often, the physically handicapped, such as Kalasa Giri, who wore the robes of an ascetic as a means of livelihood, were devoid of religious feeling or training.

Summary

Gaura Dasa, the bhakta, was a Madhva Gaudiya who knew no Sanskrit. He was neither an intellectual nor a social activist nor an able administrator. He had been a failure in the business world, but the intensity of his religious

---

2. The name Kalasi is actually a title assumed by shaman-like religious curers throughout Orissa who devote themselves to the worship of the goddess Kali. The Kapileshwar Temple is noted as a pilgrimage centre for the cure of leprosy. See James Freeman, "Power and Leadership in a Changing Temple Village of India."

devotion at daily worship communicated the depths of his religious feeling to all of those who participated with him in the presence of the deity.

The Troubadour was in many respects like Gaura Dasa. He communicated the intensity of his religious feeling through devotional songs. Like Gaura Dasa, the Troubadour had been a failure in the business world, but whereas Gaura Dasa's father had secured patronage for his monastery, the Troubadour was dependent upon donations from his clients. The Troubadour, therefore, had some characteristics of the solitary ascetic.

The only distinction between Bhavani Shankara, the Solitary Ascetic of this chapter, and a religious mendicant or an ordinary beggar posing as one was that Bhavani Shankara was sedentary and was supported by regular clients. The solitary ascetics in Bhubaneswar in 1964 seemed to provide lower socio-economic groups with sacred centres where gregariousness was tempered by a "folk" version of the ascetic tradition. The wide range of ascetic lifestyles encountered in this chapter and the one just preceding can be taken as an example of the difficulty, and even the artificiality, of attempting to make a classification of Indian ascetics.

Chapter 3

Three

Atypical

Life

Histories

Although we lack any systematic study of the
variety of resident ascetics in an Indian community, we may assume that the preceding six life
histories could be duplicated in any major pilgrimage centre. In this sense, they are "typical,"
even though they represent a considerable range.
The three histories described in this chapter are
all atypical in the sense that they include unusual characteristics and that they are considered
atypical by the lay community. Nevertheless all
three ascetics whose histories appear in this
chapter perceived themselves as sincere followers
of a religious path and so described themselves
to the interviewer. Only subsequent observations suggested a discrepancy between their
self-perceived roles and the estimation of the
community. The sobriquets given to these three
atypical ascetics are the Fun-Lover, the Mendicant, and the Babaji.

The Fun-Lover and the Mendicant represent
two very different personalities residing in the
same monastery of a Vairagin order. The Fun-
Lover enjoyed singing *kīrtanas* and holding
private festivals inside the monastery, whereas
the Mendicant said that he was concerned with
austerities and mystical knowledge. This kind
of situation is not in itself unusual; it is possible
for a wide range of personalities to co-exist
within the same institution. What is unusual in
this situation is that the two ascetics engaged in
a power struggle for headship, with the loser
returning to secular life. Although Vairagins
are generally free to return to secular life at any

time, this is the only instance that we encountered of anyone doing so. The story of the Fun-Lover is especially atypical in its ending.

The Babaji was, strictly speaking, not an ascetic at all. He still retained his family of procreation and had taken no vows. Nonetheless, he had abandoned his vocation in order to devote himself to "the welfare of humanity" and spent much of his time in the company of a solitary ascetic at a monastery near his home.

He was a marginal man living between worldly and ascetic realms. Despite his self-estimation, he enjoyed less respect from the lay community than any of the other eight individuals described in these chapters. Individuals like the Babaji are in contemporary terms self-appointed welfare workers who appear to unsophisticated observers as holy men.

The Fun-Lover and the Mendicant (Kamakara Brahmacharin and Arthadushana Brahmacharin of the Hari Krishna Matha)

The absence of absolutistic controls within Hinduism allows individuals of very different temperaments to co-exist within the same order, though inter-relationships are not without friction.

Occasionally two ascetics with divergent origins, motives, and personal characteristics find themselves living in the same monastery. The situation may lead to the kind of conflict described in the following sketch. Because the resolution of the conflict is distinctly atypical of ascetics resident at Bhubaneswar, pseudonyms are used to protect the identities of the two disputants and their monastery.

The Hari Krishna Matha was a branch of a Madhva Gaudiya sub-order with its headquarters in Calcutta. In October 1963 the only resident ascetic was a twenty-nine-year-old Bengali: Kamakara Brahmacharin. As his title indicates, Kamakara was still a novice ascetic whose head ascetic in Calcutta had not admitted him to full vows, even though this man had placed Kamakara in charge of the Bhubaneswar branch monastery. Kamakara spoke fluent English, but at first was unwilling to talk about himself. All he would divulge was that his guru had instructed him that upon taking monastic vows "his past deeds were forgotten and he now had the virtues of a child." Music proved to be the interviewer's chief method of contact. A follower of the bard Chaitanya, Kamakara enjoyed playing the harmonium and was willing to sing for the interviewer some songs of Rabindranath Tagore in exchange for being taught some Western songs. Within two months Kamakara had overcome his reluctance to talk about his past, though his stories varied from time to time as he polished certain episodes to make a more acceptable version.

On one occasion Kamakara said that he had a B.A. from the University of Calcutta; on another occasion he stated that he had not finished the degree course, although he had completed three years of university work. In any case, during his college days K. C. Banarji, as he was known then, must have been a fun-loving, light-hearted fellow who would rather sing than study. In our conversations he made no mention of his academic studies. Rather he noted with pride that as a college student he had played bit parts in three movies filmed in Calcutta. We were told that during the same period he began to "take up with prostitutes."

After college he became a manager at one of his father's five factories, which he said manufactured hand tools, shovels, and hammers. He indicated on several occasions that his father had been extremely wealthy, but after 1950 had lost a considerable sum in the failure of two banks. In despair, the father sold his factories and gave Rs. 100,000 to build four monasteries. According to Kamakara, his father then "lived like a *sannyāsin*." Finally, after a five-month illness, his "lungs burst." Within two years after the death of his father, Kamakara's mother and sister died.

Kamakara was then forced to take a position in the import department of the Calcutta Customs Office. He claimed that his salary was Rs. 500 per month but that he and four other inspectors often received as much as Rs. 3000 in bribes given by wealthy Calcutta importers who sought to bring contraband goods into India. Sometime in the late fifties he became implicated in a customs scandal and consequently lost his job. When pressed for details, he changed his story and said that he was laid off because of a slowdown in imports.

In 1959 he became a part-time movie actor and played minor roles in four Bengali films. When we knew him, he still took an active interest in the "bathing beauty" pictures in Bengali movie magazines.

By 1960 his personal crises had become overwhelming. In search of a way out of his troubles, he went to a renowned *sādhu* resident in Calcutta and requested admission into his monastic order. The *sādhu* initiated him and sent him to his Bhubaneswar monastery for "rest and meditation." He took the religious name Kamakara Brahmacharin and had been at the monastery for three years before we met him.

Kamakara was actually an apprentice *brahmacārin* who had never taken the final vows of a *naiṣṭhika brahmacārin*. He claimed that either his guru in Calcutta or his own conscience would decide when he was prepared to take final vows. It became clear that he believed that he had not yet passed the "test of a true *sādhu*" which he believed was complete sexual control under any conditions. He also believed in abstaining from killing. To illustrate the point, he kept in his kitchen a glass jar containing a scorpion nearly two inches long, about which he told the following story:

> One day I was sitting on the verandah of my *āśrama* entertaining several guests with music from my harmonium. A cry from a man nearby warned me that there was a scorpion with tail arched ready to strike, poised on my left thigh. I remained motionless and called for a glass jar. I talked softly in Bengali to the scorpion, coaxing it to enter the jar, where it now lives happily on a diet of mud and water. The scorpion has grown larger since its capture and seems to be fond of Bengali music. This scorpion is the symbol of my life as an ascetic. I will never destroy the scorpion, since I am opposed to all forms of killing.

Kamakara was an easy-going, fun-loving ascetic who enjoyed smoking *gañjā* and gossiping. He was serious, however, about his vocation as a singer of religious songs. In February 1964 he organized and presided over a Sarasvati Puja, a festival in honour of the goddess of art and learning, held at his monastery. The festival drew a sizable audience and created much good will for the monastery among the Bengali community.

Kamakara enjoyed a few comforts that, while not luxurious, surpassed the limits customarily expected of an ascetic. On one occasion he asked the interviewer to bring him a transistor radio worth Rs. 36 from Calcutta. On another occasion he ate fish in the monastery, breaking a dietary rule. On the whole, however, he represented the joyful, outgoing, artistic aspects of his order rather than the austere, intellectual, or meditative aspects.

In February 1964 a wandering mendicant forty-eight years of age named Arthadushana Brahmacharin arrived in Bhubaneswar. After attending the Sarasvati Puja at the Hari Krishna Matha he stayed on. Kamakara had been head ascetic and only resident for over three years. Now he was host to a visiting mendicant of the same order who had appeared by accident and who was tired of wandering. Arthadushana decided to settle down in Kamakara's monastery. Conflict was inevitable, for the two were of opposite temperaments and widely differing ages.

Arthadushana was born and raised in East Bengal, now known as Bangladesh. His mother and father died before he was eleven years old, but with the assistance of his paternal uncle he managed the family cloth shop. Located near his shop was a monastery where he claimed he often went for "spiritual uplift." In his early twenties he married, and in 1950 he, his wife, and two children went to Calcutta, where they stayed with his wife's father. For a short time he worked in a cotton mill, but soon lost his job, and one year later, at the age of thirty-five, he decided to enter monastic orders. He left his wife and children with his father-in-law. A major reason for his adoption of the ascetic life was his inability to support his family. His wife became a domestic servant. He did not concern himself about his children's education. The same Calcutta *sādhu* who nine years later admitted Kamakara into his order initiated him. For the next thirteen years Arthadushana wandered about India begging. He arrived in Bhubaneswar a few days before the 1964 celebration of Sarasvati Puja. When we met Arthadushana Brahmacharin, he was still wearing the ochre cloth characteristic of a mendicant; his hair and beard were disheveled and his body odour indicated that he had not bathed for several days.

Sometime during the week of 22 March 1964, Arthadushana left Bhubaneswar for Calcutta. There he told his guru that Kamakara had eaten meat and drunk wine at the monastery, squandered money that was to be used for the maintenance of the monastery, and engaged in sexual intercourse with the daughter of the doctor who had attended Sarasvati Puja. The guru immediately wrote Kamakara informing him of Arthadushana's charges and requesting him to come to Calcutta in order to clarify matters. The guru made no mention of disciplinary action that might be taken against Kamakara. On 30 March, Kamakara received his guru's letter and was greatly disturbed. He left the monastery, stating that he was going to Puri and would not return. In the second week of April the guru placed Arthadushana Brahmacharin in charge of his Bhubaneswar branch.

We knew that the charge of eating fish at the monastery was true. We doubted, however, that Kamakara Brahmacharin had been guilty of all charges. He neither served us liquor nor did he ask us to purchase it for him. When asked if he had any evidence to support his charge that Kamakara had engaged in sexual intercourse, Arthadushana replied that Kamakara and the doctor's daughter had been seen together, walking down Kotitirtha Road, an avenue that was heavily travelled during the daytime. Kamakara, however, did not return; he was, therefore, guilty in the estimation of his guru.

In a series of interviews, Arthadushana made several statements that were pietistic glosses of his accusations against Kamakara Brahmacharin. On one occasion he said:

Sādhus who sing and beat a drum do not satisfy the deity. Rather, the deity is only pleased with meditational prayer, the recitation of a *mantra* at every breathing.

If anybody has a desire [*kāma*] in his heart, then that desire should be fulfilled; if he has a desire for sex, then he should fully satisfy it. The desire will not come again. Kamakara gave much importance to wine, sex, and musical performances. Until these are completely satisfied, he will not have *darśana* [the vision of the deity].

The new head ascetic, Arthadushana, was anxious to talk about a problem that he was having with an exploratory engineer who continued to board at the monastery. On 10 July the boarder and three of his friends "travelled across the verandah floor with their shoes on." They thus broke a rule that Artha-dushana had enforced since the departure of Kamakara. Arthadushana reminded his boarder about the rule, but the engineer and his friends ignored the ascetic and continued across the verandah. Later in the day the engineer angrily confronted Arthadushana and said: "The next time you attempt to embarrass me in front of my friends I will pull out your beard and send you to the hospital."

One hour after he had threatened Arthadushana, the boarder became ill with a high fever. Arthadushana interpreted this illness as a punishment for one who committed evil acts. He said: "When he rebuked me, then he rebuked my chosen deity. If I am wrong, I will be punished, but if he, then he will suffer. I want to keep to all the rules of my guru. If anyone violates a rule, then he becomes a sinner."

The boarder admitted that he had threatened the ascetic and that later in the day he had had fever. He did not believe that the two events were related.

In July Kamakara Brahmacharin returned to Bhubaneswar. He had shaved his beard, cut his hair, and adopted modern dress: a gray sports shirt, black slacks, and light gray loafers. He shook hands and said, "I am a changed man. Can you recognize me? My name is K. C. Banarji once again." He introduced his female travelling companion as Nani Bala Devi from Calcutta, and he said: "Arthadushana blamed my name! He saw what a good life I was leading, and he told lies, all lies. Now he is living very well. But I am free, free as a bird. I am like a lark in the open sky. During the period of my *sādhu* life I was like a caged bird."

When he had received his guru's letter, he had first thought of going to Calcutta but decided to go to Puri instead. An old friend sheltered him for several days and eventually talked to him into leaving his ascetic life and enter-ing into the business world. With the friend's financial support Banarji became a fountain pen salesman. This lasted for less than a month. Then he met Nani Bala Devi, whom he had known before he entered monastic orders in 1960.

Nani Bala was selling medicated salves, labelled Kaviraja Oil and Ring Worm Ointment, and she persuaded him to become her partner. In the past two months they had made a considerable profit. Kamakara hinted that they might marry in the near future. Nani Bala said she had been influenced by the teachings of the Ramakrishna Matha. She said, "It is vague, monotonous, and boring to sit in a monastery and worship the deity all day without doing any social duty. It is better to perform some daily duty and to earn a livelihood." She had advised Kamakara, "Do not spoil your young life by becoming a *sannyāsin*." She also believed it proper to be a family man first: "An old man can always worship the deity." Nani Bala Devi summarized her views on the ascetic life in one sentence: "It's for old age." Banarji was less talkative than he had been in the past, and soon he asked to leave. That was the last we saw or heard of K. C. Banarji, the former Kamakara Brahmacharin.

The next day Arthadushana said that K. C. Banarji had visited his monastery. He seemed relieved that the former ascetic had left monastic orders without confronting his guru in Calcutta. Furthermore, his guru had written that if a boarder did not conform to the monastery rules, Arthadushana should call in the police and eject him. He was now confident of his position as head ascetic.

When we saw Arthadushana for the last time, he had returned from Calcutta wearing a heavy yellow-coloured cloth that his guru had presented to him. His hair and beard had been combed and in all respects he looked and acted the part of a head ascetic. He offered us rice that had been presented before the *lingam* at the Lingaraja Mahaprabhu Temple earlier in the day. The rice was cold and lumpy; nevertheless it was believed to be the most sacred food that one could eat in Bhubaneswar. The young boy who served it used the title Thakur (Bengali, chief) whenever he addressed Arthadushana.

Thus in the space of one year a wandering ascetic who was a complete newcomer to Bhubaneswar had overturned and driven out an established head ascetic who liked to enjoy himself but was not as guilty as charged. The former head ascetic had cheerfully returned to secular life and appeared to be making a try at both career and marriage. He would have undoubtedly continued life as an ascetic, a role that he enjoyed, had Arthadushana not carried at least partly false tales to their guru.

The struggle between the Fun-Lover and the Mendicant was the only case of this sort which came to our attention in the monastic life of Bhubaneswar, though similar rivalries undoubtedly appear all over India. Kamakara's simple, child-like enjoyment of *gañjā*, movie magazines, his harmonium, and his scorpion "pet" are probably characteristic of many solitary ascetics who enjoy an independent way of life. Kamakara's mistake was to enter a monastery in which he was subject to discipline by a superior. Kamakara's eventual return to secular life is unusual, although both spiritually and socially admissible. At least one other ascetic in Bhubaneswar had contemplated such a return.

The Babaji ("Dr. Refugee")

The term *bābājī*, literally "old man," is generally applied to any grizzled, bearded, rather eccentric individual with a leaning towards the religious life. A *bābājī* may be a solitary ascetic residing in a small monastery, like Bhavani Shankara Babaji or the three other solitary ascetics living under similar circumstances. A *bābājī* may also be someone who lives a fringe existence somewhere between the ascetic and secular ways of life. Such a person may spend many of his waking hours around a monastery and may maintain close relationships with several ascetics. At night, however, he returns to his wife and children. The Bhaktas' monastery, for instance, played daily host to a Shudra cowherd from a neighbouring village who spent most of his time in devotions instead of herding cows and thus acquired the nickname *bābājī*. Sometimes a man of this character would leave his family of procreation entirely to the care of another relative and would take the vows of an ascetic, as had Mauna Babaji of the Chintamanishvara Mandira.

The most interesting *bābājī* in Bhubaneswar was Dr. Refugee, a man whose religious energies expressed themselves primarily in the area of "social welfare." Dr. Refugee had no real desire to take the vows of a *sādhu*, which would require him to spend too much time in the formal worship of the deity and would cut him off from the dozen or so secular committees of which he claimed to be a member. He definitely believed that "social work" on behalf of mankind was the most worthwhile form of worship and he was continually seeking new causes to espouse. Because he had dedicated his life to "the welfare of mankind" in rather poorly defined terms, and because of his somewhat limited mind, he could not grasp political realities on a national or even provincial scale. He was potentially an unwitting agent for any faction or group that wished to stir up discontent among less educated people. Although he was one of the least attractive personalities whom we encountered, his life history is in some ways representative of those who live on the margins of the ascetic life without ever taking vows.

"Doctor" Refugee, as he chose to style himself on the basis of several years as a travelling drug salesman, was about five feet tall, weighed ninety pounds, had flowing hair, a straggly beard, a worn *dhoti*, and a peculiarly intense expression reminiscent of the face of Jesus in some old Gospel films. At one point Refugee, who was no advocate of non-violence, had tried to join the Home Guard and had been rejected for refusing to trim his beard.

Dr. Refugee had no brothers or other family who could support his wife and four children, so he returned to them every night but made little or no attempt to provide for them. In 1964 he was living with his family in a two-room unfurnished shack in a sparsely populated area between the Chintamanishvara Mandira and the village of Lakshmisagara where he spent much of his time. After Dr. Refugee had been evicted from several houses in Lakshmisagara for non-payment of rent, a patron had given him use of this shack rent-free in order to have someone around to protect his house from robbers. Dr. Refugee used one room as his "homeopathic dispensary"; this consisted of a bench, a note-book, and a chest with perhaps a dozen patent medicines. He claimed to make fifteen to twenty rupees a day by treating patients, but during the many after-noons we spent there we saw no patients. What little money he received prob-ably came from distributing propaganda leaflets of various sorts and from the sporadic support of occasional clients. His standard of living was even lower than that of the poorest solitary ascetic in Bhubaneswar. The solitary ascetics could at least count upon regular contributions from clients, but Dr. Refugee and his family often awoke with neither food nor money.

Professor Cora Du Bois held a series of six interviews with the informant in 1963.[1] We followed these up in 1964 with some day-to-day observations of his life in the community. There was a considerable gap between the ideal self that he tried to project in interviews and his activities in reality. During the inter-views he persistently refused to answer questions pertaining in any way to his childhood or present family life. Instead of claiming that he had renounced his past, as most ascetics could legitimately do, Dr. Refugee became incoherent and started to repeat long series of place names or committee names in a high, sing-song voice. Dr. Refugee blocked in this manner every time he was questioned about personal relations involving intimacy; he also blocked sometimes when he tried to tell a story that was obviously a lie. For instance, the pilgrimages "all over India" that he had never made turned into an incoherent repetition of place names.

In practice, much of his "piety" was unctuous and hypocritical; he made a point of bowing elaborately before every image he passed. He described youth

1. Much of the material of this biographical sketch is taken from Cora Du Bois, "Interviews with Dr. Refugee, July 25–August 27, 1963" (notes in the files of the Harvard–Bhubaneswar Project, Cambridge, Mass.).

clubs that he had founded, committees of which he was president, and important people with whom he had close relations. The following life-history has been reconstructed from interviews.

Like Arthadushana, Dr. Refugee was born in 1921 or 1922 in East Bengal, of Bengali Vaishya parents. He claimed that his grandfather was a Tantric Yogi Sannyasin and that his father was a landowner, a tax collector, a member of the village council of elders (*pañchāyat*), and also a "social worker." A social worker, in Dr. Refugee's terms, is one who does favours for others. The family apparently received considerable revenue from its landholdings until the partition of India in 1947, when the extended family unit was "splintered like a bomb" by the Muslims. The partition did not affect Dr. Refugee directly, however, because he had moved to Calcutta some years before.

The overwhelmingly traumatic event of his childhood was the death of his mother when he was seven. He never recovered from this loss and ever afterwards sought a "mother." (A female interviewer was continually addressed as "mother" and was asked to love and protect him.) More importantly, the goddess Buddheshvari, whose partly buried image he claims to have unearthed from three feet of dirt near the railway station in 1953, has become his mother–protector. When the family wakes up without food or money, his answer is, "The goddess Buddheshvari is our mother, and she *must* provide for us."

Dr. Refugee claims that his father neglected him in order to do social work, just as he is now neglecting his own family. He blames parental neglect for his own failure to pass the matriculation examination after Class 11. At the age of thirteen, he moved to his maternal uncle's house in Calcutta, but says that his uncle did not support him and that he had to make his own way. He describes his youth thus: "From childhood I was very daring and never cared for anyone. I was a dangerous boy. If I wanted to kill a man, I killed. Also, I was a hunter. So I didn't get educated. Mother died when I was a boy. Father neglected me sometimes. He was a social worker and very busy." This self-description actually applied well to Dr. Refugee's oldest son, a young rebel of thirteen who refused to attend school, did not respect his father, and wandered around town looking for trouble.

In Calcutta, the informant held various jobs, first as an usher at a movie theatre, then as a clerk in the Government Ration Bureau, as a laboratory assistant, and finally as a travelling salesman for a drug company.

When he was twenty-two, his father died. He collected rents from the family land to gather Rs. 1,000 for the funeral, said farewell to his sister, and thereupon ended all ties with his parental family. A year later a distant relative arranged a marriage for him in Calcutta. A year or two after his marriage, a drug firm asked him to represent them in both Orissa and Bihar, but Dr. Refugee refused, saying that if he were to cover two states, he would have to neglect his wife, and more importantly, his social work. After a dispute with his boss about whether or not he should obey the company's orders, Dr. Refugee quit, saying he would "obey only the deity."

He then settled near Bhubaneswar, in housing provided by the government for Bengali refugees from East Pakistan on the outskirts of the village of Lakshmisagara. First, he started a stationery shop in the railway station, using all his wife's ornaments as capital, but this failed within a month. Next, he entered into partnership with a pharmacist as an assistant. This relationship ended after a dispute, and his former partner succeeded in evicting Dr. Refugee from his lodgings because he had failed to register as a refugee. He then became an assistant at the Ramakrishna Mission Dispensary for a few months, but was asked to leave. He set up his own homeopathic dispensary in the house of a former patient in Lakshmisagara, where he treated various minor ailments. He referred serious cases, like tuberculosis or cholera, to the hospital in the New Capital. By 1964 he had moved his "dispensary" to his own two-room shack.

While in Calcutta, he had come under the influence of the Ramakrishna Mission and had been greatly impressed by their humanitarian and non-sectarian point of view. He also read some of Vivekananda's writings, which he was very fond of quoting in order to impress the interviewer. In addition, he had some garbled notions of Shankara's philosophy and of the life of Jesus, whom he admired as "a great medical man." He claimed that he had no guru to help him find his way in life and that he had to struggle alone. When pressed, he would admit that the humanitarianism of Vivekananda had influenced his activities. He would repeat stentoriously the following quotation reportedly from Ramakrishna: "Life is strength, weakness is death. Strength is felicity, life is eternal, immortal. Weakness is constant strain and misery. There are no Christians, Hindus, Mohammedans. We are all brothers."

After settling in Lakshmisagara, Dr. Refugee immediately became involved in a variety of social welfare activities that took most of his time. He identified with youth, with the Scheduled Castes, and with the poor. He was continually looking for minority grievances to adopt as "causes." Sometimes he seemed to enjoy meddling for its own sake. His most notable achievement was the elimination of the illegal production and sale of toddy (a hard liquor made from palm sap) in Lakshmisagara, a "moral success" that the people of the village did not exactly appreciate, though it was Dr. Refugee's major claim to fame. He helped the refugees from East Pakistan by writing letters on their behalf to government officials. He also organized the poor to halt an urban renewal plan that would have destroyed their mud huts in order to build more substantial housing for wealthier groups. He said he was not opposed to "slum clearance" as long as housing was provided for the poor. His name appears alongside the names of many prominent and wealthy men as a member of the Managing Committee that repaired the Chintamanishvara Mandira.

These were Dr. Refugee's visible achievements; his claimed achievements, however, far exceeded anything we could discern in 1964. He claimed to have started evening adult classes in Lakshmisagara, a school for Scheduled Caste members that failed after two months for lack of attendance, and spinning classes for women. The spinning classes only lasted six months. The project collapsed because nobody could afford to buy a spinning wheel. He also started a women's club (but could not remember the president's name) and three "youth groups" to oppose liquor. There was no evidence of any of these projects in 1964. He did take an active interest in the nearby Buddheshvari Temple and School, and in the government Depressed League Training School where boys from Scheduled Castes learned stone-cutting.

These are the positions he claimed to hold in 1964: doctor in a charitable dispensary; Secretary of a local social committee; secretary, Buddheshvari Temple Committee; Secretary, Buddheshvari Primary School; President, Buddheshvari Youth Club; Director, Stone-Cutting Society at the Depressed League School; Mandal Congress Party committee member; General Director, All-Orissa Refugee Association; Secretary, New Capital Motor Drivers' Association; organizer of sixteen youth clubs.

Many of these positions, particularly the last few, existed only in the informant's mind. We accompanied him throughout Lakshmisagara and noticed that people did not treat him with any particular respect, although he considered himself the most highly esteemed person in the whole village. When we visited the Depressed League School together, the Scheduled Caste boys with whom he so closely identified himself were not eager to see him. The directors of the school greeted his solitary ascetic friend warmly, but paid no attention to Dr. Refugee. Actually he did not receive the respect accorded even the lowliest solitary ascetic. Nevertheless, he derived satisfaction from his welfare activities. While neglecting his personal family, he regarded "the whole world" as his family. "I cannot look after my three sons and my daughter. Every day people come, poor people, people with tuberculosis, patients; some come for help because their house burned, some come from other villages because of quarrels which they want arbitrated. When they come and cry in front of me, I forget my family affairs. As I told you, our inside problems and our outside problems, all are our sins." All India became his "mother"; the interviewer became his "mother"; the children in the Buddheshvari School became his children; a business partner became his "father" or "brother."

There was nothing particularly unusual about Dr. Refugee's loss of his mother at an early age or his inability to relate to his wife and children. Many people with this kind of background would simply abandon their families and become full-fledged ascetics. Dr. Refugee, however, did not take vows, and when asked whether he had even considered becoming a *sādhu*, he went into incoherency about a celebrated call-girl scandal in England that currently was making headlines in the Indian press, Jesus Christ, and prostitution, and ended with a garbled version of the Mary Magdalene story. He admired the saintliness of ascetics who withdrew from the world, but identified himself only with those ascetics, like Vivekananda, who devoted their lives to the welfare of humanity. He associated committee work, rather than rituals or meditations, with religion; for him, the committee, not the monastery or temple, was the modern institutional vehicle for religion. Education was to be the key to social change. He said, "I believe in the deity; I believe in education. They are like the sun and the moon. We cannot live without the sun and the moon."

Here was an ironic combination of a rationalistic, activistic, and progressive orientation in a man who was an irrational talker rather than a doer. He genuinely identified with the poor and the outcast, yet was pitifully unable to relate to others, even to the extent of listening to their questions. He had devoted himself and all his resources to generalized "others" and to "causes." His one emotional outlet occurred at *kīrtanas*, when he fainted if his feelings became too strong to control. On the other hand, he helped some people and was a potential agent of social change. The somewhat neurotic tendencies exhibited by Dr. Refugee are not altogether atypical of some "holy men."

Dr. Refugee stood at the bottom of the scale of "resident ascetics" in terms of the traditional expectations of learning, charismatic qualities, and performance of austerities. Nonetheless, more men like him may appear in the future; instead of channeling their needs for affection, recognition, and security into the traditional role of the ascetic who withdraws from the world and devotes himself to a search for personal salvation, thereby acquiring qualities of "holiness," such men may turn increasingly toward works of social concern and may even reject the ascetic role as "selfish." The man who fails completely in secular life and uses asceticism as a way out may earn respect once established as an ascetic. The man with neither learning nor charismatic qualities who "devotes himself to humanity" without the protection of ascetic garb may be simply regarded as a failure. Until and unless a new role becomes established for humanitarians who do not wish to become ascetics in the traditional sense of withdrawal from secular life, existence will be difficult for self-appointed "social workers," even those who do not have grave psychological handicaps.

Chapter 4

The Development of the Monastic Career

The autobiographies of the previous chapters have provided glimpses of the monastic careers of eight ascetics and of one who lived on the fringe of asceticism. In this chapter we shall present a summary of the monastic career, looking at the motives for entrance, the initiation rites, ranks of ascetics and finally peak religious experiences, which are sought as the culmination and indeed the validation of the religious quest.

Table 17 presents the eleven categories of personal information that we have been able to secure for thirty-two ascetics and compares these with the social structure and monastic order of the monastery to which the ascetic belongs. Tables 3 and 4 taken together give a general picture of the kinds of socio-religious backgrounds from which ascetics tend to come.

Our informants enjoyed storytelling for its own sake and tended to exaggerate or at least to stress their childhood misdeeds, the hardships of the ascetic life, and the importance of dreams or divine interventions. Often the same story changed considerably over the course of four or five interviews. Later versions of a story, though more elaborate, were not necessarily more accurate. Certainly the ascetics' sense of chronology was often casual. Similarly, what theoretically should be, often took the place of what actually was. For example, one ascetic listed all the medicines in his homeopathic dispensary. On checking the dispensary shelves, we found only aspirin and a few patent medicines. The same ascetic claimed that his dispensary served 150 patients a day, representing his ideal, while the resident homeopath claimed thirty patients, and the true number was probably even fewer. Another ascetic listed the scholarly books that were in his personal library. In actuality, the library shelves were almost bare, and the ascetic's level of reading tended to be newspapers and popular books. Neither ascetic was lying by his own standards; both had simply confused the ideal and the real.

Ascetics were undoubtedly sincere in descriptions of visions of the deity. These visions were regarded with utmost seriousness and gave the beholder hope of release from the cycle of rebirth. Thus there was no ultimate profit to be gained by falsely claiming a vision one had not had. Indeed, such a claim might produce an evil *karma* leading to rebirth in a lower form of existence.

Table 3
A Comparison between Shankara and Vairagin Orders

	SANNYASINS OR SHANKARA BRAHMACHARINS (15 INFORMANTS)	VAIRAGINS (15 INFORMANTS)
Socio-religious group	Mostly Brahmans	All socio-religious groups represented, including one Shudra
Type of schooling	5 attended Sanskrit school 10 attended public school	1 attended Sanskrit school 14 attended public school
Previous occupation	Sanskrit students and teachers, Ayur-vedic practitioners, a *hotṛ* priest, one landowner, a few merchants (most come from traditional occupations connected with religion)	Merchants, artisans, civil servants, draftsman, two tenant farmers (most are from secular occupations and are less schooled in tradition)
Average age	55 years	43 years
Average years of residence in Bhubaneswar	16 years	7 years—5 arrivals in 1963–64
Distribution by social structure of monastery	4 in endowed monasteries 8 in patronized monasteries 3 in non-corporate monasteries	0 in endowed monasteries 11 in patronized monasteries 4 in non-corporate monasteries
Property rights	Forbidden to own or transmit* property to heirs, except in cases of hereditary headship	May own and transmit property; may be a householder
	No correlation for marital status, age at entrance, mother tongue, or years of schooling.	

* *At Shankarananda Matha legal transfer of property is possible.*

Table 4
Backgrounds of Ascetics Related to Social Structure of Institution

| | CORPORATE | | NON-CORPORATE |
	Endowed	Patronized	
Socio-religious group	5 Brahmans	12 Brahmans, 5 Kshatriyas, and 2 Vaishyas	3 Brahmans, 3 Kshatriyas, 1 Vaishya and 1 Shudra
Education	2 Sanskrit school Range: 4–10 yrs. Average: 7 yrs. 3 public school Range: 3–10 yrs. Average: 7 yrs.	4 Sanskrit school Range: 6–10 yrs. Average: 9 yrs. 15 public school Range: 3 yrs. to B.A. Average: 9 yrs. Highest education	No Sanskrit school 8 public school Range: 3–11 yrs. Average: 6 yrs. Least education
Birthplace	5 Orissa	16 Bengal, 2 Orissa, and 1 Nepal	2 Bengal, 5 Orissa, and 1 Gujarat
Age in 1964	Average age 54, only one under 35	Average age 47, evenly distributed between young, middle-aged, and old; includes six young ascetics	Average age 50, most between 35 and 60
Average years of residence at Bhubaneswar	23 years	7 years; six ascetics had arrived within the past year	25 years

No discernible differences in prior occupation, marital status, or age at entrance.

Psycho-Social Factors Motivating Entrance, According to Age

An ascetic's self-perceived reasons for entering a monastery often overlook important psycho-social factors that appear as side-lights in his autobiography. In some cases ascetics have so reinterpreted their pasts that they remember only the positive religious quest that resulted from a socially embarrassing or economically hopeless situation. The following section is our attempt to reconstruct from the ascetics' life-histories the various psycho-social factors affecting motivation toward the monastery.

Although only one ascetic entered as a child (age ten) upon appointment by an uncle to headship of a large monastery, childhood experiences are mentioned by some ascetics as influential. We were struck by the frequency of their early experiences with death in the family; however, it is impossible to assess the effects of early encounters with death on our informants, because in India death is a frequent experience in the childhood of most segments of the population. Some ascetics claim to have been raised by loving parents in a harmonious atmosphere; others were raised by relatives after their parents died and felt that they were a burden to these relatives even though they were loved. All had brothers and sisters; most had from two to five siblings, and one had as many as eleven. Almost all were middle children in the order of birth. If a boy were the eldest or only son, family pressure to marry and to carry on the family name made it almost impossible for him to enter a monastery as a youth. There was one exception, an eldest son who entered orders just before the marriage arranged by his parents.

The head of a large, heavily endowed monastery made the following statement about his childhood:

> My family consisted of fourteen members. The income (in 1936) of my father was up to one hundred rupees a month. I was only nine years old when my father died. The death of my father did not create any emotional upset in my mind because every day in this world somebody comes and somebody goes. Birth and death is the natural way of the world. I cannot remember any strong feelings, either for or against my parents, in my childhood. When I was ten years old, my joint family broke, and I, my mother, and my youngest brother lived with my eldest brother. My eldest brother died when I was fifteen years old. I disliked all of my brothers except the eldest one, because they were all involved in selfish interests. They did not pay attention to anyone's sorrows or sufferings. After being separated they did not take care of my mother. They are only anxious to make money. They do not know the meaning of love and affection. My joint family broke because of the misunderstanding between my two brothers.

Another recurrent feature of ascetics' accounts of their childhood is the anecdotes about minor pranks or misdeeds accompanied by an exaggerated feeling of guilt towards parents or siblings.

> I was never punished in childhood; so I did not feel insecure in any way. When I was about eleven years old I had long locks of hair, which my parents had promised to cut in a sacred place on an auspicious day. But I didn't like such large locks. I cut off my hair without telling my parents. When I came back from the barber, my friends told me that I would be severely beaten because of my disobedience. Out of fear I remained in a tree for three days

without taking food or water. I passed stools and urine there, and at night tied my waist to the trunk of the tree.

When I was eleven, I stole some money from the cash box at my uncle's shop. When my father saw me, he wanted to beat me. I ran to my uncle, who said to my father, "Is this an appropriate punishment for a child?" So I was not punished.

Although there may be a disproportionate feeling of self-reproach concerning failures in personal relationships, there seems to be no feeling of "sin" against the deity, nor of "original sin" in the Christian sense. Not one informant recounted an experience of feeling "sinful" or "evil" in relation to a supernaturally invoked ethic.

Many informants felt that their formative years had been blighted by tragedies within the family, such as death, lingering illness, and loss of money or social position. Such misfortunes are commonplace in India and are not in themselves predisposing factors. The ascetics, however, saw them as increasing the weariness of the world that precedes conversion.

Seven ascetics had proceeded directly from Sanskrit or public school into the monastery at ages ranging from twelve to twenty-two. These individuals apparently entered orders without facing the adolescent crises of marriage and occupational choice, since nothing in their biographies indicates any attempts by their parents to arrange for either a wife or a job. One of the youngest entrants (age twelve) had taken the occasion of his sacred thread ceremony, when the young initiate symbolically becomes an ascetic and renounces his parents and relatives for a day, as an opportunity to renounce them permanently and to run away, not as part of the ceremony, but in earnest. According to his account, his family did not try to find him. His case is unusual, however.

Many life-histories indicated that the narrator had displayed in adolescence positive talents for religious practices that were actively encouraged by relatives or teachers. Eight informants were highly gifted singers of religious songs even in high school, and two had acted leading roles in religious plays. Four displayed gifts for meditation and the ability to enter into trance quite early in life. Thus, when these people entered the monastery, they were putting their major talents to use and choosing a vocation for which they seemed suited from early adolescence.

Two other young adults had entered monasteries primarily because they feared sexual experience and marital responsibility, though all gave "religious" explanations for their behaviour. For a youth unaccustomed to intimate relations with women and unsure of his ability to sustain a potentially growing family economically or emotionally, a marriage arranged by his parents may present a major crisis from which he is only too happy to escape.

> Since I was the eldest son, my father wanted me to marry and lead the life of a householder, but even from early childhood I had decided not to marry. Consequently, at the age of twenty-four I rebelled against my father's wishes and took upon myself the vows of a *brahmacārin*.
>
> The purpose of life is to worship God because we have all come from God. If we want to worship God, then we will have to serve humanity. The home is not a proper place to serve humanity and to pay homage to God. This is the highest principle. The duty of a *brahmacārin* is to call upon God (recite the names of God) for humanity. The *brahmacārin* is not worried about personal pleasure and happiness. The family is the centre of selfishness. Sacrifice is not possible there. To avoid the selfishness of the family the son should cut all social and familial bonds, become a *brahmacārin*, and serve humanity and God.
>
> I have never thought of marriage, because to think of marriage means to deviate from the peaceful life of a *sannyāsin*. A man may not get a full meal every day in the ascetic life, but there is peace of mind if he is devoted to God. A man will forget his hunger and thirst if he can fully concentrate on God. It is better to remain away from the family. A lonely life leads to full satisfaction of one's religious aim. When I first became a *sannyāsin* I took a vow that I would not marry, and that vow is now stronger than ever.

Nine adolescents and young adults, ranging in age from seventeen to thirty, had entered out of fear of a worldly occupation. Six of these had tried and failed at various occupations and had then given up and entered orders. Two of the best examples are the Bhakta, Gaura Dasa, and the Fun-lover, Kamakara.

Another informant states: "Throughout my early years I had experienced the sufferings and sorrows of poverty. I had witnessed my father's futile attempts to feed his family on a handful of rice per day. I thought it was painful to remain in such a condition, surrounded by the sufferings and sorrows of others. Thus, at the age of twenty-three I renounced all worldly ties and took the vows of a *sannyāsin*."

One youthful entrant, who is quoted as the boy with eleven hungry siblings and in the second of the two cases of refusal to marry earlier in this chapter, had never attempted a worldly occupation. Now head ascetic at a heavily endowed monastery, he openly declared that his reasons for entering orders were to escape the poverty of his youth. The objects in his spacious room (thirty feet by twelve feet) indicated that he had succeeded. His possessions included a large wooden-framed bed with mosquito netting, a kerosene stove, an altar to his guru (his uncle) that was decorated with peacock feathers, and a radio, a major status symbol in the Old Town, encased in orange velvet, the same material with which he had covered his ascetic's staff (*daṇḍa*). On the wall hung two enlarged photographs of him taken in a Cuttack studio; the first showed him in a shirt and was labelled with his birth-name while the second showed him in ascetic robes as "Maharaja," head of the monastery. With a guaranteed annual income of Rs. 35,000 a year for the monastery and Rs. 100 a month for himself, plus fringe benefits, the informant had come a long way from the poverty of his childhood.

For one informant the difficulties of earning a living were so overwhelming that he was forced out of economic life before marriage or work even became possible. A goldsmith's son with defective eyesight was unable to carry on the family trade, which requires flawless vision. The son went to Puri with his father to seek a cure from Lord Jagannatha Krishna. When this failed, he dedicated himself increasingly to Jagannatha in order to rid himself of his eye troubles. In this process his attachment to Jagannatha became closer and closer. Eventually he dedicated himself completely to the deity.

Four of the five individuals who entered monasteries while in their thirties had failed either in marriage or at earning a living or both. Economic failure sometimes led to the abandonment of a man's family of procreation or to a general weariness of life, which turned his thoughts to eternity. Marriage in India has traditionally included the burden of the successive births of many children. Although it is not unusual for half to die in infancy, the survivors may be too numerous for their father to feed. Thus, oppressive social factors may drive men to ascetic escapes, with or without conversion experiences.

The following taken from the life-history of Arthadushana, the Mendicant, is an example of failure in middle life. Arthadushana and his wife worked in a Calcutta cotton mill. In the early 1950s the mill ran into financial difficulties, and Arthadushana and his wife were laid off. She moved into her father's house and soon found a job in a chemical company. Arthadushana was unable to find work and began to perform meditations in a burial ground. Eventually he ran out of money, but was given free room and board at a monastery. His financial troubles ceased, and he "took his place under the cool shade of a tree."

Although Arthadushana left his wife, son, and daughter, he does nothing for them because, according to him, "The world is full of relatives, and every child I see is like my own child." Whenever he goes to Calcutta, he does not visit his wife at her home because, "They eat fish and meat, and, after all, an impure home is polluted with sins and falsehood. Home is not a suitable place for the *brahmacārin* or *sannyāsin*." However, if by chance Arthadushana meets his wife, he "talks and behaves like a friend with her, not like a husband." He claims that his wife is not in financial difficulty because she has a job. He is not concerned about the education of his son: "He is not my son, but the son of God."

In another report of marital failure, the informant at the age of thirty-two, became tired of the endless, petty quarrels that had turned the whole of his extended family into "a den of snakes." Consequently, in order to gain peace, he renounced all family relationships including his wife and became an ascetic.

Entrance into orders is often the socially acceptable way out of marriage in a country where divorce is still associated with scandal and where the difficulties of providing a livelihood may become intolerable. Seven informants left their wives and children. Five of these did so at retirement age when their children were already grown, but the other two abandoned wives with small children. Though the ascetics are likely to say either "God will provide for my wife and children" or "It doesn't matter who provides, because life is ephemeral anyway; it is better for me to seek the eternal, even if my family dies, because death is also ephemeral," in practice the ascetic's older or younger brother is expected to support his ex-wife and children. Ideally, and usually in fact, contact with his family of procreation remains distant and unemotional, though he may visit his grown children. According to our informants, such families harbour little or no resentment for the choices that have been made. Since the families were not available for interviews there is no way to verify these informants' reports.

A very different outlook on marriage was put forward by a Shankara Dashanami who had been strongly influenced by Tantric Yoga. He assured us that a wife was absolutely essential for Tantric practice. He had married at fifty-five. His wife was then thirty-five and had been a widow since age nine. The scandal was not that an ascetic had married, nor even that he had many "lovers" before marriage, but that he had married a lower-caste woman and thus had to have a civil rather than a religious marriage. He had no children, but about fifteen members of his extended family lived in the monastery amid continual bickering.

He justified his marriage thus:

I am a Tantric *sādhu*, not a *sannyāsin*. *Sannyāsins* say that man and woman should be separated, but Tantric Yoga says they should be attached. This will lead you to the ultimate goal. *Sannyāsins* say that a woman is not a good thing, but all the human incarnations of Vishnu have married. I cannot understand life-long celibacy. A woman is needed for the study of the Tantric path. Krishna and Radha represent to me ideal man and woman, not God. I draw inspiration from their lives. When I am reborn I should receive favor from them and be born an ideal man.

Fourteen ascetics claim to have entered orders on account of conversions occurring at a wide variety of ages ranging from fifteen to fifty-two. A conversion may be an overwhelming experience of the presence of the divine, which causes a man to lose consciousness. Jagadananda, the Preacher, had such an experience of conversion as a youth while in Sanskrit school.

A significant dream may also change the course of a man's life. Bhavani Shankara, the Solitary Ascetic, entered orders at the age of thirty-nine in response to a dream appearance of Durga. Sometimes an informant reports a series of dreams and visions occurring over a period of several years while he is still in secular life. The life-history of Nibaran Mukharji, the Bhakta, is a good example of the gradual conversion of a successful cloth merchant who preferred *kīrtana* singing and pilgrimages to the continuation of his worldly career and who responded to his dream visions by becoming a full-time ascetic at the age of forty-seven.

Most of the fourteen conversion experiences reported, however, do not include a positive vision of the deity. Instead, they parallel the conversion of the Buddha in reporting incidents that led to a weariness of the world and a search for the eternal. In most cases oppressive social factors or the individual's failure led him to seek escape in the religious life, and he later interpreted these factors as a conversion. In two cases, however, this kind of conversion seems to have authentic religious origins. The Troubadour's autobiography details a series of events occurring over several years that led the youth to give away his remaining possessions and enter orders at twenty-two. Sometimes disasters have a delayed effect; one informant mentioned that a flood that he witnessed when he was twenty-two predisposed him to enter orders thirteen years later.

One informant reported a sudden conversion upon hearing of some misery totally unrelated to his own family, as if the shock of someone else's death had suddenly brought home his awareness of the passing character of all visible reality. Such a conversion was almost exactly the contemporary equivalent of Buddha's conversion. This ascetic relates:

During the Second World War I became a close friend of a British officer in charge of a company at Tata. One splendid morning while we were taking breakfast together, this British officer received a telegram that announced that his eldest son had been killed in an air battle over Germany. It was then about 6:00 A.M. At about 1:00 P.M. this same officer was presented with another telegram which stated that his middle son had been killed in North Africa. Later in the day he received word that his home in England had been totally demolished by German bombs. Utterly heartbroken and totally demoralized, the British officer died at 6:00 P.M. I was terribly shaken by the death of my friend and became convinced that attachment to one's family ultimately leads to grief. Consequently, I broke all ties with my family and renounced worldly affairs to become a *sannyāsin*. My wife, my brother, my grandson, and my great-grandson have all remained at my home village, but I no longer go there. Thus I became a *sannyāsin* at the age of fifty-two.

The *āśramas* or traditional stages of life require entrance into the ascetic stage (*vānaprastha*) after one's earthly duties have been fulfilled. Seven informants had entered orders upon retirement at ages forty-seven to seventy-three, but three of these, two Ayur-vedic practitioners and a *hotṛ* priest, carried on their former activities within the monastery. The other four retirees were two former administrative officers in civil service, a sculptor of religious images, and a cloth merchant, Nibaran Mukharji, whose major concern in 1964 was preparation for death.

The two civil servants had led exemplary lives, retiring from the civil service with records of distinction. Prajnananda Sarasvati Svami, founder of the newest monastery at Bhubaneswar, and a B.A. from Calcutta University, held various posts in the Orissa administrative service for nearly thirty years. Retirement from active life brought some of the most competent men into ascetic orders.

Initiation

Once an individual has decided to enter the ascetic life, his first task is to find a guru who will accept him as a disciple. The guru may be an ascetic from the disciple's home village or a well-known religious teacher with a monastery in Calcutta or Puri. Occasionally the guru is a relative, such as an uncle. The guru recognizes a would-be ascetic as his disciple by administering *dīkṣā*, a rite of initiation that separates the disciple from his former life. Ideally only the head ascetic of a monastery, a man who has himself taken final vows of renunciation, can administer *dīkṣā*. There are two forms of *dīkṣā*: one is administered by a guru to lay disciples and one is given only to ascetic disciples. Some ascetics receive lay *dīkṣa* long before they decide to enter an order. At entrance they receive a second *dīkṣā* reserved for ascetics. Others have taken only the ascetic *dīkṣā*, because they were not previously lay disciples. Four of thirty-two respondents claimed that they had never taken *dīkṣā*; by this they meant that they had received only lay *dīkṣā* and at a later date had simply decided to don the robes of an ascetic without the permission of their gurus.

Before taking ascetic *dīkṣā*, a Shankara Sannyasin disciple must cut all remaining ties to his family of orientation by performing death ceremonies (*śrāddha*) for his parents. After taking *dīkṣā* he will no longer be permitted to perform any household ritual and thus must perform his parents' death ceremonies in advance. Occasionally, monks report favourable visionary experiences when performing this ritual. These, in turn, are interpreted as reaffirming their vocational choice and implying the assent of their parents. For example, before Jagadananda, the Preacher, became a *sannyāsin*, he went to the bank of the famous Phalgu River at Gaya to make the funeral offering (*śrāddha*) to the spirit of his mother. While he was offering this *śrāddha* he saw an indistinct figure of his mother moving further and further away from him. Suddenly he noticed a four-armed figure like Vishnu, but it soon vanished. At last he saw the red cloth of a *sannyāsin* hanging before him.

The rites accompanying ascetic *dīkṣā* are seldom witnessed by a non-Hindu observer. However, the Calcutta head ascetic of a Vairagin Madhva Gaudiya sub-order that had a Bhubaneswar branch was willing to provide written descriptions of both the lay and ascetic *dīkṣā* ceremonies that had been given to his guru, which is paraphrased below.

On the day of the initiation in 1886, Kuladakanta Banarji arose at 3:30 A.M. and took his morning bath. He then went directly to the Dacca residence of his guru. The guru took his seat, facing west, and instructed Kuladakanta to take a position in front of him. Kuladakanta began by reciting a long prayer to Vishnu, ending with a request for initiation. The two men joined hands and the guru chanted the following hymn in Bengali: "I bow down to Him, to Him, to Him alone I bend down my head indeed—to the supreme Deity who dwells as tranquility in all living beings." The guru repeated the Gayatri (a hymn to the Sun God) several times, recited a short prayer, and shouted, "Jai Guru! Jai Guru!" (Hail to the Guru!). Several minutes of silence followed before the guru said: "Receive your *mantra* [sacred verse], the mystical name of Vishnu, which my guru, the Great Paramahansa, pleases to give you."

The guru whispered the secret *mantra* to his pupil and explained its inner meaning. Finally the guru taught his pupil a method of breath control (*prāṇāyāma*) that he had devised. The initiation ceremony was concluded, and Kuladakanta became a lay disciple.[1]

1. Benimadhab Barua, *Brahmachari Kuladananda* (Puri: The Thakurbadi Committee, 1938), pp. 75–77.

Five years later, Kuladakanta came to his guru and requested an ascetic *dīkṣā*. On the next day, after Kuladakanta had completed his morning bath, he was instructed by his guru to separate 108 *rudrākṣa* beads, sacred to Shiva, into the following strands: thirty-two for a necklace, twenty-two for a head-band, six for each ear, twelve for each wrist, eight for the upper arms, and two as a hairpiece. Next the guru held up a new sacred thread, and after reciting the Gayatri twelve times, he placed it about Kuladakanta's neck and chest. Silently reciting another *mantra*, the guru handed his disciple a yellow cloth (*yogapaṭṭa*), which Kuladakanta wrapped about his waist. Then, the guru picked up the *rudrākṣa* beads, one strand at a time, and placed each strand on the part of the body that he had designated earlier. Finally, he concluded the ceremony with the words: "This is the garb of Nilakantha." Nilakantha ("blue-necked," an epithet of Shiva) was the nickname by which Kuladakanta Banarji was known thereafter; the name he chose as a Madhva Gaudiya Vairagin was Kuladananda Brahmacharin.[2]

Although the order into which Kuladakanta was being initiated is a Madhva Gaudiya Vairagin order, a degree of syncretism is evident from the *rudrākṣa* bead necklace and the nickname Nilakantha, both of which indicate Shaiva rather than Vaishnava orientation.

The *dīkṣās* for both the laity and the ascetics require the initiate to bathe and to fast before the ceremony. In the lay initiation ceremony the initiate is not symbolically reborn, although he is infused with the power (*tapas*) of his guru when he is given a sacred verse (*mantra*) and told its secret meaning. In the ascetic initiatory rite, the initiate is symbolically reborn; he is given a new sacred thread, new clothing, and a new name. The guru intensifies the infusion of his power into the initiate by touching his body with sacred objects. Often the initiate is given special beads or clothing; a Dashanami Sannyasin may be given a bamboo staff (*daṇḍa*).

Upon taking *dīkṣā*, a Shankara Dashanami ascetic always takes a religious name ending with the name of his sub-order, such as Sarasvati in the case of the Guru or Tirtha in the case of the Preacher. He is allowed to choose his personal religious name, although his guru may suggest one. What he is neither allowed to choose nor to reveal is the sacred verse (*mantra*), including a special name of the deity, that his guru whispers in his ear during the initiation ceremony. This may be a Vedic or Puranic verse, or simply one of the thousand names of Shiva or Vishnu. A Vairagin ascetic may or may not take a religious

2. The second section is from: Brahmacharin Gangananda, "Nilkantha," *The Mother*, vol. 2, no. 11 (Calcutta: Sri Ramgopal Banerjee Press, July 1960), pp. 501–7.

name at initiation; if he does so, he is likely to take the name of his chosen deity with the suffix *dāsa* (slave), indicating that he is the slave of that deity. An example is Gaura Dasa, whose name means Slave of the Light-Skinned. Gaura means light-skinned and is an epithet of Chaitanya.

Ranks of Ascetics

The titles given to various stages of the monastic career reflect the traditional Hindu doctrine of the four *āśramas*, or stages of life, with some important changes.

The term *brahmacārin*, or "novice," has several different meanings: a member of a Shankara order who has received from a guru a special rite of initiation reserved for ascetics, and who is undergoing a period of apprenticeship that may last anywhere from one to twelve years, during which he is free to return to secular life; a member of a Vairagin order, who may be either an apprentice *or* who has taken final vows; and a self-styled Shankara ascetic who has not joined an order and who has taken only the rite of initiation administered to lay-disciples of a guru.

The *gṛhastha*, or "householder," has no place in the Shankara orders, but may join a Vairagin order, particularly the Madhva Gaudiya, as an ascetic and still maintain normal family relations. As in the case of Nibaran Mukharji, the whole family participates in the daily routine of monastic life.

The *vānaprastha*, or "forest hermit," is an older person who has retired from his economic career and sought peace and refuge in a monastery; he may take ascetic *dīkṣā* and join a Vairagin order or he may take only lay *dīkṣā* and style himself as a follower of Shankara.

A *sannyāsin*, or "final renouncer," is a resident ascetic member of a Shankara order, who has taken final vows after a period as a *brahmacārin*, and who may no longer return to secular life. The Vairagin equivalent of a *sannyāsin* is a *naiṣṭhika brahmacārin*, who has also taken final vows after a period of apprenticeship as an *upakurvāna brahmacārin*.[3] Thus the person joining a Shankara order must first receive ascetic *dīkṣā* from his guru; he then becomes a *brahmacārin*, entitled to wear dress and facial markings that distinguish him from a full-fledged *sannyāsin*. The length of his apprenticeship depends either upon how soon he succeeds, by appointment or inheritance, to the headship of a monastery, or upon when his guru decides he is ready to take final vows.

---

3. *Naiṣṭhika* means "fixed" or "firm" or "vowing perpetual abstinence and chastity." *Upakurvāṇa* is derived from the verbal root $\sqrt{kṛi} + upa$ which means "to finish with"; hence, to finish with the period of studentship and to pass on to the stage of the householder.

A Shankara Brahmacharin or Shankara Vanaprastha, having not formally entered an order, does not proceed to the final vows of a *saṅnyāsin*.

Levels of spiritual progress in the Vairagin orders are somewhat different; one may join as an *upakurvāna brahmacārin* (novice), as *gṛhastha* (householder), or as a *vānaprastha* (retired man). In each case one takes ascetic *dīkṣā*. The distinction between one who has taken final vows and one who has not is not so pronounced as in Shankara orders, partly because one still retains the title *brahmacārin*. Table 5 compares titles given to members of the two orders.

Table 5
Ranks of Ascetics

| Form of Initiation | Order | |
	SHANKARA SANNYASIN	VAIRAGIN
Ascetic dīkṣā	*saṅnyāsin* (final vows) *brahmacārin* (novice)	*naiṣṭhika brahmacārin* (final vows) *upakurvāṇa brahmacārin* (novice; may be a student in a monastery school)
Lay dīkṣā	*vānaprastha* (ascetic-retirement) *gṛhastha* (lay only) Shankara *brahmacārin*	*vānaprastha* (ascetic-retirement) *gṛhastha* (can be religious householder or ascetic–*sādhu*)

Religious Experiences

The satisfactions derived from the monastic life are varied. For some informants who have experienced a hungry childhood, a quarrelsome family life, or economic failure with the attendant inability to support wife and children, the monastery means a refuge from burdensome struggles for existence. Such men often seek no more. Some undoubtedly enjoy the leisure and the support provided by some of the wealthier monasteries. Others find satisfaction in the individualistic, independent way of life provided by the monastic career. A few find outlets for their musical talents by becoming professional singers of devotional songs. Still others have succeeded to their present positions by inheritance and have only a hazy notion of their calling.

Whatever the gratifications, for many informants the religious quest is undoubtedly sincere and sometimes so compelling that they have abandoned moderately successful careers in order to seek release from the cycle of birth and death. This desire is often expressed as a wish "to see the deity" since a vision of one's chosen deity at some time during one's life is considered a guarantee of final release. Six out of thirty-two informants claim that they have had an experience of "seeing" (darśana) the deity. To be deceitful in such a serious matter is considered an unforgivable sin that would cause a major setback on the road to release. Informants are unquestionably sincere in these descriptions. The three most important visions of the deity have been described in the life-sketches. The life-sketch of the Guru provides the most vivid detail in describing such an experience, although this vision of Lakshmi–Narayana occurred thirty-five years earlier. Such visions are not necessarily overwhelming in their power. For example, Gaura Dasa, the Bhakta, related this experience:

> Once I was drawing water from the temple well. I heard the sound of a wooden sandal and suddenly saw a man wearing a white *dhoti* and a white shawl going towards my house. When I went to receive him, the white-robed figure vanished. I believe that this was a Vaishnava saint or perhaps Chaitanya, himself.

Nibaran Mukharji, Gaura Dasa's father, has had visions of several different deities. The first was a dream-vision of Durga, far away and hidden by clouds. He was astonished to see her and begged her to give him love for each and every living creature. His most wonderful dream was a vision of a man with very long arms, no hair, a shining face, and a red-ochre cloth, who he says was either Svami Vivekananda or Shri Krishna. He offered food to the figure, who placed a garland around the ascetic's neck. His third experience was a weird and powerful auditory one. In 1940, after Nibaran had built a temple to Chaitanya at Bhubaneswar, he and a friend decided one evening to visit the Bhaskareswar Temple, which at that time was approachable only through paddy fields. Upon entering the temple they were awed by the presence of the Shiva *liṅgam*, which was over ten feet tall. After paying respects to the deity they went out and walked around the temple. Suddenly a very frightening, groaning sound, "ooooh" came from within. Both Nibaran and his friend began to tremble. The sound came again and again, each time more frightening. They ran from the temple as fast as they could. Nibaran had heard about the solemn and rhythmical sound that is known to come from the Bhaskareswar Temple, but had never believed the story until he heard the sound for himself. That night Nibaran's wife went into labour. The baby was born with very little pain before he returned with the mid-wife. He emphasized that the easy birth was due to the grace of Shiva, whose voice he had heard earlier that night.

Bhavani Shankara Babaji, the Solitary Ascetic, on first arriving in Bhubaneswar, threw himself in front of the reclining stone image of the goddess

Parvati in a small, seldom-used temple, and swore that he would remain there until the goddess provided him with food and shelter. He fell asleep and dreamed that Durga appeared to him and promised him that she would take care of him. The next day he was given patronage by two merchants in the Old Town. Durga (not Parvati) became his chosen deity.

All these informants have had theistic experiences of the deity. Certainly they were surrounded by a wealth of visual representations of deities which may have been conducive to their religious experiences. Jagadananda, the Preacher, explained the reasons for the different kinds of theistic visions thus:

> It is written in the Arya Shastra that God is personal. Some may see Shiva, some may see Krishna, some may see Kali, but on the whole they see God according to their own *sampradāya*. There are four main *sampradāyas*, namely, Shakta, Shaiva, Ganapatya, and Vaishnava. The man who belongs to a Shakta *sampradāya* will see Kali; a Shaiva will see Shiva; a Ganapatya will see Ganesha; a Vaishnava will see Vishnu or Krishna. God is only one, but he appears according to one's *sampradāya*. There is a God-consciousness in every man's heart, which is the same but takes a different form according to one's beliefs.

Jagadananda said that once he meditated before the image of Jagannatha in Puri, but when he opened his eyes he could see only the image of Krishna. Krishna and Jagannatha are both incarnations of Vishnu according to the local Jagannatha cult. Often Jagannatha is identified with Krishna, although some informants believe Jagannatha to be a separate incarnation.

The non-dualistic (*advaita*) philosophy of Shankara has perhaps affected the tendency of some ascetics to claim that a theistic vision of the deity, encompassed by glowing light, surrounds and enters into them until they go into a state of unconsciousness in which all differences between self and objects are obliterated. The prototype of this vision was experienced by Ramakrishna Paramahansa.

The closest any report came to a non-theistic experience is Jagadananda's own description of absorption (*samādhi*).

> *Samādhi* can neither be induced nor resisted. It is involuntary. As an adolescent I was eager to experience *samādhi*, so I took my posture for meditation (*āsana*) and began to chant OM. Then I had an exciting experience! I felt as if I was no longer a man of flesh and blood but was present everywhere. This feeling started from my toes and rose to my head until I felt I had burst out of the upper part of my skull. It was as if my skull was

hit by hammers. Then I lost all consciousness. I was in *samādhi* for three days and three nights, with no feeling of the external world. When I returned to my senses, I was uttering the sound *ma*, which means mother. I found that I had placed my head on the lap of an old lady, who gave me orange juice and told me that the pleasure of a mother's lap could be experienced in *samādhi* and in the grave. She said that people had been crowding around me for three days to obtain blessings from my feet, and that the doctor had declared me dead.

This was only one of many such experiences for Jagadananda, who was practiced in extended trances. He claimed that if a man does not get back his senses for fifteen days and his body starts to rot, he attains liberation (*mokṣa*) from rebirth. If the body does not rot, his senses will probably return. For Jagadananda, *samādhi* itself is similar to death.

After that first *samādhi*, Jagadananda has gone into trance while on the street or even on the toilet, whenever he remembers *brahman*. For two years he wandered the streets of Calcutta, weeping and crying: "Mother, Mother." When prostitutes passed him, he would run after them crying: "Oh, Mother, Mother, take me to you. Do not leave me alone!" Finally, a guru-mother (*sannyāsinī*) took him away to save his life, because she was afraid that he would jump into the river or touch an electric wire while in *samādhi*. Although such an account suggests periods of mental abnormality, there was no evidence of mental disturbance in the informant's behaviour during our interviews.

Most informants pointed to instances in which deities had intervened in their lives in extraordinary ways, but such interventions were too commonplace in the Old Town at Bhubaneswar to be considered miracles. Dreams of a prophetic or telepathic nature are frequently reported and are considered sacred manifestations. For example, on one of his missionary journeys, Jagadananda encountered the three sons of his host, who all fell down at his feet, exclaiming that he was the *sadhu* who had appeared to them in a dream the previous night. When Jagadananda was robbed by a disciple, the guru-mother dreamed that very night that a young man had killed him. Examples of such dreams are almost endless, and tend to become exaggerated in the telling.

Rescues from danger are also interpreted as supernatural intervention. Often the danger is exaggerated, particularly in favourite stories of tigers in the jungle and of wandering ascetics rescued just in time by a kindly villager. Indeed, a journey would hardly be worth describing without a tiger story or some other comparable hardship or danger. Sometimes the rescue is more prosaically but possibly more realistically from the police or from angry Muslim villagers.

"Cures" are also reported by some ascetics. Jagadananda spoke of a swift and painless childbirth produced on the spot by his preaching on the birth of Krishna. Most cures are of a gradual nature and range from the slow and apparently actual cure of "a mad boy" living in the monastery to Jagadananda's unsubstantiated claim of an eventual cure for a leprous disciple who had deceived him into accepting him for initiation (lepers are ordinarily denied initiation).

It is evident that the ascetic life has definite religious rewards. The fact that six ascetics, almost a fifth of the thirty-two, have had decisive visions of the deity which entitle one to *mokṣa* at death means that a surprisingly high percentage of ascetics have attained their final goal. Not all of these have attained the same respect from the lay community, however.

Apparently the ascetic in contemporary Bhubaneswar is a man who has entered monastic life out of mixed motives: he *may* have displayed an early talent for the religious life or have entered after seeing old age, sickness, and death, as did Gautama. Mingled with those having genuine religious motives are a number of failures in marriage or occupation. A surprising number report direct religious experiences, but the ascetic's life apparently has other rewards apart from the attainment of visions of the deity.

Chapter 5

The Laity's Perception of Ascetics and Contemporary Hinduism

The Laymen's Opinions

The ascetics' views of their roles are undoubtedly affected by the prevailing opinions of the laity about the prestige and value of asceticism as a way of life. After all, every ascetic was once a layman, and the perpetuation of the role of ascetic depends upon the quality of lay expectations. Our own estimations of lay attitudes are mostly derived from participant observation in the Old Town, not from formal interviews. Laymen's opinions about monasticism generally fall into three groups: extreme opponents of monasticism, the noncommittal middle ground, and patrons or clients of a monastery.

The opponent of monasticism is the rare individual who rejects any and all ascetics categorically. He considers ascetics as tough, corrupt, ill-mannered, ignorant rogues. His major attack is usually a charge of either sexual activity or drunkenness, an accusation he makes against even the two most respected religious leaders in the Old Town, the Guru and the Preacher. We encountered only two or three such extremists in eighteen months. All were newcomers to Bhubaneswar, and may simply have said what they thought "secular" Westerners wanted to hear. One was an Oria employed by the government to supervise reconstruction of a temple. Some experience in his past had completely soured him on ascetics. None of the opponents of monasticism was able to prove the charges he levelled against ascetics, though it is quite possible that the head ascetic of one endowed monastery was indeed visiting the houses of prostitution near the railway station. This ascetic had lost the respect of the community already because of his mismanagement of funds.

The majority of citizens in both the Old Town and the New Capital are not associated with any one monastery, though they may occasionally attend one on major festivals. These people form the great "middle ground" and take a neutral attitude toward the existence of monasteries and ascetics. They tend to have strong ethnic loyalties and judge an ascetic according to whether or not he belongs to their linguistic group. Thus many Orias have nothing good to say about Bengali ascetics and even repeat the extremist charges of sexual irregularities. This attitude reflects the Oria antagonism against the Bengalis as intruders into Oria politics and economic life. The Bengalis of Bhubaneswar, who still own much land and in 1964 still held many important positions in the Oria civil service, definitely consider themselves superior to Orias in education, standard of living, and style of life. Consequently, they also consider their ascetics superior to Oria ascetics. Both Orias and Bengalis usually point to one or two of their monasteries, usually the Shankarananda Matha or the Arya Rishikula Bhuvaneshvari Ashrama, as ideals.

The newspapers, such as the *Samaj*, also take the middle ground and judge a monastery on a secular basis, such as good management of funds and efficient administration of lands and personnel. Thus the *Samaj* issued charges against one head ascetic for budgetary corruption and for discontinuation of the daily rituals that the laity expected performed. The *Samaj* would also occasionally print an article favourable to a monastery. For instance, the head ascetic of the Shiva Tirtha Matha was commended for his good administration, which had made the manager appointed by the Orissa Hindu Religious Endowments Commission no longer necessary and had regained him the prerogatives of sole administrator.

Finally, the third group of laity, a minority of the population, are patrons or clients of some monastery. Patrons or clients not only respect their own guru, but are tolerant of most other ascetics. Of the approximately 48,000 residents of the Notified Area of Bhubaneswar in 1964, perhaps as many as 1,000 were patrons or clients of monasteries. The Guru had three hundred patrons visit on Guru Purnima, the Preacher has almost as many, and the Ramakrishna Mission probably had more; on the other hand, the Solitary Ascetic had only the five or six clients necessary to feed him. Thus perhaps one out of every forty-eight persons in Bhubaneswar is related to a monastery in some way.

Patrons and Clients

In addition to our participant observations, we are fortunate to have access to the interviews conducted by Professor Richard P. Taub of the University of Chicago with influential men in the civil service, politics, and business, some of whom were mentioned by head ascetics as prominent patrons of their monasteries.[1] A patron is one who supports a monastery financially but does not necessarily worship there or visit the head ascetic. A client visits the monastery but does not regularly support it. The seven men whose responses to Taub's interviews are quoted below are described as patrons rather than clients because their names were taken from the monastery's list of donors. In some cases, we observed the patron attending public ceremonies at the monastery. In other cases, we do not know whether or not the patron ever visited the institution that he supported. Indians, of course, would not in general make our distinction between patron and client.

All of the seven influential patrons named by our informants and interviewed by Taub claimed that religion was on the decline in India and stated that they themselves did not participate in traditional rituals. With one exception, none admitted having any relation to a monastery. Undoubtedly the presence of a secular Westerner influenced many of their answers in a non-religious direction. However, these same people who had denied participating in ceremonies not only were on the guest lists for various festivals held in monasteries, but all had their own household altars. They claimed that these were only for the use of the female members of the household; it is quite possible, though, that Taub's informants may have performed *pūjā* themselves when a Westerner was not around. Their responses to a question about the growth or decline of religion in the modern day were as follows:

> I don't think that at any time in Indian society religion played an important role in doing day-to-day business or in caste. I think the workings of religion were always in the background. If a Brahman had high status, it was because he had high responsibility, not because of his caste. As it was, Brahmans were responsible for doing the daily *pūjās,* and the people only attended the temples on special occasions and holidays. It is the same way today. Religion is still not deeply involved in society and has never intruded too much into people's lives.[2]

1. The quotations that follow are from Richard P. Taub's unpublished field notes in the files of the Harvard–Bhubaneswar Project. See also, Richard P. Taub, *Bureaucrats under Stress.*
2. Statement by an Oria Brahman, age 54, a patron of the Guru. The words seem somewhat inconsistent with the informant's behaviour because we observed him worshipping at Guru Purnima.

India is divided into two classes: the sophisticated and the conservative natives. The conservatives are worried about observing ritual, but I am not. I pay no attention to them. Hinduism is fine for an agricultural economy, but is not much use in an industrial economy. But some people need the fear that religion puts into them so they'll be moral. The present decline in ritual is good, but the decline of moral standards is bad.[3]

People don't attach as much importance to religion as they once did. But it still plays a part, a smaller one, with the people. This decline is not good. People should not make many decisions without consulting their religion first.[4]

Religion is that which gives men fixed principles of life to contemplate. Our philosophy of life remains as firm as always. But if you mean the externals of ritual, they are vanishing and they were a strait jacket.[5]

[An Oriya Kshatriya, age 51, a patron of a new monastery founded in 1964, whose head ascetic the informant named as the most important religious leader in town, feels that religion is becoming less fanatic, less dogmatic, and "more sensible."]

The awareness and regard for tradition are still there, but the real old time religion has gone. This is good. There should be spiritual strength in a country as distinct from religious fanaticism.[6]

Religion has always been foremost in India. Everybody has religion, and everybody takes it seriously. Even the Christians are more devout here than they are anywhere else in the world. Of course they got a lot of encouragement under the British, but aside from these recent converts, we have had Christians in India since the first century (Syrian Christians) who are real Christians. The recent converts are sometimes really still more Hindu than Christians. You can never convert a Hindu. We do have a Ramakrishna Mission here, but I have no contact with it. We have no leadership as such in our church, so you just go to somebody who suits you. If you wish to do service, you go to the Ramakrishna Mission. If you wish to learn yoga, you go to another person. If you wish to approach god through the erotic route, you find another person. There are ascetics who attract many disciples and

3. Statement by an Oria Brahman, age 50, Ph.D., another patron of the Guru.
4. Statement by an Oria Kshatriya, age 43, a patron of the Preacher, whose counsel and advice he actively sought.
5. Statement by an Oria Kshatriya, age 51, a patron of the Preacher.
6. Statement by an Oria Kshatriya, age 65, a patron of the Preacher.

acquire great reputations living elsewhere in India, but to my knowledge there are not any in Bhubaneswar.[7]

This last paragraph probably summarizes the attitude held by most patrons and sophisticated clients of the local monasteries.

Although the Preacher and the head ascetic of the Nigamananda Ashrama were Bengalis, their five patrons quoted above were all Orias. The Preacher listed the man quoted in the next to the last extract as one of ten contemporary people "who had lived their lives according to philosophical principles," along with Tagore and Bertrand Russell. This particular patron liked to describe himself as a follower of Gandhi, as a philosopher, and, when it was politically advantageous, as a staunch defender of tradition. These claims, plus substantial monetary contributions, had endeared him to the Preacher. Certainly as a public figure and a devout man, this patron had only advantages to gain from the Preacher's favourable opinion.

On the whole, these responses of influential patrons, none of whom admitted to Professor Taub that he had any connection with a monastery, betray somewhat ambivalent feelings toward traditional Hinduism. Once born into a Hindu culture, it is almost impossible to cease being a Hindu. At the same time that they disavow tradition, informants maintain a household altar at which someone performs *pūjā*, and they also contribute to the upkeep of a monastery.

The Du Bois Value Guide

It is not unusual to encounter similarly mixed and even conflicting attitudes in some of the individuals interviewed in 1965 in Professor Cora Du Bois' study of the values of three hundred citizens of Bhubaneswar who were interviewed in 1965.[8] The informants were divided into fifteen socio-economic groups: high government officials; government technicians and overseers; government clerks; government-employed peons; college students; school teachers; big businessmen; small businessmen; temple servants; cultivators; milkmen; rickshaw pullers; woodcutters; Bauri (a Scheduled Caste of wage labourers, sharecroppers, and stonecutters); and sweepers.

When asked the question, "What is an ascetic?" some of the uneducated proved to be unfamiliar with the word *sādhu*, which had to be rendered *bābājī*

---

7. Statement by an Oria Brahman, age 44, a patron of the Guru and of the new 1964 monastery. His ancestors had been *purohitas* for a large landowner.

8. The following data is taken from: Cora Du Bois "Study of Values, 1965" (interview guides in the files of the Harvard–Bhubaneswar Project).

for them. The responses of the 197 people who understood the word *sādhu* differed markedly from the answers of the 103 uneducated people who responded to *bābājī*.

The ten salient characteristics of a *sādhu* as given by 197 persons who understood the word are summarized in table 6. Of the total of 308 responses from

Table 6
Responses to the Word Sadhu
(total number of responses given = 308, total number of respondents = 197)

Types of Characteristics	PER CENT OF TOTAL	NUMBER OF RESPONSES
*Leads a god-centred life; meditates, worships, thinks about god	22.0	68
‡Has a good character; high-principled, unselfish, dutiful	13.9	43
‡Has integrity; honest, trustworthy	12.0	37
*Possesses spiritual powers, an untarnished mind, and is free from worldly bondage	11.7	36
Other—includes erudition, also respondents' negative feelings	11.4	35
*Renounces the world or worldly desires; lives in lonely places and has no home	10.7	33
†Concerned with social welfare	8.6	26
*Partakes of sanctity; has divine or supernatural characteristics	3.9	12
†Teaches; promulgates religion, leads others to god, discusses religion	3.9	12
†Gives good advice on religious and secular affairs	1.9	6
Total	100.0	308

† *socially oriented characteristics*
* *essentially traditional characteristics*
‡ *personal attributes*

these 197 subjects, 48.3 per cent dealt with traditional characteristics, such as leading a god-centred life, performing meditations, possessing spiritual powers, and renunciation of the world. One-fourth of the responses, or 25.9 per cent, described the personal attributes that differentiate "true" from "false" *sādhus*. Of the 308 responses, 14.4 per cent dealt with social welfare activities.

The replies of the 103 uneducated subjects who responded to the word *bābājī*, as summarized in table 7, presented a very different picture. Of the total of 165 characteristics named, 84 per cent referred to the traditional role of an ascetic and none applied specifically to social welfare. While the 197 better-educated laymen expected social activities from an ascetic, the 103 uneducated clung to the traditional idea of an ascetic as someone who wears distinctive dress and facial symbols and renounces a worldly occupation. These answers reflected the fact that the wealthy and better-educated laymen patronized some

Table 7
Responses to the Word Babaji
(total number of responses given = 165, total number of respondents = 103)

Types of Characteristics	PER CENT OF TOTAL	NUMBER OF RESPONSES
*Leads a god-centred life	16.4	27
*Lives apart	16.4	27
Other, including negative responses	14.6	24
*Wears distinctive clothing	13.9	23
*Depends upon charity	12.1	20
*Practises celibacy	10.9	18
*Wears a beard and long, matted hair	10.9	18
‡Has a good character	2.4	4
*Has spiritual powers, practises divination, and is a seer	2.4	4
Total	100.0	165

* *essentially traditional characteristics*
‡ *personal attributes*

of the larger institutions which engaged in welfare activities, whereas the less educated were apt to be clients of a solitary ascetic of their own caste or ethnic group.

When asked to name three ascetics, about two-thirds of the respondents (197) could name at least one *sādhu* or *bābājī*, about half of the respondents (142) could give two names, and only one-third (103) were able to list three. Some said plainly that it was not their business to know who was a *sādhu* or *bābājī*.

442 positive responses were given by 197 respondents naming either *sādhus* or *bābājīs*. These have been categorized and summarized in table 8. The 442 responses were first divided among contemporary (nos. 1, 4, 5, 6, and 7), historical (nos. 2 and 3), or mythological (no. 9) figures. Contemporary figures accounted for 68.9 per cent of responses. These were further subdivided into

Table 8
Categories of Holy Men Named

Category of Person Named	Summary of Responses Naming a Person		Summary of Order of Responses					
			First		Second		Third	
	PER CENT OF TOTAL	NUMBER OF RESPONSES	PER CENT	NO.	PER CENT	NO.	PER CENT	NO.
Contemporary individuals in the local community (mostly ascetics)	38.2	169	31.0	93	15.3	46	10.0	30
Reformers and revivalists of non-sectarian or Vairagin traditions, such as Ramakrishna or Chaitanya	16.5	73	11.3	34	8.0	24	5.0	15
Historical religious figures, such as Buddha, Guru Nanak, or Shankara	11.3	50	5.3	16	6.3	19	5.0	15
Social or political figures—Nehru, Kennedy, Gopabandhu Das	10.0	44	3.0	9	5.3	16	6.5	19
Gandhi	9.0	40	6.0	18	4.0	12	3.3	10
Contemporary individuals *not* in the local community (mostly ascetics)	9.0	40	5.7	17	5.0	15	2.7	8
Respondents' relatives or gurus	2.7	11	2.0	6	1.3	4	0.3	1
Other	2.0	9	0.7	2	1.0	3	1.2	4
Mythological figures, like Krishna	1.3	6	0.7	2	1.0	3	0.3	1
"Don't know any"	—	—	34.3	103	52.8	158	65.7	197
Totals	100.0	442	100.0	300	100.0	300	100.0	300

individuals with a following limited to some community in India (nos. 1, 6, and 7) and internationally known figures (nos. 4 and 5). Contemporary individuals with a limited following accounted for half (49.9 per cent) of the total number of responses. Of these responses, 169 (38.2 per cent of the total) named persons residing in or near Bhubaneswar, but at least three-quarters of these were not connected with monasteries in Bhubaneswar and were not known to the authors. Another 40 responses (9.0 per cent of the total) referred to individuals not resident in or near Bhubaneswar. These were usually holy men living in the respondent's natal village. Only 11 responses (2.7 per cent of the total) named a person intimately related to the respondent either by blood or spiritual advisorship. Of the 84 responses naming internationally known figures (19.0 per cent of the total), almost half (40) referred to Mahatma Gandhi, who seemed important enough to be given a separate category (no. 5). The other 44 responses listing persons of international reputation included such diverse political figures as Kennedy, Nehru, and Krushchev. A historical religious leader was indicated in 27.8 per cent of the responses. These responses seemed to fall into two groups; leaders of the reformist–revivalist tradition, including the Vairagin Chaitanya of the sixteenth century and the nineteenth-century reformers such as Ramakrishna (16.5 per cent of the total), and religious leaders of earlier times such as Buddha and Shankara (11.3 per cent). Only 1.3 per cent of responses indicated a mythological figure.

Again the replies of subjects responding to *sādhu* and *bābājī* differed significantly. Only a few of the educated subjects named a local contemporary *sādhu*, while considerably more of the answers of the uneducated named a contemporary local *bābājī*. The educated groups, with more elaborate standards for ascetics, including the desirability of social service, perhaps found it difficult to name a local *sādhu* who measured up to their standards, whereas the uneducated had less difficulty in pointing to someone who simply wore a distinct dress. The educated tended to find local ascetics less satisfactory in fulfilling their ideals and tended to point to famous men.

When we examine the numbers who responded in terms of a "local contemporary," we find 93 names given as the first response, 46 as the second response, and 30 as the third response, a total of 169 instances of the naming of "local contemporaries." Of these 169 responses, 136 named individuals unfamiliar to us, mostly ascetics from the respondents' natal villages near Bhubaneswar. The other 33 responses named 14 individuals directly connected with twelve Old Town monasteries. This list included eleven monasteries extant in 1964 (one Oria solitary ascetic, named five times, had left the Old Town before the inquiry began) of which eight were Oria and three Bengali. Since 90.4 per cent of the 300 people interviewed claimed Oria as their mother tongue, it is not surprising that most of the Bengali institutions were not named. All but three of the eleven Oria monasteries were named. The three not named were an endowed monastery that had collapsed (the medieval Kapali Matha), an initially patronized home for retired people (Harihara Satsangha Ashrama), and a small non-sectarian monastery established in 1964 (Trinatha Gosvami Matha) that had only a handful of clients. The three Bengali monasteries named were the Ramakrishna Matha, the Nigamananda Ashrama, and the Nimbarka Ashrama.

Most of the respondents did not identify an ascetic by his exact religious name, because he was usually known by his title, Svamiji or Thakur, or by the name of his guru or the founder of his monastery.

The following sample groups did not identify any specific Old Town ascetic: college students, schoolteachers, big businessmen, small businessmen, milkmen, woodcutters, and sweepers. The uneducated, lower-caste groups were more readily willing to give the names of Old Town ascetics, partly because they did not have the education to give more famous names. An analysis of the addresses and birthplaces of the respondents who named Old Town ascetics shows that they were apt to name one who lived nearby, not necessarily anyone whom they respected.

The following respondents named an identifiable Old Town ascetic or monastery: one high government official; one government technician; one government clerk; one government peon; eleven temple servants; two cultivators; three Scheduled Caste Bauri; and thirteen Oria and Telegu rickshaw pullers. Out of the 197 respondents who gave the name of at least one ascetic, 33 respondents named an Old Town monastery or ascetic. Five of these respondents, all rickshaw pullers, named an Oria monastery that had ceased operations before the inquiry began. The frequency with which the names of the other eleven monasteries appear does not produce any pattern of relevance. The Ramakrishna Matha and the Shiva Tirtha Matha were each named five times by members of Scheduled Castes. This may mean that the Ramakrishna Matha and Mission is living up to its claim to be reaching out toward the lower castes. No other monastery was named more than three times, and three were only named once. The monastery of the Oria religious leader (the Guru) was only named twice, and the monastery of the leader of the Bengali religious community (the Preacher) was not named at all.

The following are some typical comments about ascetics made by respondents who named an Old Town ascetic or monastery.

A *sādhu* keeps away from all worldly affairs, speaks the truth, and serves people. Considering present times, meditation has no value.[9]

9. Statement by a government technician who named the Nigamananda Ashrama.

A *sādhu* has a deep understanding of life's philosophy and believes in god. *Sādhus* are the force that keeps society going.[10]

Sādhus must consider the welfare of others. A *sādhu* is one who worships the deity, participates in religious discussion, and gives good advice in worldly matters.[11]

An ascetic has no worldly cares and anxieties. He recites the name of the deity and speaks the truth.[12]

A *bābājī* has long hair, a beard, a moustache, and a red ochre cloth. He is always smoking *gañjā*.[13]

Sādhus today are very selfish and do not work. *Sādhus* are doing good work. They have faith in god.[14]

Sādhus today are not real *sādhus*.[15]

The rest of the 169 replies coded as "local contemporaries" were the names of ascetics from the respondents' villages in either Puri or Cuttack districts. The temple servants, as expected, produced the greatest number of names, since they were familiar with the medieval endowed monasteries whose heads officiated in certain temple-connected festivals.

Nevertheless, the prestige of the ascetic's role still outranks dedication to the welfare of humanity in a secular role. When asked, "If a young man does not marry, in order to dedicate himself to noble purposes, is it better to serve the government in an important position, or to become a very respected holy man?", the answers were as found in table 9. Perhaps the career of holy man outranks that of government service because the latter is often viewed with disaffection by both the citizenry and the civil servants. Those who preferred government service tended to have little education, be low-caste, and have dissimilar occupations for grandfather and father, but similar occupations for father and respondent. Government service still appears as an avenue of social mobility for the less privileged groups, whereas the more educated tend to find government service less rewarding.

10. Statement by a government clerk who named the Ramakrishna Matha.
11. Statement by a government-employed peon who named the Shankarananda Matha.
12. Statement by three temple servants who named the Shiva Tirtha Matha.
13. Statement by two temple servants who named the Sadavrata Pitha.
14. Statement by two rickshaw pullers who mentioned the Vishrama Ghatta Matha.
15. Statement by a rickshaw puller who named the Gopala Tirtha Matha.

Table 9
Preference for Government Service
versus the Ascetic Life (total number of responses given = 300)

Preference stated	PER CENT OF TOTAL	NUMBER OF RESPONSES
Prefer holy man	63.7	191
Prefer government worker	26.7	80
Rejected question, equivocated, or said, "don't know"	9.6	29
Total	100.0	300

When asked whether or not religion is dying out in India, the responses were almost evenly divided, with a slight edge in favour of those who thought religion was *not* dying out. The feeling that religion *is* dying out correlates with high education and occupational level, high caste, and youth. Attitudes associated with the response that religion *is* dying out include preference for conscience over sacred tradition, a confidence that the poor can succeed, sympathy for human beings, and a feeling that institutional priests and family priests (*purohitas*) retard progress.

Responses about religious practices demonstrate a similar ambivalence in attitudes. When asked *why* the respondents preferred a certain festival, almost half of the 300 gave reasons like "important," or "traditional," or "part of my worship." The other half listed such reasons as family reunions, merry-making, new clothes, food, dances, music, and vacations.

Table 10
Frequency of Temple Visits
(total number of responses given = 297)

Frequency	PER CENT OF TOTAL	NUMBER OF RESPONSES
Within last month	41.1	122
Within last six months	22.9	68
Not at all	18.2	54
Within last year	16.5	49
Rejected question	1.3	4
Total	100.0	297

Table 11
Household Puja Performance
(total number of respondents = 237)

Performers	PER CENT OF TOTAL	NUMBER OF RESPONDENTS
Not done	54.5	129
Performed by respondent's generation	37.5	89
Performed by older generation	8.0	19
Total	100.0	237

Most of the informants had visited the temple within the last year, as shown in table 10. Persons who visit the temple infrequently tend to have little education, a low level of occupation, low caste, no intergenerational mobility, and a long term of residence at Bhubaneswar. Some Scheduled Caste groups are not allowed to enter beyond the temple courtyard, but are welcome at a few non-sectarian monasteries.

Those who visit the temple are likely to be those who also perform household *pūjā*. Of 237 respondents, almost half still had *pūjā* performed in their houses, as shown in table 11. Performance of *pūjā* correlates with: high level of education for respondents and their two preceding generations of forebears; high level of occupation; high caste; high income; being married; and being part of a large household. The correlation between high educational level and household worship occurs because the families best able to provide an education are traditionally privileged and conservative. Associated attitudes for those who come from households in which *pūjā* is performed are preference for community over family, education over status, sympathy for human beings, and preference for individual conscience over sacred books.

Apparently the same sample groups who are patrons or "sophisticated" clients of monasteries are also those most apt to visit the temple or to perform *pūjā*. These are the educated, upper-caste families of wealth and high-level occupations. In other words, the same upper castes who have traditionally been the supporters of religious institutions remain so today. While actual patrons or clients of monasteries are likely also to uphold other religious institutions, such as the temple, the reverse is not the case. The majority of those who visit the temple regularly are not necessarily connected with a monastery.

These same upper-caste groups who have traditionally upheld religious institutions tend to feel that "religion is dying out" (in response to the question on the strength of religion today) and are also unable or unwilling to name a local Old Town ascetic. The general impression is that the traditional elites remain elites and that they support traditional values, but that they have added new values such as modern education and social service while questioning the surviving institutions and roles associated with Hindu religiosity in the past.

The uneducated, on the other hand, are less likely to perform *pūjā*, visit the temple, or become resident ascetics. More of them would choose government service as a way to economic security and social mobility.

Plate 1. The Kedara Gauri Temple complex, located on the north-east border of the Old Town, is characteristic of Oria architectural style with an audience hall (the smaller structure) adjoining the sanctum which houses a Siva *lingam*.

Plate 2. The magnificent Lingaraja Mahaprabhu Temple complex, completed during the reign of the Somavamsha kings (950–1065), is one of the major architectural monuments on the east coast. Still in active use, the main tower of the temple houses a stone *liṅgam* that represents the dual powers of Shiva (Lingaraja) and Vishnu (Mahaprabhu). (Courtesy of the Archaeological Survey of India.)

Plate 3. An aerial view of the Old Town, looking northward, with the Lingaraja Mahaprabhu Temple complex in the foreground. Directly north of the main tower or sanctum of the temple and along the main road of the town are the two medieval-built monasteries pictured in the frontispiece (photographer unknown).

Plate 4. The Sadavrata Pitha, the oldest of the endowed monasteries, was built in the seventh century A.D. as a guest house for wandering ascetics. The residential quarters are similar to those at the Shankarananda Matha, the monastery of the Guru. (See plates 6 and 17.)

Plate 5. The main residential building of the Ramakrishna Matha, built in 1919 at the north end of the Old Town, is the largest monastic structure at Bhubaneswar. It houses five ascetics.

Plate 6. Saccidananda Sarasvati, the Guru, and head of the Shankarananda Matha, exemplifies the austerity of the traditional follower of Shankara. The three horizontal markings across his forehead, the large *rudrākṣa* beads about his neck, and the single-pronged bamboo staff identify the Guru as a Dashanami Sannyasin. Highly respected by all who knew him, the Guru is the religious leader of the Oria community in the Old Town.

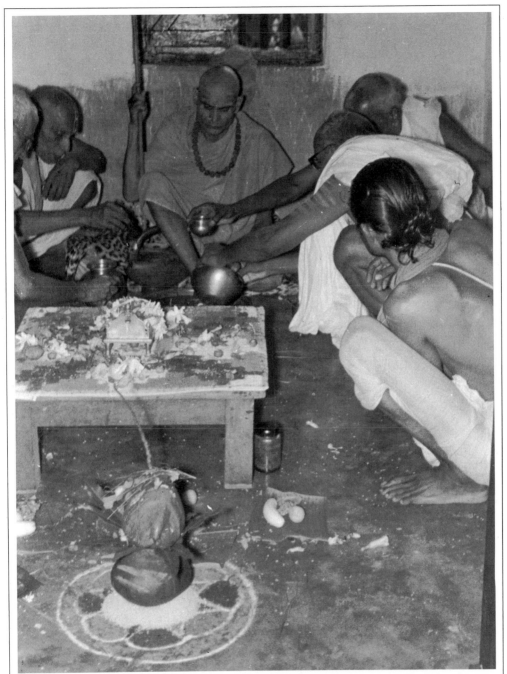

Plate 7. On Guru Purnima (the full-moon day of July) Saccidananda Sarasvati is honoured as the Guru of the Shankarananda Matha. Part of the ceremony is the solemn rite of washing the Guru's feet. The bench, strewn with flower petals, was used in the earlier ceremony honouring the previous heads of the monastery.

Plate 8. The Arya Rishikula Bhuvaneshvari Ashrama, the residence of the Preacher, is typical of the hermitages of Sanskrit literature; hidden within the sacred mango grove to the south of the town, the monastery grows most of its fruit and vegetables within the compound.

Plate 9. Many of those who attend Guru Purnima at the Shankarananda Matha are learned in Sanskrit and are either head ascetics at other monasteries or lay Sanskrit teachers at local high schools. Although the Guru is a Dashanami Sannyasin, three of the ascetics sitting in the second from top row are Vaishnava Vairagins, illustrating the fluidity of Hindu sectarianism even within more traditional monastic orders.

Plate 10. The guru-mother (*ma*) of the Arya Rishikula Bhuvaneshvari Ashrama silently places the first daily offering of food (*bala bhoga*) before the altar enshrining photographs of the monastery's gurus. She is a widow who waits on the head ascetic, the Preacher, and who manages the monastery's kitchen.

Plate 11. Evening worship (Sandhya Arati) is being performed before the six-armed image of Rama-Krishna-Chaitanya by Gaura Dasa, the Bhakta of Shadbhuja Chaitanya Mandira. The food (*prasāda*) placed on plates before the altar and offered before the image will be eaten by the residents of the monastery later in the evening.

Plate 12. If the ascetics of Bhubaneswar were to be ranked according to social status, these two men would be placed near the bottom; on the left is Bhavani Shankara, the Solitary Ascetic, who converted an abandoned temple into his *maṭha*, and on the right is Kailasa Tapas Giri, a former temple cook who donned religious garb after becoming stricken with leprosy. Bhavani Shankara holds a Bengali translation of the Bhagavad Gita and the staff of a wandering ascetic.

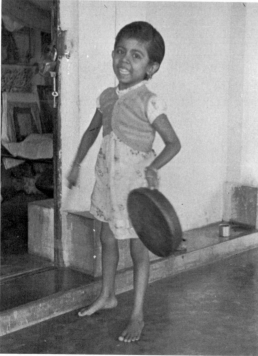

Plate 13. Virendra Natha Sadhukhan, the Troubadour, beats the drum and Kamakara Brahmachari, the Fun-Lover, plays the harmonium as they sing a Bengali devotional song. Both men are renowned in the Old Town area for their musical talents. Although the Troubadour is a Shudra and the Fun-Lover is a Brahman, they spend many hours singing together.

Plate 14. The Bhakta's six-year-old daughter, Shanti Rani, stands in the audience hall, to the right of the inner chamber, banging a gong (*ghaṇṭa*) while he conducts the evening worship of the deity.

Plate 15. At Chintamanish-vara Mandira three Brahmans assemble after completing their morning toilet. To the left is Abakash Padhi, the hereditary priest assigned to the temple, who performs the daily *pūjā*. In the centre is Mauna Babaji, the resident ascetic who, although taking a vow of silence, is the one most responsible for securing the financial aid which supported the repairs and the renovations to the temple property. On the right is Doctor Refugee in a pose of reverence before the image of Hamuman enshrined within one of the smaller temples on the compound.

Plate 16. Dr. Refugee stands at the rear of the main classroom of the Buddhasvari primary school, which he claims as one of the many social service projects that he has supported.

Plate 17. Taponidhi Sudarshana Bharati Gosvami is the head of Sadvrata Pitha, more commonly known as Bharati Matha, the oldest monastery at Bhubaneswar, built in the seventh century A.D. Although he belongs to the Bharati suborder of Dashanami Sannyasins, the image enshrined in the monastery is that of Kamakhya, normally a Shakta deity.

Plate 18. Jagadguru 1108 Shri Vishveshvarananda Tirtha Svami, head of the Shiva Tirtha Matha, moves toward a window in his bedroom. Prior to entrance into monastic orders, he was an Ayur Vedic medical practitioner, an occupation he maintains on a limited basis as an ascetic.

Plate 19. On Guru Purima, Jagadguru 1108 Shri Gopala Tirtha Svami, head of Gopala Tirtha Matha, sits in front of the altar honouring the previous head of the monastery, who was also Gopala Tirtha Svami's uncle. Again, it is interesting to note that, although Gopala Tirtha Svami belongs to the Tirtha suborder of Dashanami Sannyasins, the images enshrined in the *pūjā* room of the monastery are those of Krishna and Radha, Vaishnava deities. The images placed before his uncle's picture represent, however, his preference for Shiva and Parvati.

Plate 20. On the eve of Durga Puja, Virendra Natha Sadhukhan, the Troubadour (left, cupping the author's son underneath the chin), and Sudhir Adhikari, the head ascetic at Sadguru Nivasa Ashrama (facing camera), are shown in front of a tableau of Shiva and Parvati. Most of the endowed monasteries provide space for similar tableaux, which are constructed within their compounds for the festival. Many of the ascetics, like other residents of the Old Town, enjoy walking about the streets and the market place during the major festivals, which often last for several days.

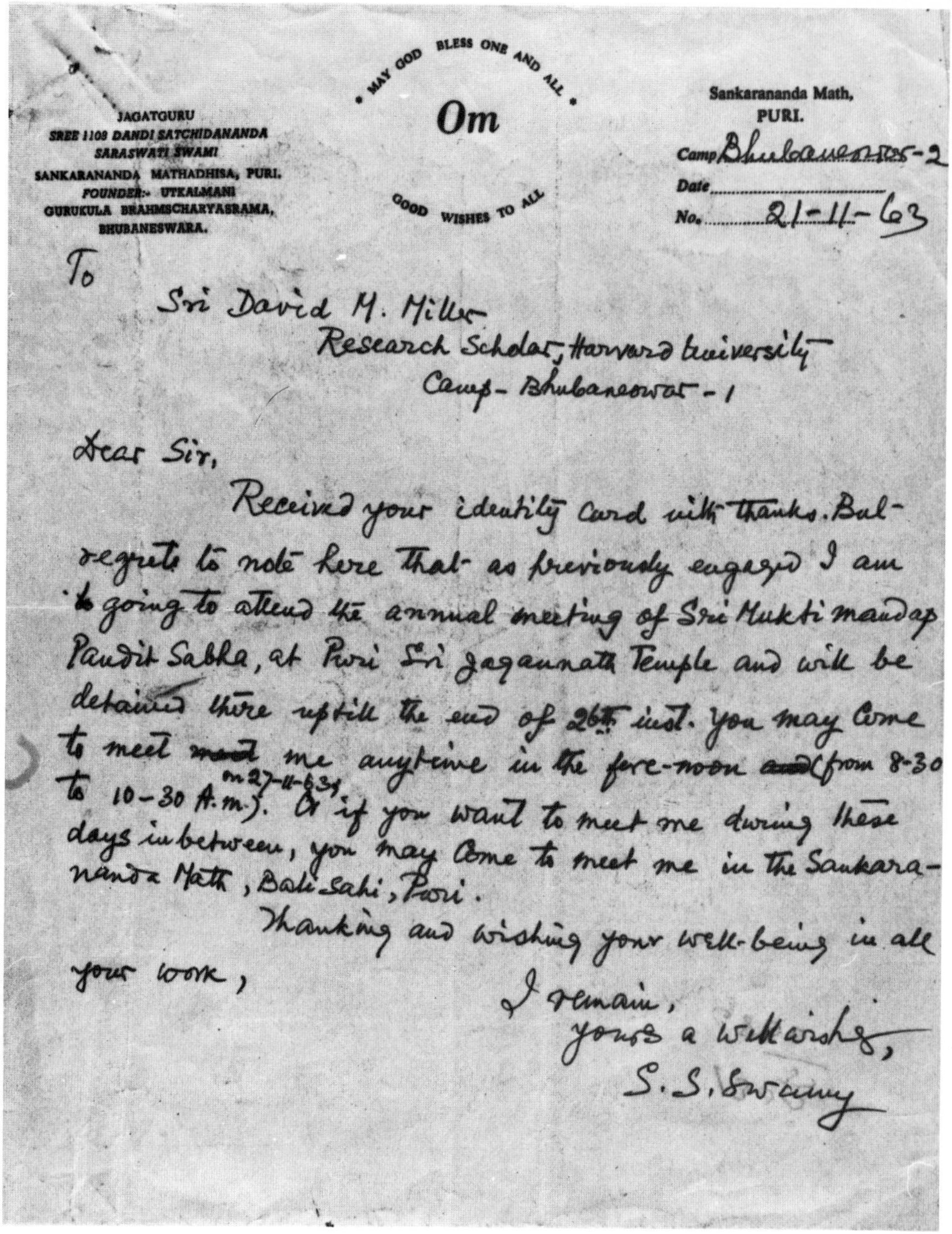

MAY GOD BLESS ONE AND ALL

Om

GOOD WISHES TO ALL

JAGATGURU
SREE 1108 DANDI SATCHIDANANDA
SARASWATI SWAMI
SANKARANANDA MATHADHISA, PURI.
FOUNDER:- UTKALMANI
GURUKULA BRAHMSCHARYASRAMA,
BHUBANESWARA.

Sankarananda Math,
PURI.
Camp Bhubaneswar-2
Date
No. 21-11-63

To

Sri David M. Miller
Research Scholar, Harvard University
Camp- Bhubaneswar - 1

Dear Sir,

Received your identity card with thanks. But regrets to note here that as previously engaged I am going to attend the annual meeting of Sri Muktimandap Pandit Sabha, at Puri Sri Jagannath Temple and will be detained there uptill the end of 26th inst. You may come to meet me anytime in the fore-noon on 27-11-63 (from 8-30 to 10-30 A.m.). Or if you want to meet me during these days in between, you may come to meet me in the Sankarananda Math, Bali-sahi, Puri.

Thanking and wishing your well-being in all your work,

I remain,
yours a wellwisher,
S. S. Swamy

Plate 21. Saccidananda Sarasvati Svami, the Guru, writes that he will be detained at Puri for meetings of the Mukti Mandapa Pandita Sabha and therefore will not be able to meet the author until later in November 1963. The letter-head calls attention to the fact that the Guru was founder of Utkalmani Gurukula Brahmacharyashrama, the Sanskrit school connected with the Bhubaneswar branch of the monastery.

SWAMI VIVEKANANDA BIRTH CENTENARY, ORISSA.

Sri Ramakrishna Math.
Bhubaneshwar-2.
18th December, 1963

Phone : 213

Dear Sir/Madam,

The concluding celebration of the Centenary of **Swami Vivekananda** will be held at Sri Ramakrishna Math, Bhubaneshwar as per programme overleaf.

You are cordially invited to attend with your relatives and friends.

Yours in Service of the Lord,

BIJU PATNAIK   **SWAMI SUPARNANANDA**
President   *Secretary*
CENTENARY COMMITTEE, ORISSA,

N. B:—An Exhibition, depicting the life of Swami Vivekananda, will be opened on 25-12-63 and will continue till 6-1-64 at Sri Ramakrishna Math, Bhubaneshwar. **Sri Biren Mitra,** Chief-Minister, Orissa has kindly consented to open the celebration.

The Exhibition will also be opened and a Ladies' Day observed at Cuttack, the details of which will be announced later.

Plate 22. The Ramakrishna Matha announces the Svami Vivekananda Birth Centenary to coincide with the Annual Meetings of the Congress Party at Bhubaneswar in January 1964. Biju Patnaik, a wealthy businessman and a powerful political figure, will assist the head of the monastery, Svami Suparananda in making arrangements.

Annual Budget Estimate of Temple or Math o

GOPALA TIRTHA MATHA

INCOME   1963-64

Heads of income	Estimat. for the succeeding year.	Total as per heads
6	7	8
	1963-64 Rs.	Rs.
1. Opening Balance—		
(a) Cash	1444.02	
(b) Current account		
(c) Price of paddy and other crops	2439.79	
Total		3883.81
2. Land— Md. Sr.		
Estimated quantity of Paddy		
Quantity of paddy required for Deba seba	153000.00	
(a) Quantity and price of Rs. surplus paddy.		
price of crops other than paddy		
Price of paddy required for Deba seba.		
(b) Price of surplus crops	200.00	
(c) Other incomes from land.	6500.00	
Total—income from land		22000.00
3. Rents and fees—		
(a) Income from house-rent	300.00	
(b) Income from shops situate within the premises of the temple.	6500.00	
(c) Fees realised from Bhog.	1000.00	
Total—income from rents and fees		7800.00
4. Veti and Darsani offered to Deity—		
(a) Cash	200.00	200.00
(b) Approximate cash value of Veti articles		
Total—income from Veti and Darsani		
5. Grants and Aids from Government		1100.00
6. (a) Interest on investments		
(b) Interest on deposits		
Total—income from interest		
7. Prasad, etc,—		
(a) Income from sale of Prasad (Excess Kotha Bhoga towards sevaks " khei ")		
(b) Income from fines on employees and servants.		
(c) Income from other sources	400.00	
Total—income from sale of Prasad and other sources.		400.00
8. Income from extraordinary sources and loans—		
(a) Deposit withdrawn		
(b) Loans refunded		
(c) Loans taken		
(d) Consideration money for sale of land		
(e) Consideration money for sale of house		
(f) Money realised from mortgage of land		
(g) Money realised from mortgage of house		
Total—Income from extraordinary sources and loans.		
9. Recoveries from advances		
Grand Total		35383.81

Plates 23 and 24. These plates are copies of Form E for the Gopala Tirtha Matha, 1963–64, from the files of the Orissa Hindu Religious Endowments Commission in Cuttack, Orissa. The Gopala Tirtha Matha has the largest income and expenditures of the five endowed monasteries. Each year the Endowments Commission is required to audit the financial records of the monastery.

GOPALA TIRTHA MATHA

Heads of expenditure	Estimate for the succeeding year.	Total as per heads
6	7	8
	1963-64	
	Rs.	Rs.
1. (a) Pay of employees and servants.	5936.00	
(b) Fixed travelling allowance		
(c) General travelling allowance of employees	314.00	
(d) Contingencies	500.00	
Total—Expenditures for pay, etc.		6750.00
2. Expenditure for general daily worship		6640.00
3. Expenditure for festivals and ceremonies.		2110.00
4. (a) Expenditure for personal cultivation and horticulture.	1700.00	
(b) Expenditure for improvement and repair of lands.	300.00	
(c) Expenditure for repair of houses.	3750.00	
Total—Expenditure for repair of lands and houses.		5750.00
5. (a) Rent payable to Government	2500.00	
(b) Tax payable to Municipality, etc.	2500.00	
(c) Contribution payable under Endowment Act.	500.00	
(d) Suit costs payable to Endowment Department.		
Total—Expenditure for revenue, tax and contributions.		5500.00
6. (a) Expenditure towards suits and cases	500.00	
(b) Expenditure for audit	1000.00	
Total—Expenditure for suits, cases and audit.		1500.00
7. (a) Personal expenses of Mahant	1250.00	
(b) Expenditure on Mahant's pilgrimages.		
(c) Medical expenses of Mahant and employees.		
(d) Expenditure on schools and libraries		
(e) Miscellaneous charitable expenses.	625.00	
Total—Expenditure towards Mahant's personal and charitable purposes.		1875.00
8. (a) Repair of conveyances		
(b) Maintenance of domestic animals	100.00	
(c) Other minor expences	100.00	
Total—Miscellaneous minor expenditures.		1100.00
9. (a) Purchase of lands		
( ) Construction of houses		
(c) Purchase of conveyances		
(d) Purchase of domestic animals.		
(e) Interest on loan		
(f) Repayment of loan		
(g) Investments other than current accounts in Banks.		
Total—Expenditure on extraordinary sources and loans.		
10. Amounts recoverable from advances.		885.61
11 Balance at the end of the year—		3273.20
(a) Cash		
(b) Current account in Bank		
(c) Approximate price of surplus paddy and other crops.		
Total—Balance amount		
Grand Total		35383.81

Farewell Address

To

Mr. David M. Miller

Research Scholar,

Harvard University, U. S. A.

Our beloved and highly-esteemed friend :

It was with great pleasure
That we first met you here,
And offered our cordial welcome
At your inner urge and self-prompted advent
To pay obeisance to Sri Sri Thakur,
Srimat Gangananda Brahmachari Maharaj,
When you got the fragrance of
Coming across His Ashrama at Bhubaneswar,
Your centre of research and culture.

We had the proud privilege to know :
From a distant part of the globe,
Very rich and illustrious as well,
Utmost trouble did you take
To come over the ancient land of ours
In search of precious gems and pearls,
Bedecked with transcedental Joy and Truth,
From the fathomless depth of Theeology.

Drifted away in that endless ocean,
Benumbed with its matchless beauty & purity,
Yourself, our ever-welcome guest,
Cast anchor at this poor but all-embracing shore ;
What have been out, you know —
We could only extend love and reverence
Throbbing in the very heart of our hearts
Towards the traveller in the realm of Religion.

Highly delighted we're to find in return
From sweet words and unsophisticated looks
Greatly inspired and enamoured you're
At the magic-wand of Sri Sri Thakur.
Thus were opened the doors of hidden treasure
When you got your ever-inviting jewels
Through a magnetic glimpse of unlimited Grace
Radiated from Sadguru Sri Sri Bijay Krishna
And other representative Saints of the soil ;
So profound was your spontaneous homage
Towards Sri Sri Kuladananda Brahmachari,
The living embodiment of Lord Nilkantha.

Equally elated and grateful we're
That you've cherished heart-felt desire
For communicating nectar-like mirth and
realisation
To the near and dear ones in the motherland
Through the publication of "Nilkantha"
And the Divine Life-history of Sri Sri Thakur.
You'll render immaculate services thereby
To the cause of humanity at large,
When the existance of the peace-loving earth
Is threatened by colossal pride and insolence ,
Deeply absorbed in studies and meditation,
You have had communion with us all
In this holy and common platform
Propagating the spirit of universal brotherhood.

Go you back to your native-land,
Rejuvenated with increasing zeal,
Revitalised with superb consciousness.
Hope, you'll have such deep regards
For our revered Sri Sri Thakur
And love for these brethren of yours.
May you be crowned with real success
In the path of your onward march
By smacking the very essence of Religion.
May God bless you with true Joy & Peace.

J A I   G U R U

60, Simla Street,
Calcutta-6.
The 3rd December, 1964.

Yours most sincerely,
Members of
SRI SRI SADGURU SADHAN SANGHA

Plate 25. Brahmachari Gangananda, head of the Sadguru Sadhan Sangha in Calcutta and of the Sadguru Nivasa Ashrama branch monastery in Bhubaneswar, presents the author with a farewell address written in the style and language characteristic of the Hindu *sādhu* who wishes to express his gratitude for the warmth of friendship he has encountered.

Part Two

The

Monasteries

Chapter 6

The

Range

of

Religious

Structures

Although the religious hierarchy, monastic order, and chosen deity are clearly ascertainable for each establishment, the inter-relations between them are highly complex. The Indian tradition of an individualized search for salvation has produced a chaotic structure of religious authority. Centuries of syncretism have weakened the original relation between monastic order and chosen deity or deities.

Fission and Intercommunication

Unlike the highly organized Christian or Buddhist monasteries, in which a religious superior can discipline or expel an inferior for heresy or breaking rules, the Hindu monastic orders usually have no effective source of religious discipline. The only firm standards of religious practice are set by Hindu custom: a monk may not eat meat, fish, or eggs, and must avoid sexual scandal. Beyond these general rules there are no real means of establishing distinctions between "orthodox" and "heretical" faith and practice. A man who wishes to become an ascetic needs the guidance of a guru but is not bound in later life by the guru's teachings. Many ascetics simply don distinctive dress and put on facial symbols. With or without formal permission from their gurus, they set themselves up as holy men, choose their own deities, and adopt their own styles of life. No one, ascetic or layman, can tell them that they are following a right or wrong path unless they break one of the fundamental rules of Hindu custom.

The only vestiges of religious authority appear among orders having branches in different towns. In such orders the head ascetic usually has the power to appoint the abbot and to exercise some financial control over branch monasteries. However, he rarely interferes with the branch monastery's daily worship or annual festivals. He usually intervenes only when there is a breach of custom so great as to cause a scandal. The only instance we encountered of any enforcement of religious discipline was that involving Kamakara Brahmacharin, the Fun-lover.

The existence of an established order with head and branch monasteries does not guarantee the continuity of the institution. The five monasteries dating from the medieval period have indeed shown a continuity of tradition on account of their landed endowments, the economic management of which required a stable succession to headship. Monastic groups without endowments tend to divide and subdivide. At the death of their guru, each of several disciples may found his own separate monastery, thereby splitting the order. The following sketch demonstrates the almost complete lack of religious hierarchy and the extreme individualism found even within monasteries founded by disciples of the same guru.

Gangananda Tirtha, a Shankara Dashanami Sannyasin of the mid-nineteenth century, was believed to be an incarnation of the Vedic seer Vasishtha, one of the stars in the Great Bear. He initiated a disciple known as Nityananda Chaitanyaghana (1862–1931), who in turn initiated two disciples, Jagadananda Bhakti Shastri Tirtha (the Preacher) and Mada Brahmarishi Pagalananda Thakur. At Nityananda's death, the order split into two major sections headed by these two disciple brothers, each of whom set up his own monastery at Bhubaneswar. Jagadananda's institution, founded in 1945, is the headquarters of one section of the order. The other section, founded by Pagalananda in 1955, has its headquarters in Contai, West Bengal, with a branch at Bhubaneswar.

At Jagadananda's establishment the chosen deities are actually the guru-founders of the order. The altar contains, in descending order from top to bottom, a drawing of the legendary Vasishtha, flanked by photographs of Nityananda Chaitanyaghana, and Nityananda's wife. Vaishnava influences also appear in the form of a print of Krishna beside the guru's picture. After Jagadananda's death, his picture may be placed on the altar below Nityananda's, adding to the chain of gurus.

On the other hand, Pagalananda the head of the other division of the order, has established himself as the "chosen deity" at the Bhubaneswar branch. His two-foot-square photograph is the only object enshrined on the canopy-covered altar in the *pūjā* room. It is somewhat unusual for the contemporary founder of a monastery to place his own photograph on the altar as the one and only object of worship. Jagadananda was shocked to learn that no other guru besides Pagalananda is worshipped in his disciple-brother's monastery. He refuses to enter Pagalananda's monastery or to accept the food offered to the deity, since the "deity" is in fact his "friend" and disciple-brother.

According to an article in the 6 April 1959 issue of *Nihar*, a weekly published in Contai, Pagalananda was the object of an attack by "mischief-mongers," perhaps inspired by local Communists. The rumour spread that he was sacrificing children in the ritual fire ceremony (*homa*). Public indignation exploded when the skull of a baby was found near the monastery early one morning. A mob led by college students fired the *āśrama*, severely beat Pagalananda, and threw him into the bathing tank. The police finally dispersed the mob and removed the head ascetic from the tank. To their amazement, he was still alive, a feat of survival that he attributed to the yogic practice of feigning death. An investigation proved that someone had taken a dead baby from a nearby hospital and had placed the body near the monastery. The ascetic took the students to court, but withdrew the charges when his attackers repented.

Pagalananda has been influenced by Tantric practices, which arouse the suspicion of many Hindus. Jagadananda, the Preacher, on the other hand, has never been influenced by Tantra. He is the acknowledged leader of the Bengali religious community in the Old Town.

Monasteries of different orders often have little intercommunication and only a scattered knowledge of each other's existence. In 1962 a resident of the Old Town provided a list of eighteen monasteries then operating, of which four had ceased to function as religious establishments by 1964. The authors asked the head ascetic of each of the fourteen extant establishments whether he knew of any other monasteries in the Old Town. The average head ascetic could name the five oldest monasteries clustered around the Temple in the centre of town, but none could name more than ten institutions besides his own and most were quite surprised to see a list of fourteen. Occasionally a head ascetic would add another name to the list, which eventually grew to twenty-one. The twenty-second establishment (Trinatha Gosvami Matha) was unknown to any other head ascetic and was discovered through an accidental encounter with its founder in a tea-stall. Although one head ascetic might occasionally criticize another during an interview, none disputed the other ascetic's prerogative in setting his own religious standards. To do so would have meant to dispute the basic principle that there are many different paths to salvation.

Chosen Deities

Centuries of syncretism have produced anomalies and complexities in the relations between monastic order and chosen deity. The individual idiosyncrasies of founding patrons or head ascetics have added to the tangle. Deities fall into five categories, listed roughly in the order of their antiquity in Bhubaneswar: Shaiva; Shakta (Tantric); Vaishnava; gurus; non-sectarian (see table 2).

The Shankara tradition is originally Shaiva. Even today in the folk tradition Shankara is considered to be the incarnation of Shiva. The central object of Shaiva worship is the Shiva *lingam*, an upright column of stone that may range from a few inches to several feet in height, representing the creative power or phallus of Shiva, surmounting an oval pedestal (*yoni*) signifying the genital organ of his female consort. Of the ten monasteries following the Shankara tradition today, only two preserve the *lingam* as symbolic of their chosen deity. At the one endowed institution preserving its original Shaiva image (the Shiva Tirtha Matha, founded in the medieval period), the eight-inch *lingam* is completely overshadowed by a life-sized Vaishnava wall mural of Jagannatha (Krishna), Balarama (Krishna's brother), and Subhadra (Krishna's sister). At the Gopala Tirtha Matha, the sister organization of the Shiva Tirtha Matha, the principal deities are Krishna and Radha and no image of Shiva is present, although the monastery is part of the Tirtha sub-order of Dashanami Sannyasins.

Seven of the eight monasteries that follow the Shankara tradition have been so affected by syncretism that they cannot be considered purely Shaiva. The oldest institution at Bhubaneswar presents an interesting example of early syncretism with the Shakta or Tantric tradition.

The Sadavrata Pitha, founded in the seventh century, is the oldest of the eight Bhubaneswar monasteries whose head ascetics belong to Shankara orders. The name, a combination of *sadā*, "always," or "at all times," and *vrata*, "vow," refers to its medieval function of promising always to feed wandering ascetics and pilgrims. *Pīṭha* means the "seat of a deity," and in this case designates the place where, according to a Bhubaneswar legend, the vulva of Parvati fell after she had been cut to pieces by Vishnu's discus. Sometime during the seventh century, the rulers of Orissa built this monastery as a home for ascetics of the Pashupata sect, an early, austere Shaiva order which, after its introduction to Bhubaneswar at about this time, quickly overcame the earlier Jain and Buddhist groups. The legendary founder of the Pashupata sect, Lakulisha, appears in a stone carving of the late sixth century in the classic post-Gupta

Buddhist style that was later built into the monastery wall. Lakulisha, who lived around A.D. 100, is regarded as the guru-founder of the monastery. The chosen deity of the Pashupatas was Shiva; yet, at some point Shiva was replaced by an image of Kamakhya (Durga), who according to a Bhubaneswar legend is a Tantric deity symbolic of the vulva of Parvati. This image of Kamakhya, who remains the chosen deity today, was probably first installed at some time in the eighth century, when other archaeological evidence of the Tantric–Shakta tradition appears in Bhubaneswar. During the next century the Shankara tradition spread northward to Bhubaneswar absorbing both the Shaiva Pashupatas and the Tantric Shakta influence. Thus the history of the Sadavrata Pitha probably includes, within two centuries of its founding, a synthesis of three different traditions: the austere Shaiva Pashupata, the Tantric–Shakta, and the Shankara cults. The monastery has retained a Tantric deity although it does not belong to the Tantric monastic order and is not today influenced by Tantric beliefs and practices.

Monasteries following Vairagin monastic traditions all worship either forms of Vishnu or their own guru-founders who trace their linage to divine figures related to Vishnu. Vaishnava deities include Lakshmi–Narayana, Radha–Krishna, Sita–Rama, Jagannatha, and Chaitanya. The dual images of Narayana (Vishnu) and his wife Lakshmi symbolize the unity of the godhead and are analogous to the well-known Tantric unity of Shiva–Shakti. Vishnu represents the male principle or static ground of being, while Lakshmi represents the female principle or dynamic power of creation. However, the concept of the macrocosmic union of the male and female principles can be traced to Rig-vedic times, and is therefore not limited to the Tantric tradition. The dual images of Krishna and his consort Radha, and Rama and his wife Sita are similar in import. Jagannatha (Lord of the Universe, often identified with Krishna) is the name of the deity whose temple at Puri, thirty-five miles from Bhubaneswar, is one of the four major Vaishnava pilgrimage centres. Chaitanya is worshipped as an incarnation of both Krishna and Radha, and is sometimes pictured with the physique of a man yet with the breasts and hair of a woman.

The temple to Chaitanya at the Shadbhuja Chaitanya Mandira, founded by Nibaran Mukharji, the Bhakta, is characteristic of Vaishnava monasteries. A recently built (1941) and well-kept shrine, it is located at the southern edge of the Old Town, near a mango grove of legendary import. Its compound has gardens with mango trees, papayas, vegetables, a grazing area for the cow, a *tulasī* plant sacred to Lakshmi, a well, and a very small four-room residence. The temple to Chaitanya is the most striking feature in the compound. A handsome building in Bengali style with open verandahs and repeated pyramidal towers, it is decorated in Puri-style coloured paintings with vividly active figures. Chaitanya is pictured preaching to the wild animals in the heart of the Orissa jungle. Within the ten-foot-square inner chamber, guarded by two demons whom the saint converted, stands the four-foot-tall, six-armed image of Shadbhuja Rama–Krishna–Chaitanya. Shadbhuja means "six-armed." The upper two arms of the image are green; the left hand holds a bow and the right hand holds an arrow, which are symbols of Rama as a warrior. The middle two arms are blue and the hands hold a flute, the symbol of Krishna the lover. The lower two arms are yellow, as is the body of the image, characterizing Chaitanya as Gauranga (yellow-limbed). The lower left hand holds a water pot and the lower right hand a staff, symbolizing Chaitanya as a *sannyāsin*. According to the founder, Chaitanya is regarded as the incarnation of Vishnu for this age, the Kali Yuga (dark age), whereas Rama and Krishna were incarnations of Vishnu for the two previous ages.

There has been continual accumulation of influences among Shankara Shaiva, the Tantric–Shakta tradition, and Vaishnava tradition. Finally, syncretism has sometimes been carried to the extent of complete eclecticism and the worship of non-sectarian deities. A typical example of eclecticism was observed in the shrine of a solitary ascetic who is head of the Pashupatinatha Gita Ashrama. Although he is a Vaishnava, he retains both the original Shaiva name of the monastery and his predecessor's shrine. He has moved the former ascetic's Shaiva pictures to the side walls and has placed an image of Sita–Rama in the centre. Above the Shaiva crescent moon stands the wheel (*chakra*) of Vishnu that must be at the top of every Vaishnava altar. The interior walls of his thatch-roofed hut are almost completely covered with pictures representing all the major deities of the Hindu pantheon.

A syncretistic temple is planned at the Arya Rishikula Vasishtha Yogashrama. The head ascetic wishes to build a shrine to "the five gods" (*pañcadevatā*); that is, Shiva, Shakti, Vishnu, Ganesha, and Surya (the Sun).

The worship of gurus is an ancient practice found at all the medieval monasteries, including those that worship Shaiva or Shakta deities, although these monasteries do not place gurus in the centre of the altar as chosen deities. The legendary founder of an order is most often an incarnation of Shiva, Vishnu, or of a Vedic sage who transmits some of his divine knowledge and supernatural power or charisma to his chosen disciple. In each generation the living head ascetic of the monastery can trace his spiritual descent back through a list of gurus (*guruparamparā*) to the divine founder and can claim to have received some degree of in-dwelling spiritual power by virtue of his succession to headship, which is usually by appointment. The guru thus becomes a living incarnation for this generation, a representative of the deity whom the laity can see and personally revere.

Usually a head ascetic's picture is not placed upon the altar until after his death, although practice varies. Most shrines to gurus include the order's legendary or historical founder at the top, with photographs of his chosen disciples descending in generational order. Sometimes gurus' wives are included. The first monastery at Bhubaneswar to make its founding guru the central object of worship is the Ramakrishna Matha (1919). The practice appears with increasing frequency after 1940, a trend that reflects a return to ancient practice. In 1963, six establishments worshipped their guru as chosen deity.

Monastic Orders and Non-Sectarianism

Of the six major teaching traditions or monastic orders currently active in India, three are flourishing in Bhubaneswar: the Shankara Dashanami Sannyasins, the Madhva Gaudiya Vairagins, and non-sectarian groups. The first represents an intellectual, austere, Shaiva tradition primarily restricted to Brahmans and to people with a Sanskritic education. The second is a devotional, non-intellectual, Vaishnava tradition that gained popularity among all castes in the fifteenth to sixteenth centuries. Its influence was then so powerful that even members of the Shankara orders began devotional practices and the worship of Vishnu or Krishna as chosen deity.

Non-sectarianism did not appear in India until the advent of the nineteenth-century reformist–revivalists such as Ramakrishna and Vivekananda. Non-sectarianism now appears in Bhubaneswar in three very different forms: the simple absence of sectarian membership; preaching of the fundamental unity of several different Hindu deities with no one deity predominant; and a world view that proclaims the unity of all great religions, Hindu and non-Hindu.

Two establishments listed in table 18 as non-sectarian were not originally meant to be monasteries at all. The Chintamanishvara Mandira was founded in 1950 by a managing committee of citizens as a "religious park" but became a monastery when two wandering ascetics, each a solitary of a different monastic order, moved into the buildings. The Harihara Satsanga Ashrama was founded in 1962 by a managing committee of prominent Oria and Bengali citizens for the special purpose of averting a disaster threatened by an unfavourable alignment of the planets. It was designed to be a place for performance of the ritual fire sacrifice (*homa*), but became a monastery when the priest bought the land and decided to stay on with his wife as a *vānaprastha*, or forest hermit. Both these monasteries are listed as "non-sectarian" only because there exists no better label. They do not advocate non-sectarianism as a way of life.

The second form of non-sectarianism seems to be increasing in popularity among both laymen and ascetics. The Trinatha Cult, primarily a lay organization, teaches the inseparable unity of Brahma–Vishnu–Shiva, represented by a crude black stone. Popular with laity of the lower castes, it is a non-sectarian movement within Hinduism. It does not preach the unity of all religions.

The Ramakrishna movement has extended non-sectarianism beyond the boundaries of Hinduism. The head ascetic of the Ramakrishna Matha at Bhubaneswar says that Ramakrishna ascetics are not followers of any Hindu teaching tradition, but are non-sectarian, accepting Ramakrishna's view that "different creeds are but different paths to reach the One God."[1] He maintains a concept of God that acknowledges the validity of Hindu, Christian, and Islamic beliefs. Unlike orthodox Christians or Muslims, however, he considers Ramakrishna the most important incarnation of God. A historian of the Ramakrishna movement relates that:

> A couple of days before the end (Ramakrishna's death), a curious thought flashed across Narendra's mind as he stood at the Master's bedside, "He has said many times that he is an Incarnation of God. If he can say it now in the throes of death, then I will believe him!" Instantly the Master turned to him and summoning all his energy said distinctly, "O my Naren, are you still not convinced? He who was Rama and Krishna is now Ramakrishna—but not in your Vedantic sense!"[2]

The same head ascetic, just mentioned, also believes that Ramakrishna's wife Sarada Devi and others such as Vivekananda and Brahmananda are embodiments of God. Photographs of all three stand on the main altar of the monastery in Bhubaneswar. Thus, even though the order formally proclaims the unity of all world religions, its symbols and images are distinctly Hindu, and there is no evidence of any strong Christian or Muslim influence on religious practice.

We have seen that Hinduism allows its monasteries great variety in choice of deity and teaching tradition. In Bhubaneswar one rarely saw evidence of any hierarchy within an order whose purpose was to enforce certain practices. An ascetic was free to choose his own deity, even if this did not coincide with his order's teaching tradition. In 1964, the trend seemed to be toward making the deity's presence more immediate to the laity through the worship of gurus. In addition, non-sectarianism in its various forms seemed to be of some importance.

---

1. Swami Gambhirananda, *History of the Ramakrishna Math and Mission*, p. 16.
2. Swami Gambhirananda, *History of the Ramakrishna Math and Mission*, p. 38.

Chapter 7

The Varieties of Social Structure

At first glance the monasteries of Bhubaneswar seem to present social structures with no easily discernible patterns. Fifteen monasteries appear to have a social structure sufficiently strong for the ritual tradition to survive beyond the lifetimes of the present ascetics. Seven other monasteries came into existence with the arrival of their present head ascetics in Bhubaneswar, and, lacking any established practice for continuing, may disappear at the death or departure of the head ascetic. The first type of monastery is designated in table 18 as "corporate," the second type as "non-corporate."

Financial Structure

The clearest distinguishing characteristics of the kinds of monasteries listed in table 18 are financial. Possession of large amounts of land that must be administered by the monastery in order to provide for the support of the Lingaraja Mahaprabhu Temple has helped to stabilize the existence of the five monasteries founded in medieval times. In the case of the Kapali Matha, where the monastery has lost its land, the loss occurred only in the late nineteenth century and has not completely destroyed a ritual tradition dating back eight hundred years. Three twentieth-century monasteries have landed endowments of seven to sixty-eight acres, but these provide only part of their incomes.

Regular donations in cash or kind from businessmen and government officials provide the mainstay for those monasteries founded in Bhubaneswar in the twentieth century that expect to survive the death of the present head ascetic and can thus be considered corporate. Money may have been provided in a lump sum by the founding patron and/or be received in annual, monthly, or weekly donations. Sometimes a monastery owns buildings or shops that it rents out for added income to insure its survival as an economic entity.

A corporate monastery, then, depends on either a landed endowment or regular monetary patronage of a substantial nature, not on day-to-day handouts. Those monasteries originally deriving their wealth from land are listed as "endowed"; those living by initial or continual cash donations are called "patronized."

Endowed Monasteries

Endowed monasteries include the five monasteries founded in medieval times (table 2), by the rulers of Orissa. Detailed statements of the initial endowments for these monasteries were not available in 1964. However, the three monasteries under the control of the Orissa Hindu Religious Endowments Commission submit annual estimates of income and expenditures to that Commission.[1]

These budget estimates indicate the size of the original endowments in terms of sources of rupee income for the fiscal year 1963–64 (when five rupees were equal to one dollar). Table 12 summarizes the principal sources of income for these three monasteries.

Table 12
Principal Sources of Income for Endowed Institutions

Institutions	INCOME FROM LAND	INCOME FROM DONATIONS	OTHER SOURCES OF INCOME	TOTAL INCOME
Gopala Tirtha Matha	Rs. 22,000	Rs. 200	Rs. 13,184	Rs. 35,384
Sadavrata Pitha	1,688	0	1,114	2,802
Shiva Tirtha Matha	8,000	0	2,275	10,275

With the exception of the ruined Kapali Matha, all the endowed monasteries are large constructions, sometimes of archaeological distinction. What follows

1. Many of the figures and quotations that follow have been taken from the files of the Orissa Hindu Religious Endowments Commission Office, Cuttack, Orissa. Permission to use the files was given by the Orissa Home Secretary and the Commissioner of Endowments.

will give the reader some idea of the typical size, ground plan, and administration of an endowed monastery.

The size and general plan of the compound of the Sadavrata Pitha (figure 2) are typical of the five monasteries founded in medieval times. The ten-foot high, laterite stone walls of the compound each measure 240 feet in length and enclose a space of 57,600 square feet. About one-quarter of the enclosure is covered by a two-story rectangular stone building (80 feet by 110 feet) with an inner courtyard where there stands a small temple to Kamakhya, with a typical Oria-style pyramidal roof. The rest of the compound includes servants' huts, a haystack, a cowpen, and a cemetery for the earth burial of head ascetics, who, unlike the laity, are not cremated. The open ground near the cemetery usually serves as pasture for the monastery's small herd of cows. Basically, the compound resembles a small, well-kept farmyard. Although the main building could easily house several dozen ascetics, the only ascetic in residence is an Oria Brahman of about 65, who in 1936 at the age of 35 inherited his position as head ascetic upon the death of his uncle. The headship of this monastery has been handed down from uncle to nephew for many generations within his family. He employs a fairly large staff: a Brahman officiant (*pujārī*), a Brahman cook, a personal servant, and several cowherds and labourers.

According to the head ascetic, when he first assumed charge of the Sadavrata Pitha in 1936, the institution was in a state of financial chaos. Naga ascetics, a militant Dashanami order, had plagued him with frequent visits, each time extorting by threats a "protection fee" of one hundred rupees. Taponidhi, a determined man, was not easily frightened and managed to eliminate Naga threats. He also initiated rigid controls over the monastery's fifty acres of land, located in a village fourteen miles away, and stationed another ascetic on the spot to oversee cultivation. In 1940 the OHREC took over financial control of the monastery. The officer-in-charge was apparently satisfied with Taponidhi's budget estimates up through 1964, and indeed the 1963–64 estimate seems to verify the head ascetic's statement that he has stabilized the monastery's financial condition. The annual income of Rs. 2,802 is modest in comparison to that of other landed monasteries. The head ascetic professes not to think about the future of his institution. He knows that the Orissa government will inevitably assume further administrative control.

Very few of the patronized and none of the non-corporate establishments approximate the Sadavrata Pitha in size and in number of servants. Only a permanent endowment of land can succeed in supporting a monastery of this size over a long period of time.

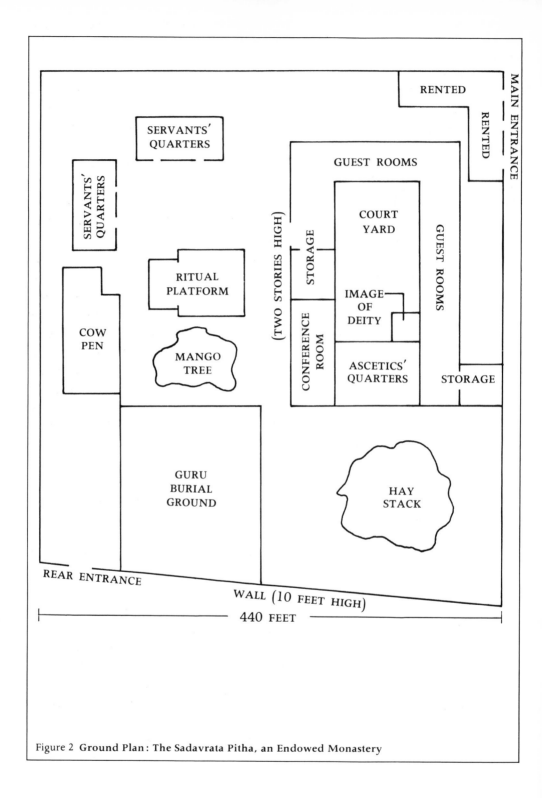

RENTED

RENTED

MAIN ENTRANCE

SERVANTS' QUARTERS

SERVANTS' QUARTERS

GUEST ROOMS

COURT YARD

GUEST ROOMS

(TWO STORIES HIGH)

STORAGE

RITUAL PLATFORM

IMAGE OF DEITY

COW PEN

CONFERENCE ROOM

MANGO TREE

ASCETICS' QUARTERS

STORAGE

GURU BURIAL GROUND

HAY STACK

REAR ENTRANCE

WALL (10 FEET HIGH)

440 FEET

Figure 2 Ground Plan: The Sadavrata Pitha, an Endowed Monastery

Patronized Institutions
The distinction between endowed and patronized institutions is not absolute, but contains some overlap. Three monasteries (table 18) have both landed endowments and continued cash donations, exemplified by the following.

The Jagannatha Deva Mandira has the second largest compound area in the Old Town (289,000 square feet), one third of which is covered by a large temple with a Bengali-style open verandah and a modern version of an Oria-style pyramidal tower. One of the most elaborately decorated monasteries established in the 1930s, the temple has marble floors and inlaid tile walls, and is well-maintained. In order to defray maintenance costs, a lay disciple of the female founder has endowed the monastery with seven acres of farm land. In recent years the head ascetic has constructed two houses across the road from the monastery and has rented them to newcomers who are working in the New Capital. The income from these properties is still not sufficient to meet expenditures, and the headquarters at Puri has had to supply additional support.

The head ascetic employs five servants: a Brahman officiant, a cook, a gardener, and two labourers to keep the buildings in repair. He is not optimistic about the future of the institution and fears that after his death people will cease to give donations. To provide financial security for the monastery, he hopes to raise vegetables for the market and also to construct some more houses to rent. A board of trustees will appoint his successor.

Six of the monasteries that depend on regular donations receive continued patronage from businessmen and government officials, and are thus listed as "continually patronized." All six continually patronized institutions are Bengali organizations, founded and financed predominantly by Bengalis, the vast majority of whom live in West Bengal and seldom come to Bhubaneswar except during the major festivals.

Information on three typical Bengali-patronized institutions follows.

The present head ascetic of the Arya Rishikula Bhuvaneshvari Ashrama, Jagadananda, the Preacher, is now recognized as the leader of the local Bengali religious community. He came to Bhubaneswar in 1945 to restore his health after many years as a travelling missionary. With the financial help of a high government official, he constructed a monastery that was so poorly built that the roof fell in during the monsoon season in 1958. Another government official raised money to repair the roof and to begin a new "temple and religio-cultural hall." Although the cornerstone had been laid in 1958, funds were exhausted and in 1964 the building remained only a shell.

This monastery is an *āśrama* in the true sense of a forest hermitage; located in the remains of an old mango forest, the monastery is so covered by a wild growth of vines and weeds that for one unacquainted with the area it is difficult to locate (see figure 3). The rickety compound wall is about six feet high; the compound itself covers only about 30,000 square feet. The laterite stone walls are not coated with cement, as are the walls at the wealthier monasteries, but the galvanized tin roof is fairly substantial. This *āśrama* has gardens with papaya, mango, and bel trees that produce most of the monastery's fruit and vegetables. The major building houses not only the head ascetic, but two *sannyāsinis* (widows who live under the same roof with the ascetic and care for him as if he were their son, hence the nickname, "guru-mother"), two *brahmacārins* or apprentice ascetics, a homeopath who runs the charitable dispensary and who considers himself a *vānaprastha* or forest hermit, and a general servant who looks after the garden and the monastery cow. The second building is a dispensary for the treatment of minor ailments. The head ascetic claims that it treats 3,000 patients a year.

The Nimbarka Ashrama is the largest one-story monastery in the Old Town, with fifteen rooms 15 feet by 20 feet. The hallways have marble floors and mosaic-tiled walls with inlaid pictures of peacocks, *tulasī* plants, and divine creatures. Names of the entire list of gurus associated with the monastery appear in tile. Crystal chandeliers, painted ceilings, plaster railings, and a monumental lion gate in Oria style provide an atmosphere of relative luxury. The marble *pūjā* room houses two life-size figures of Radha and Krishna. The builder and most important patron is a Calcutta lay-disciple, the senior partner in a firm of booksellers.

The Ramakrishna Matha has by far the largest staff and compound in Bhubaneswar, although it does not have the largest income. In 1959 the mission received a total of Rs. 4,732, mainly from Orissa government grants (Rs. 2,200), donations from Oria and Bengali patrons in the Bhubaneswar and Cuttack areas (Rs. 1,340), and annual pledges (Rs. 560).

The monastery covers four times the area of any other institution but does not farm its land. The buildings include a three-story residence, a guest house, a library, a school, and a dispensary. The head ascetic has four other ascetics as assistants; one serves as officiant, one supervises the school, one is in charge of institutional publications, and one acts as librarian. The medical doctor is assisted by two pharmacists.

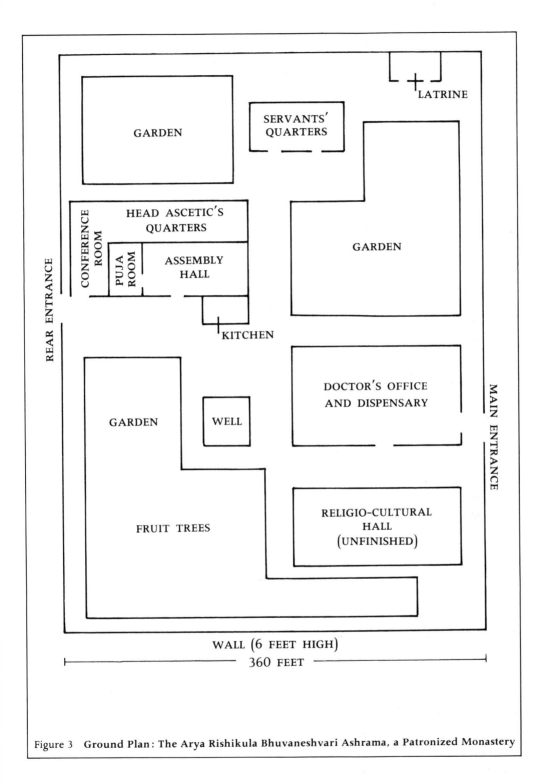

Figure 3   Ground Plan: The Arya Rishikula Bhuvaneshvari Ashrama, a Patronized Monastery

Client-Supported Monasteries

The ascetics at the seven non-corporate monasteries depend upon their personal clients for their food, clothing, and shelter. They have no patrons in the sense of absentee donors; those who give donations are those for whom the ascetics perform various services.

In time, after the original donations run out, an initially patronized corporate monastery tends to depend for support on day-to-day clients and becomes essentially non-corporate. Whether such support is forthcoming depends to a large extent on the qualifications of the head ascetic. The Radhakrishna Sevashrama is an example of a monastery now encountering this problem. Such institutions are correspondingly impermanent when compared to those with large land holdings.

In three cases the people of a given area have invited an ascetic to live among them, have provided him with a dwelling, and have given him a constant supply of food in return for leading them in devotional practices.

Occasionally, the ascetic may provide entertainment or instruction for his clients. For example, the ascetic at the Trinatha Gosvami Matha spends a considerable number of daylight hours at tea stalls located on Bhubaneswar Road entertaining the owners with mythological stories, while they provide him with tea and food. At night he often leads devotional singing (*kīrtana*) for the delight of those who live in the hamlet surrounding his monastery.

The financial structure of a non-corporate monastery is as minimal as its administrative structure, because a client-supported financial structure is more tenuous than the other kinds. The Solitary Ascetic maintains close personal relationships with his clientele that are impossible at more structured monasteries.

The following monastery is representative of the seven non-corporate establishments in the Old Town.

The name Pashupatinatha Gita Ashrama means literally "the song (*gītā*) of the lord (*nātha*) of beasts (*paśu*)." Lord of Beasts is an epithet of Shiva. The building is named after the Shaiva ascetic, Pashupatinatha, for whom it was built in 1958 by a merchant who lived nearby at the southern edge of the Old Town. The ascetic maintained himself for several years by practising Ayur-vedic medicine, then suddenly left Bhubaneswar. The merchant was eager to have another ascetic occupy the house that he had built, and in 1964 he convinced Madhava Chandra Dasa, a strikingly handsome but unassuming young man of the Ramananda order, to move into the dwelling. When the merchant met Madhava, the latter had been an ascetic for six years and was supporting himself by

running a *pān* shop in the neighbourhood in order to finance his pilgrimages to
Vaishnava shrines in northern India. After several pilgrimages, he became
convinced that to gain profit in a worldly vocation was contrary to the vows
he had taken. The merchant's offer therefore provided a solution to Madhava's
financial problems. In addition to free use of monastery properties, according
to an informant, the merchant promised to provide Madhava with twenty
pounds of rice per month. Madhava has been employed by the owner of a
nearby restaurant to perform worship three times daily before the restaurant's
image of Ganesha, the patron–deity of students and businessmen. In return for
his services, he receives tea and *chapātīs* (a type of unleavened bread). He feels
that his establishment is "a very insignificant one, with no major functions."
This is an honest and humble statement. He says that he is not in a position to
help in any way the inhabitants of the Old Town, and that his contribution to
the citizens is practically nil.

Organizational Structure

In general the corporate institutions tend to have more elaborate organizational
structures than the non-corporate monasteries. The endowed institutions have
either the most complex organizational control, that by the civil government
through the Orissa Hindu Religious Endowments Commission (OHREC), or the
simplest control, that by the head ascetic, or (as at the Shiva Tirtha Matha) a
combination of the two.

Patronized monasteries tend to prefer boards of trustees consisting of prominent laymen, a business feature in keeping with the cash nature of their
receipts. Four monasteries (two corporate, two non-corporate) have a less
permanent form of organization called a managing committee, usually an *ad
hoc* group assembled to found or repair a monastery but lacking a charter or
rules to provide permanence.

The Orissa Hindu Religious Endowments Commission (OHREC)
The tradition of government regulation of financially ailing monasteries goes
back to the British establishment of the Board of Revenue in 1810, followed by
a succession of regulatory acts, culminating in the establishment of the Orissa
Hindu Religious Endowments Commission in 1936. Between 1939 and 1941 the
government placed three endowed institutions, the Gopala Tirtha Matha, the
Sadavrata Pitha, and the Shiva Tirtha Matha, under the jurisdiction of the
OHREC (table 18). From then until Independence, the OHREC remained
primarily concerned with finances, leaving all other aspects of administration

to the discretion of the head ascetics. The Orissa Hindu Religious Endowments Act of 1951 (Act II of 1952) broadened the powers of the OHREC.[2]

A "scheme" is a court-approved legal document under which the OHREC can assume *all* the administrative powers over a religious institution. The case of the Gopala Tirtha Matha best describes the establishment of a scheme.

In 1958, the Commissioner of the OHREC required that an audit be made of the finances for the Gopala Tirtha Matha. Since the monastery's annual income exceeded Rs. 10,000, the Act of 1951 required that the auditors be selected by the Accountant-General's Office to insure a more objective audit than auditors from the Endowments Commission might conduct. In one section of an extensive report the auditor stated:

> Budget estimates were not prepared correctly. Variations were especially noticed from the provisions under personal expenditure of Svamiji (the head ascetic). The provision under personal expenditure from 1954 to 1956 was Rs. 1,000 each year, but for 1955 it was raised to Rs. 2,900. It was not known how this was raised to such extent when income for 1955 did not show any rise but was reduced from Rs. 26,144 to Rs. 20,831.[3]

Shortly after the publication of the audit, the head ascetic of the Gopala Tirtha Matha directed two of his servants to burn three bags of records that he said were useless. The next day the clerk of the monastery informed the Endowments Commissioner who immediately investigated the report. The commissioner felt that the situation was critical, and using the powers granted him under Section 7 (2) of the Orissa Hindu Religious Endowments Act of 1951, he appointed an interim custodian for the Gopala Tirtha Matha.

The head ascetic initially agreed to cooperate with the custodian, but in March 1960 the ascetic stopped performance of the daily worship. This act angered the residents of Puri and Bhubaneswar, and the commissioner placed the custodian in charge of maintaining the ceremonies. The head ascetic then applied for an extended leave of absence, and the commissioner granted him permission to leave Orissa for one year. While the ascetic was absent, the commissioner initiated procedures under Section 42 of the Endowments Act that would give the Endowments Commission even more effective control over the administration of the Gopala Tirtha Matha. On 21 August 1961, the commissioner finalized the scheme for the Gopala Tirtha Matha.

---

2. Srinibas Misra, *The Orissa Hindu Religious Endowments Act, 1951.*

3. P. Venkatesvarulu, *Audit Report Number 119, 1958–59*, "A report of the Audit of Gopala Tirtha Matha, Puri," 2 December 1958 (a report in the files of The Orissa Hindu Religious Endowments Commission).

On the basis of the scheme, the administrative structure of the Gopala Tirtha Matha can be diagrammed as in table 13. Within this administrative structure, the head ascetic is little more than a religious figurehead salaried by the government. The executive officer administers through the board of trustees, although in matters of ritual he is to act upon the advice of the head ascetic. The scheme makes it quite clear that the executive officer, acting on behalf of the commissioner, is the supreme authority in all matters, including ritual.

Table 13
Organizational Structure of the Gopala Tirtha Matha

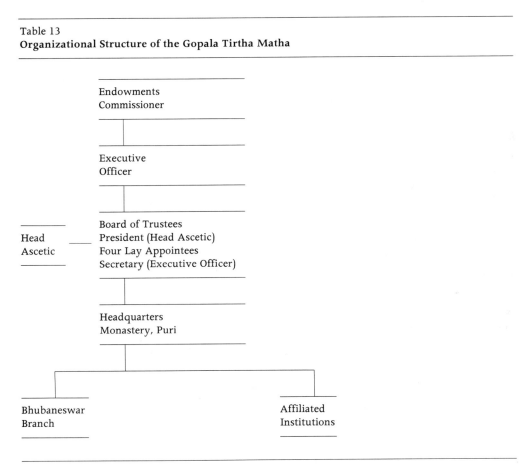

The original endowments were made to support the ritual functions of the monasteries. Today, however, a large portion of the monastery's income is used to pay for government-imposed financial supervision. The result is a diversion of the monastery's funds from ritual to administrative procedures. Table 14 represents a breakdown of principal expenditures for 1964, based upon budget estimates for that year, for the three monasteries under OHREC control.

Table 14
Principal Expenditures for Endowed Institutions

Institutions	FOR RITUAL	FOR SALARIES, GOVT. FEES, AND TAXES	OTHER	TOTAL
Gopala Tirtha Matha	Rs. 8,750	Rs. 13,500	Rs. 13,134	Rs. 35,384
Sadavrata Pitha	1,180	750	872	2,802
Shiva Tirtha Matha	4,342	2,405	3,528	10,275

Although the government has had no alternative in trying to correct the mismanagement of the Gopala Tirtha Matha, the action of the OHREC is quickening the process of spiritual deterioration. The head ascetic has lost any respect that he might have had in the community. Under government control the institution has become further estranged from the laity.

The two other endowed monasteries under the control of the OHREC in 1964 have less complex administrative structures than does the Gopala Tirtha Matha. Managers who are solely concerned with finances have been assigned by the OHREC to the Sadavrata Pitha and the Shiva Tirtha Matha. The manager works directly with the head ascetic, who maintains responsibility for performances of rituals and discipline of employees without a board of trustees.

The Board of Trustees
Eight patronized corporate institutions, mostly branch monasteries with headquarters located elsewhere, are managed by boards of trustees (table 18). Since all the trustee-administered institutions are Bengali, most of the headquarters monasteries are located in West Bengal. The lay members of the board of trustees generally live near the headquarters monastery. The presidents of all the trustee boards, except the Nimbarka Ashrama, are the head ascetics of their respective organizations. The board of trustees holds certain legal powers granted to it by a statute of the state where the headquarters monastery is located. For example, the board of trustees for the Sadguru Nivasa Ashrama is constituted according to Act 21 of 1860 for the state of Bengal.

To illustrate the composition and powers of a typical board of trustees, the organizational structure of the Nigamananda Ashrama is described in table 15.

The head ascetic and founder of the Nigamananda Ashrama at Bhubaneswar is appointed the president of the headquarters and its branches in accordance

Table 15
Organizational Structure of the Nigamananda Ashrama

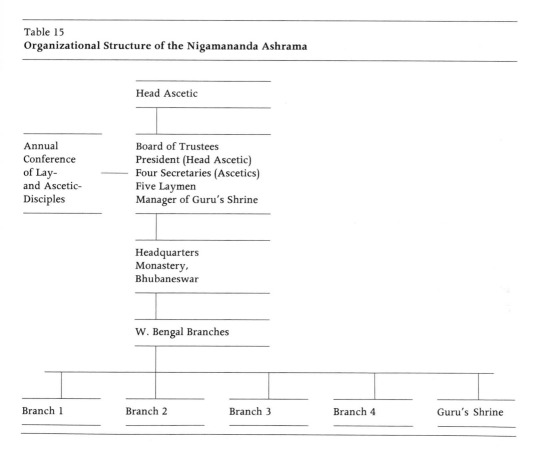

with a deed of trust that his guru, Nigamananda Sarasvati Svami, registered in 1930 under a statute of the state of West Bengal. The board of trustees consists of: the president, who must be the head ascetic at the headquarters institution; the head ascetics of the four branch monasteries, who are known as secretaries; the manager of the shrine at Nigamananda's birthplace; and five laymen. The president and the heads of the various branches initially select the five laymen from disciples who live in the area of the headquarters monastery. Thereafter, if a layman terminates his post, a majority of the remaining trustees can appoint his successor. The president alone appoints the head ascetics or secretaries of the various branches. The secretaries are responsible for the ascetics and lay employees assigned to their respective monasteries and for the maintenance of traditional rituals and ceremonies. The president annually appoints zonal representatives for the four monastic branches. The zonal representatives are lay supervisors who report directly to the president, who in this way maintains a check upon the secretaries who head the branch monasteries.

The board of trustees is required to meet at least once a year and to draft at this meeting a budget estimate of income and expenditures for the coming fiscal year. The budget is then submitted for approval to an annual gathering of the ascetic-disciples and lay-disciples of the Nigamananda organization. The board also considers such long-range plans as the maintenance and construction of buildings and the establishment of schools and charitable dispensaries. The day-to-day operation of the headquarters monastery and its branches remains the function of the president and the secretaries. The board of trustees, however, holds the right to bring a "no confidence" vote against the president if he breaks the rules of the trust. By such action, the board can force the president to retire. The president, however, maintains the right to dismiss any ascetic-disciple for breach of discipline.

The structure characteristic of patronized institutions allows control by the head ascetic, but insures considerable lay participation in administration. The head ascetic is the principal administrator, but in matters of finances or plans for expansion, he has to act through the board of trustees with the consent of the total membership of his organization. The interaction between ascetic and lay members involves more direct personal relations than are possible under the administrative structure forced upon the endowed institutions by the OHREC. Since the deed of trust has been sanctioned by the state as a legally binding document, the board of trustees can enforce its decisions by court action if necessary.

The Managing Committee
A managing committee administers four monasteries (table 18). Two of these are patronized corporate monasteries and two are non-corporate.

Usually the managing committee is an *ad hoc* advisory board, consisting predominantly of laymen who voluntarily offer their administrative services to create a new monastic institution or to guide an old one. It does not possess legal powers to enforce its decisions. The lay members of the four managing committees are all from the Bhubaneswar–Cuttack area and are men prominent in either business or politics. An illustration of the *ad hoc*, informal organizational structure of the managing committee is that of the Chintamanishvara Mandira. This was set up in 1950. It was composed of laymen who wished to reconstruct a temple that had fallen into disrepair and develop it into a religious park. Initially, they were little concerned whether or not any ascetics would live there. It was by chance that Mauna Babaji, a wandering ascetic, arrived in town in 1957 and actively encouraged the managing committee to construct a small temple, a bathing tank, and a recitation hall. Furthermore, it was by chance that in 1963 Virendra Natha Sadhukhan, the Troubadour, joined those reciting the *mahāmantra* and stayed on, adding new life to the Chintamanishvara Mandira. Once the reconstruction had been completed, the temple area became self-sustaining. Every ascetic and layman who came to the Chintamanishvara Mandira to worship, sing, or bathe left a contribution in a small box near the main temple.

The managing committee has little to do except to maintain the buildings. On the one hand, the two resident ascetics play no part in the organizational structure of the temple, but, on the other, the managing committee has no legal control over them. Like other solitary ascetics, the ascetics at the Chintamanishvara Temple are free to do as they please.

A managing committee, because it is a voluntary association of interested laity without powers of legal enforcement, is the least effective type of administrative structure. Its principal function is to assist in the initial phases of establishing a monastery. After the buildings have been built and the ascetics occupy the monastery, the establishment becomes self-sustaining and the managing committee becomes non-functional. The highly personal and informal structure of a managing committee is both its strength and its weakness. Through participation the laity can manifest their interest in the establishment of monastic institutions. However, without legal powers the committee cannot implement its decisions. Institutions that once began as "patronized corporate" tend to become "non-corporate" in their organizational structure when the original managing committees lose effective control.

The Head Ascetic

At seven monasteries the head ascetic holds all administrative responsibilities. Two of these are endowed institutions and five are non-corporate establishments (table 18). These monasteries range from the Shankarananda Matha, one of the largest endowed institutions, to the Bhavani Shankara Matha, the smallest, poorest non-corporate establishment.

A difference in the conception of the responsibilities of the head ascetic distinguishes between administrations at the endowed monasteries and at the non-corporate monasteries. At the Shankarananda Matha the head ascetic is an exemplary administrator who has the support of influential politicians and businessmen. Consequently, his institution has not been taken over by the OHREC, although, according to the head ascetic, the gross income of the monastery is over Rs. 30,000, a figure almost as large as the annual income of the Gopala Tirtha Matha. If the effectiveness of the head ascetic decreases, the

OHREC is entitled to assume administrative duties. The head ascetic is therefore under considerable pressure to provide an effective administration.

The head ascetics at the non-corporate monasteries maintain themselves at a minimal level of subsistence and are free to leave Bhubaneswar at any time. They are therefore characterized as "solitary ascetics," responsible to no one but themselves.

The head ascetic fulfils the oldest conception of administrative structure. In medieval times, he was "all in all," meaning that he combined the roles of administrator, teacher, philosopher or mystic, disciplinarian, and ritualist. The only head ascetic who continued to exemplify this traditional conception in 1964 is Saccidananda Sarasvati Svami at the Shankarananda Matha. The contemporary conception of the head ascetic demands that he share administrative responsibilities, especially financial concerns, with the laity.

Succession to Headship

An established practice of monastic succession to headship after the death or retirement of a head ascetic is probably the most important characteristic that differentiates corporate from non-corporate monasteries.

Appointment of a Kinsman or Disciple by the Head Ascetic

The commonest process of succession is for the head ascetic to appoint his own successor, to whom he transmits both his ritual and managerial obligations and powers. In some cases a decision originally left to the ascetic's choice may have automatically devolved upon a kinsman, usually a nephew, occasionally a son. Thus at two of the endowed monasteries of medieval date (the Kapali Matha and the Sadavrata Pitha) the head ascetic is expected to appoint his nephew as his successor, continuing a long "hereditary" tradition. At the patronized Shadbuja Chaitanya Mandira, which has no such tradition, it is likely that the present head ascetic will transmit the property and the headship to one of his sons who is already an ascetic. At the Radhakrishna Sevashrama headship will probably devolve upon the ascetic's brother. Appointment of a kinsman does not necessarily rule out the sincerity of this kinsman's religious vocation. It does mean, however, that headship is regarded as a position in which one receives income and controls property. From this point of view, appointment of kinsmen is the most successful method of maintaining an institution over a long period of time.

In Bhubaneswar in 1964, however, most head ascetics with the power of appointment selected, not kinsmen, but favourite disciples. Three endowed monasteries and eight patronized monasteries practise appointment by the head ascetic of a disciple as his spiritual heir. In these cases headship is seen as a continuation of the teacher–disciple relationship, not as a means for the perpetuation of property or ritual duties. Appointment of disciples is a less stable means of continuation than appointment of kinsmen, for if the head ascetic dies before making a choice, two or more disciples may dispute the claim to headship.

Appointment by Lay Managers

If the head ascetic fails to determine a successor, one can be appointed by the OHREC if it is in control. The Orissa Hindu Religious Endowments Act, 1951, Section 36, gives the commissioner the following power:

> When a vacancy occurs in the office of the trustee (head ascetic) of a matha or specific endowment attached to a matha . . . and there is a dispute respecting the right of succession to such office or when such office cannot be filled up immediately or when the trustee (head ascetic) is a minor and there is no recognized guardian willing to act as such or when there is a dispute respecting the person who is entitled to act as such guardian, the Commissioner, after being satisfied that an arrangement for the administration of the matha and its endowment or of the specific endowment, as the case may be, is necessary, shall make such appointment and arrangements as he thinks fit until the dispute is settled or another trustee (head ascetic) succeeds to the office, as the case may be.[4]

At patronized institutions a board of trustees may choose a successor if the head ascetic has not made the appointment. The following statement from the deed of trust for the Nigamananda Ashrama grants such powers of appointment to its board of trustees:

> But the right of selecting a Mahanta (head ascetic) will rest only with the Mahanta (to preserve the relationship of teacher–disciple). But however, in case of sudden death or missing of the Mahanta or if he quits the post as a result of his disobedience of the rules of the Deed of Trust, then as a general principle, a Mahanta can be selected from among the Sannyasin trustees by majority consent.[5]

Managerial appointment is a secondary method of selection used only if the

---

4. Misra, *Orissa Hindu Religious Endowments Act, 1951*, pp. 47–48.
5. Svami Nigamananda Sarasvati, *Trust Deed of Assam–Bengal Sarasvati Matha*.

primary ones, inheritance or appointment by the head ascetic, somehow fail. Corporate institutions possess both stability and continuity because they deal effectively with the problem of succession.

The Lack of Succession at Non-Corporate Establishments
Perhaps the principal defining characteristics of a non-corporate monastery are the lack of a clearly defined method of succession and its administration by a solitary ascetic. Normally, the non-corporate monastery disappears with the departure or death of the solitary ascetic, who is responsible to no one but himself.

The endowed structures represent the Shankara Dashanami Sannyasin and Tantric traditions of their medieval founders. The patronized institutions may represent Shankara, Vairagin, or non-sectarian traditions, but all have chosen to worship Vaishnava deities or gurus. The non-corporate monasteries continue to depend for their religious structures on the individual preference of the solitary ascetic and upon shrines left by prior occupants of the building.

Chapter 8

The

Range

of

Religious

Rituals

The rituals in Hindu monasteries vary greatly both in type and in importance. Their range includes participation in public annual festivals, specifically sectarian celebrations, special-purpose rituals to ward off disaster, and daily worship (*pūjā*). Although the five monasteries endowed by Oria kings in the medieval period were built partly to assist in certain annual ceremonies connected with the Lingaraja Mahaprabhu Temple, their roles in these annual festivals have shrunk in importance either because the monasteries are increasingly mismanaged and impoverished, or because the festivals themselves have lost popularity. Some of the patronized corporate monasteries, particularly those of Vairagin orders, hold their own celebrations that may be specific to the sect or that mark national holidays. Such occasions may attract sizable gatherings. Expenditures for public festivals account for the major portion of the budgets of the larger monasteries. They also represent some of the monasteries' most important contacts with the laity and may be the only occasions when the population is aware of a monastery's existence.

For the monastery, public celebrations mean a rationale for scheduling the year's activities, a welcome break in daily routine, and an opportunity to collect money. The only monastery where public ritual is dominant is the Harihara Satsangha Ashrama, which was founded exclusively for the performance of the ritual fire sacrifice to avoid planetary disaster.

Within most monasteries, the performance of daily ritual (*pūjā*) is the most important religious function. Laymen do not necessarily expect a monastery to perform annual ceremonies unless such observances are required by ancient tradition. They do expect every monastery, regardless of its spiritual or financial condition, to perform daily worship. This expectation persists even if no layman is present. Cessation of daily worship at a monastery may even provoke comment in the newspapers, such as the following in the *Samaj*, an Oria-language daily published in Cuttack: "Bhubaneswar, November 17, 1961. It is heard that all the rituals of the temple and the deity have been discontinued on account of the negligence of the manager of the local Gopala Tirtha Matha. We hope that the concerned authority will take remedial action in these matters."

Public External Festivals

Various monasteries in Bhubaneswar carry out certain observances, usually processions, outside their walls, or take part in some way in widely observed religious celebrations. Such festive occasions outside the monastery walls provide one way in which the monastic community is visible even to those who do not regularly visit ascetic institutions or contribute financially to them. At present the popularity of a given national or provincial festival appears, at least in Bhubaneswar, to be inversely related to the amount of active participation by the monasteries. The two most popular festivals, Durga Puja and Ashokashtami Yatra, are street parades with images of the deities publicly carried on floats through the streets. Both involve much lay participation. The monasteries do little more than provide services, such as space for the images, offerings of food for the deities, or money. At no time does an ascetic play an active role in these two popular observances.

At the opposite end of the scale of popularity, two similar ceremonies, Prathamashtami Yatra and Yamadvitiya Yatra, also involve carrying images of the deities through the streets, but these images are concealed from public view. The audience, if any, is not permitted to participate. In both ceremonies the heads of endowed monasteries and the priests of the Lingaraja Mahaprabhu Temple play the leading roles, but they have lost their audiences, leaving the two festivals empty and deteriorated survivals of medieval pageantry. In 1872, 10,000 people attended these festivals.[1] In the intervening century, the endowed institutions involved have consistently mismanaged funds, leading to economic decay, and for several generations many of their head ascetics have not commanded respect. Furthermore, a covered deity approachable only by

1. Rajendra Lala Mitra, *The Antiquities of Orissa*, p. 134.

priests and ascetics no longer has the popular appeal it held in 1872.

Mitra lists for the year 1872 fourteen major and twelve minor festivals at Bhubaneswar, all of which technically remain in the religious calendar, though only seven remain popular (Durga Puja, Ashokashtami Yatra, Dola Purnima–Holi, Shivaratri, Janmashtami, Ganesha Puja, and Sarasvati Puja).

To illustrate the nature of such festivals and give some idea of the monasteries' involvement in them, we give brief descriptions of five public festivals as observed in Bhubaneswar, listing them in order of decreasing popularity: Durga Puja, Ashokashtami Yatra, Dola Purnima–Holi, Prathamashtami Yatra, and Yamadvitiya Yatra.

Durga Puja

Held in mid-October (the Hindu month of Ashvina), immediately preceding the end of the monsoon and the harvest of the summer rice crop, Durga Puja is a ten-day carnival which has many elements of an ancient fertility celebration. It commemorates the victory of the goddess Durga over the buffalo-demon Mahishasura, and celebrates the deity's triumph over the forces of chaos. For several weeks before the festival, the craftsmen who traditionally make religious images are busy constructing large and elaborate clay figures of Durga and Shiva. These are carefully painted and gilded to appear lifelike and form tableaux portraying some story connected with Durga's life. The tableaux are installed on raised platforms (*maṇḍapas*) in front of monasteries in the Old Town and in squares in the New Capital. Monasteries, businessmen, and government officials contribute to the costs of construction. A prize is awarded for the best display. On the final night of the festival the clay images are taken with noisy ceremony to the river for immersion.

In 1964 over 10,000 people from all parts of Orissa came to Bhubaneswar on the ninth day of the festival, to see the displays and to renew family ties. In the evening they walked around the town to appraise the tableaux, to shop for toys, ribbons, and various luxuries in temporary stalls, and to patronize carnival performers, such as snake charmers, sword swallowers, and fortune tellers. After midnight the images in the New Capital were removed from their platforms and placed on flat-bed trucks. They were immediately surrounded by noisy groups of young men playing gongs, drums, and cymbals. The six or seven trucks carrying the images from the New Capital arrived in the Old Town in a convoy, accompanied by monumental noise, at about 1:00 A.M. Men in the crowd swung firebrands and some, wearing women's clothing, did a stiff-legged phallic dance accompanied by obscene songs and dirty jokes reminiscent of harvest festivals throughout the world. Many of the lower caste members drank considerable amounts of toddy, a liquor made from palm-sap. At about 3:00 A.M. the images from the Old Town were also loaded onto flat-bed trucks and the whole crowd proceeded to the Daya River, where the figures were immersed to dissolve gradually.

Although the endowed monasteries of medieval date contribute money for the festival, none of the ascetics participate actively, and all avoid the immersion ceremonies. They consider themselves too sophisticated for the festivities, because the ordinary rules for proper behaviour are relaxed during the ten days of public celebration.

Ashokashtami Yatra

The Ashokashtami Yatra is celebrated on the eighth day (*aṣṭamī*) of the waning half of Chaitra (April). A car (*ratha*), carrying the movable bronze images of Shiva, Parvati, Durga, and Vishnu, is pulled from the Lingaraja Mahaprabhu Temple to the Rameshvara Temple, nearly one-and-one-half miles to the northwest. The images, which are about twelve to fourteen inches high, represent the sacred *liṅgam* housed inside the temple. The images remain at the Rameshvara Temple two nights before being returned. Panigrahi believes that the Rameshvara Temple may have been built upon the site of an earlier Buddhist shrine and that "these festive visits . . . to these places on special auspicious days might be in the nature of the deity of a later shrine paying homage to the earliest ones."[2] However, the local interpretation connects the festival with the visit of Vishnu's incarnation Rama to Bhubaneswar before the war with Ravana, the demon-king of Ceylon. At the site of the Rameshvara Temple, it is believed that Rama worshipped Lord Lingaraja. Hence the ceremonial visit commemorates Rama's act of worship. This five-day celebration is held during the extremely hot, dry season before the monsoon and is the last major public festival before Durga Puja in mid-October. The wood for the car that carries the image of Shiva, Lord Lingaraja, is traditionally cut from a mango forest owned by the Shiva Tirtha Matha, one of the endowed monasteries. According to legend, it was in this mango grove that the eight-foot natural stone *liṅgam*, now enshrined in the temple, was found. The grove has long since disappeared, but a commemorative sapling is still cut ceremonially. Also the car is no longer made anew each year; instead, the four eight-foot wheels and some other pieces are saved and reassembled.

The festival as observed in 1964 used a car forty-two feet tall, which was pulled by two huge ropes five inches thick and fifty yards long. Before the

---

2. K. C. Panigrahi, *Archaeological Remains at Bhubaneswar*, p. 190.

images were placed in the car, anyone in the crowd, regardless of caste, could climb a stairway and circumambulate the car's platform in a clockwise direction. Once the deities had been placed upon the platform, however, police cordoned off the area and permitted only Brahmans to ride the car with the images. The young Brahman "charioteer" mounted one of the two wooden horses affixed to the front of the car and chanted obscene songs or made indecent remarks, finally pointing to someone in the audience as the butt of his jokes. Then the crowd, consisting mostly of young men, broke into laughter and began to heave on the car's massive ropes, moving it about twenty yards, until it was stopped for another act by the charioteer. This movable street comedy began at about 2:00 P.M.; by 6:00 P.M. the car had moved only one-third of the distance to the Rameshvara Temple. The procession took another full day to reach its destination. The images of Shiva and his family remained in the Rameshvara Temple for two days, then made the return journey in a single day. Whenever the procession was moving, the police cordon functioned as a safety guard to prevent anyone from falling, getting pushed, or throwing himself under the wheels of the car.

In 1964 over 10,000 people watched this procession in spite of the intense heat, though fewer came from the New Capital than had attended Durga Puja. Again, the monasteries' role was limited to providing food offered before the images. The Gopala Tirtha Matha, the richest endowed monastery of medieval date, contributed Rs. 150, considerably less than it contributed either to Ganesha Puja or to the Car Festival at Puri. The Sadavrata Pitha, another old endowed monastery, gave only Rs. 5.

Dola Purnima Yatra

Dola Purnima is observed on the full moon day (*pūrṇimā*) of the Hindu month of Phalguna (March), at the beginning of spring ploughing. Images of Vishnu–Krishna and sometimes Radha are placed in a swing (*dola*) and gently rocked back and forth. The festival includes a procession that carries the movable images of Shiva, Parvati, Vishnu, and Durga from the Lingaraja Mahaprabhu Temple to a stone platform (*maṇḍapa*) near the entrance of the Shiva Tirtha Matha. Since the Dola Purnima Yatra is primarily a Vaishnava festival, the image of Vishnu receives special attention.

In Bhubaneswar on Dola Purnima in 1964, a crowd of perhaps five hundred gathered at the main entrance of the temple shortly before 2:00 P.M. The procession was led by a Shudra gong-beater followed by a Brahman carrying a large black umbrella, a symbol of medieval royalty, and more than twenty priests of the Lingaraja Mahaprabhu Temple holding a brilliant red canopy

shielding the movable images. Behind the canopy was another Brahman holding a white umbrella. Scattered among the crowd were drummers and
trumpeters.

The procession bore similarities to Ashokashtami Yatra; it halted frequently
for the band to perform while many of the onlookers danced. Since this festival
is immediately followed by Holi, a carnival period during which the social
order is temporarily suspended, anyone in the audience could throw coloured
water or coloured powders at anyone else, regardless of caste or sanctity.

At the Shiva Tirtha Matha the procession turned and circumambulated the
platform three times clockwise. The priests then placed the image of Vishnu
in a swing hung from a stone arch. The images of Shiva, Parvati, and Durga
were carried across the street and installed on a platform beside the wall of the
temple compound. The onlookers could reverence the images and receive some
of the *prasāda* (food which is considered blessed with God's grace by having
been presented first to the deities). The priests remained on duty until 7:00
P.M. Later in the evening half the temple servants ate their dinner at the Shiva
Tirtha Matha while the other half ate at the Gopala Tirtha Matha.

The endowed monasteries' contributions remained limited to providing food
for the deities and temple servants and to building Vishnu's swing. Only the
temple priests, not the ascetics, took an active role. According to its budget
records for the year 1963–64, the Gopala Tirtha Matha contributed Rs. 123,
about one-quarter of the amount spent on festivals during that year.

Two Less Popular Festivals: Prathamashtami Yatra and Yamadvitiya Yatra
Those public festivals in which the ascetics *do* play an active or even leading
role are ceremonies that rarely draw the attention of even a handful of the laity.
Two of these festivals, Prathamashtami Yatra and Yamadvitiya Yatra, closely
resemble Durga Puja and Ashokashtami Yatra in so far as the movable images
are carried in a procession through the streets. In 1964 fewer than a dozen
laymen attended Prathamashtami Yatra, mostly barren women hoping to be
cured by drinking the water in which the images were bathed. The major
differences in performance between these two neglected festivals and the Car
Festival or Durga Puja are that the images are concealed from public view by
a covering, and that the laity are not allowed to participate. At both Durga Puja
and Ashokashtami Yatra the laity can ride on the truck or car beside the deities
and can dance, sing, or pull the car. At Prathamashtami Yatra and Yamadvitiya
Yatra the laity can only watch a ceremony restricted exclusively to ascetics and
priests.

The Yamadvitiya Yatra is a processional through the streets of the Old Town, with the temple priests carrying the movable images of Shiva, Parvati, Vishnu, and Durga from the Lingaraja Mahapraphu Temple to the Yameshvara Temple and the Sadavrata Pitha, the oldest endowed monastery in Bhubaneswar.

A popular folk explanation for the processional is that if a sinful individual worships at the Yameshvara Temple during the month of Kartika (November), he need not fear punishment at death. The head ascetic of the Sadavrata Pitha dismisses the folk explanation as "mere superstition." Rather, he says, the proxy of Lingaraja Mahapraphu visits the Sadavrata Pitha because the goddess Kamakhya (Durga), the chosen deity of the monastery, is his sister. This explanation points to a still-popular social custom associated with the festival, which celebrates the day on which Yami, the sister of Yama, the god who rules the abode of the dead, provides a feast in honour of her brother. In imitation of Yami's act, sisters invite their brothers to their homes for dinner on this day in November.

In 1964 the festival was scheduled to begin at 8:00 P.M. However, the priest in charge of worship (*pūjā paṇḍā*) and the head cook became involved in a dispute that delayed the celebration. Finally at 9:15 the procession formed, and led by trumpeters and gong beaters, two palanquins bearing the movable images arrived at the back gate of the Sadavrata Pitha. The priests carried the images inside the compound of the Yameshvara Temple and placed them on a *maṇḍapa* in front of the temple entrance. The officiating temple priest (*pūjā paṇḍā*) arranged four plantain leaves and sugar-coated rice balls before the images. Two attendants held a white cloth curtain across the front of the platform, shielding the images from the view of the audience, so that the deities could have privacy as they symbolically ate the food. After a few minutes the curtain was lowered, and the priests picked up the movable images and proceeded to the entrance of the Yameshvara Temple. The officiating priest performed a brief ritual and led the whole procession out of the temple compound and into the Sadavrata Pitha monastery. Servants of the monastery had removed the plantain leaves and rice from the platform and had placed the food before the image of Kamakhya-Durga within the inner compound of the monastery. After the procession reached the image of Kamakhya, the officiating priest conducted another ritual after which a morsel of the offered food (*prasāda*) was given to the onlookers.

At this point, a heated argument broke out between the officiating priest and the head ascetic of the monastery. The intermittent shouting of the *pūjā paṇḍā* and the other temple priests was almost completely subdued by the lion-like roar of the head ascetic, who told the priests that they could keep the *prasāda* as their payment. The priests, however, demanded Rs. 1.00 per individual, and the *pūjā paṇḍā* declared that the movable images could not be removed from the monastery until the temple priests had received the full amount. If the images were not taken back to the Lingaraja Mahaprabhu Temple, the temple services would be disrupted and the monastery would be blamed for this. The head ascetic countered by stating, "If you wish to leave the images in my monastery, I have no objection." Further debate forced the head ascetic to concede that he would provide a larger quantity of rice and a total of Rs. 2.00 to be divided among the seven temple priests present. This was still short of the *pūjā paṇḍā*'s demand. Finally the ascetic raised the total to Rs. 5.00 to be paid to the temple priests on the following morning. That satisfied the priests, who quickly formed a procession and noisily made their way back to the temple. We asked an Old Town informant whether or not he thought the head ascetic would fulfil his promise. His answer was, "If the ascetic fails to do so, the temple priests will have him beaten by the Old Town toughs."

Although the Orissa Hindu Religious Endowments Commission administers the finances of the Lingaraja Mahaprabhu Temple, its priests are not satisfied with their traditional recompense, and many of the younger men who have sufficient education aspire to government employment in the New Capital. The temple is, therefore, understaffed and the staff is underpaid, at least according to New Capital standards. The previously described argument between the head cook and the *pūjā paṇḍā* was over payment; the head cook had refused to prepare the offered food until he was assured of a salary increase. Financial troubles alone, however, do not explain the decline in the festival's popularity. Apparently the ceremony does not fulfil the laity's demands for the immediate presence of the deities, for audience participation, and for the expression of emotion, either joyful or penitential.

Internal Monastic Celebrations Held Annually

Although monasteries play only a minor role in the most popular contemporary public festivals, the private annual festivals celebrated inside some monasteries present a different picture. Three examples which illustrate such celebrations are Janmashtami, Sarasvati Puja, and Guru Purnima. Although these festivals are celebrated in other parts of India, the descriptions that follow represent Bhubaneswar practice.

Janmashtami (Krishna's birthday) is primarily a Vaishnava ceremony and is celebrated in all fifteen monasteries belonging to the three Vairagin monastic orders and in some of those adhering to the Shankara tradition. Institutions that enjoy lay respect are assured of a good attendance by laymen who come prepared to participate in the singing and other devotions. On Sarasvati Puja, Sarasvati, the goddess of learning, is worshipped; it is a popular festival among Bengalis. Guru Purnima is an ancient rite that honours the living guru as the embodiment of sacred tradition. It was performed at fifteen of Bhubaneswar's monasteries. While no one observance is attended by large numbers of people, there are many such festivals in the community with many sponsors, lay or religious.

Janmashtami

Janmashtami celebrates the birthday of Krishna on the eighth day of the waning half of the Hindu month of Bhadra (mid-August, during the monsoon). Although the Lingaraja Mahaprabhu Temple ritual calendar classifies Jan-mashtami as a minor festival, it is actually a major annual festival at patronized institutions belonging to Vairagin teaching traditions. The four endowed institutions belonging to Shankara orders apparently also celebrate it due to the influence of Vaishnavism since the medieval period. Janmashtami festivals vary greatly from one sponsoring institution to another. The following is an example of its performance in one monastery, but should not be regarded as typical of all such festivals.

We observed the festival in 1964 at the Shadbhuja Chaitanya Mahaprabhu Mandira, founded by the Bhakta, Nibaran Mukharji, a patronized monastery of the Madhva Gaudiya tradition. Although this was a Bengali institution, the non-resident audience included four Orias and three Bengalis. The Orias were a London-trained medical practitioner, the solitary ascetic of the Pashupati-natha Gita Ashrama, a goldsmith, and a cowherd. They represented a socio-economic range from a wealthy Brahman (the doctor) to a poor Shudra (the cowherd). Three Bengali government workers were present: the office manager and a clerk from the Geological Survey of India, and the head clerk at the Accountant General's Office. They were Brahmans and had brought their families. The special guest who presided over the festival was a noted leader of devotional songs (*kirtana*) from Dum Dum in West Bengal. He was referred to as *Prabhu* (powerful one).

At 5:00 P.M. the *Prabhu* blessed a Bengali translation of the tenth chapter of the Bhagavata Purana, which describes the life of Krishna. He then sprinkled water on a *tulasī* plant symbolizing Lakshmi, following the custom that salutations should be presented to Lakshmi before worshipping Vishnu-Krishna. Next the *Prabhu* asked a layman to assist him in administering sandal paste (*gopīcandana*) to the foreheads of those present. He chanted a prayer and several passages from the Bhagavata Purana in Bengali. Then he arose and began to chant devotional songs, strutting and pacing back and forth; after a verse or two he stopped, and the audience responded with a refrain, after which he resumed his animated narrative of the life of Krishna. The following is a translation of a portion of the *kīrtana*:

> O what a form I saw! Such a charming and sweet appearance. The best essence of love.
>
> The peacock feather waving in his locks and a sandal paste mark—the beauty of moonlight—drawn upon his forehead, provide a source of unending pleasure.
>
> The beauty of his face outshines the radiance of the full moon. Such beauty alone hypnotizes the whole world.
>
> The waving garlands of multicoloured flowers that adorn his neck fill the air with heavenly fragrance. Seeing those garlands swaying from side to side, I sacrifice myself at his beloved feet.
>
> Smiling, he utters a few soft words, and then with a radiant face he places that wondrous flute between his honey-sweet lips.
>
> Upon seeing such a beautiful appearance the devotee [*bhakta*] must sacrifice himself, as Kaviraja Dvija Bhima [the author] has declared.

The *kīrtana* continued for over an hour.

At 7:00 P.M. the *Prabhu* began the second phase of the ceremony. While one man played the harmonium, two others played the drums and Nibaran Mukharji the cymbals. For over two hours the *Prabhu* led the participants in devotional songs. Gaura Dasa, Nibaran's son, conducted the last ritual of the day, the Saya Arati, and everyone ate the *prasāda*, which consisted of a vegetable curry.

At this particular celebration of Janmashtami, those present, regardless of age, sex, or social status, participated in singing the *kīrtana*. The leader was a religious specialist trained in the art of devotional songs, but he was not considered either a dispenser of grace or an intermediary between the deity (Krishna) and man.

The purpose of the *kīrtana* is to create an ecstatic atmosphere in which Krishna is spiritually present, dancing and singing among his devotees. The *kīrtana* is popular both at patronized institutions and at non-corporate establishments. Its popularity dates back to the time of Chaitanya in the sixteenth century and seems to be increasing.

Sarasvati Puja

Sarasvati Puja, held in mid-February during the Hindu month of Magha, honours Sarasvati, the goddess of learning, and is popular among Bengalis. It is not sectarian and is thus not confined to monasteries of any one teaching tradition. Unlike Janmashtami, which is primarily a *bhakti* or devotional celebration, Sarasvati Puja lays more stress on the intellectual side of life and allows some of the young people in the audience an opportunity to demonstrate their talents and learning.

In 1964 Sarasvati Puja was held at the Sadguru Nivasa Ashrama, which housed two ascetics and supported itself by taking in paying guests. Nine of the twenty Hindus attending the ceremony were temporary residents of the monastery; four were vacationing from Calcutta and three had government positions (two in the Old Town, one in the New Capital). The two resident ascetics and Bhavani Shankara Babaji, the Solitary Ascetic, were present, as were the doctor (educated in Western medicine) from the Ramakrishna Mission Dispensary and his family. All twenty were Bengalis, ranging from the highest to the lowest in the economic scale.

The celebration began at 11:30 A.M. but little attention was paid to the morning rituals. A few people casually wandered in and out as one of the ascetics performed the waving-of-light ceremony (*ārati*), threw flower petals, and offered *prāsada* before a small plaster image of Sarasvati surrounded by a black backdrop decorated with stars and a crescent moon. A Bengali layman chanted from texts sacred to Sarasvati. At 1:00 P.M. about twenty-three people ate a meal provided by the monastery. The main part of the ceremony began at dusk. First a layman read a translation of the guru-founder's diary. One of the resident ascetics, Sudhir Adhikari, gave a long, animated lecture on the teachings of his guru. Finally the son and daughter of the Calcutta family vacationing at the monastery performed. The daughter, a girl in her late teens, recited passages from the Bhagavad Gita with the aid of some prompting from her father. The son then recited and acted out some of Tagore's writings. After the formal ceremony ended, some of the audience stayed on to sing songs.

Guru Purnima

It is in the worship of the guru (*guru pūrṇimā*) that monastic institutions come into their own. At least fifteen institutions at Bhubaneswar celebrate Guru Purnima, including all five endowed monasteries of the Shankara and Tantric traditions and ten patronized monasteries of Vairagin monastic traditions. The non-corporate establishments do not have an enduring tradition or history and therefore have no guru-founder whom they can worship. Many famous gurus, from the middle ages until the present, have considered themselves incarnations of Shiva or Vishnu, or have been regarded as incarnations by their followers even if they themselves made no such claim. By worshipping the living guru, the disciples are simultaneously venerating all past gurus of their particular order and expressing their belief in the continuity of Hindu tradition.

Each monastery chooses its own day for Guru Purnima; some immediately follow a major festival, such as Dola Purnima; some have no relation in time to other festivals. All are held on the day of a full moon, hence the title *pūrṇimā*. The ceremony at an endowed monastery of the Shankara tradition maintains traditional ritual procedures and forms of worship, with the guru himself remaining austerely silent. Many patronized monasteries, especially those of Vairagin traditions, have developed newer conceptions of guru worship that include a moral sermon by the head ascetic and a *kīrtana*, as well as a banquet.

At Shankarananda Matha, whose head ascetic Saccidananda, the Guru, stands high in the esteem of the laity, the participants are numerous. The ascetics of the Ramakrishna Matha also have a well-attended ceremony celebrating the birthday of Shri Ramakrishna. At seven other institutions, particularly four of the five endowed monasteries, Guru Purnima has become a celebration as empty and ignored as Prathamashtami Yatra and Yamadvitiya Yatra. Thus, while Guru Purnima is potentially the most lively and best attended internal festival directly related to the monasteries, its success depends almost entirely upon the personal qualities of the incumbent head ascetic, and lay attendance over the years will fluctuate as head ascetics change.

The way Guru Purnima is celebrated at an endowed monastery can be illustrated by this account of the Guru Purnima festival at the Shankarananda Matha. It occurs on the full moon day (*pūrṇimā*) of Ashadha (July). Before the Guru Purnima ceremony began, the officiant (*pujārī*) of the Shankarananda Matha arranged a design of *rudrākṣa* nuts and white flower petals upon a wooden bench, in the centre of which was a small replica of the guru's throne. Forty-two nuts were placed along the edges of the bench, symbolizing the forty-two gurus of the monastery, beginning with the founder, Shankarananda

Sarasvati. In front of the bench sat a retired postmaster and the head ascetic of the Harihara Satsangha Ashrama. These two men conducted the first phase of the ceremony, assisted by the head teacher (*pandita*) of a Sanskrit school at Puri. For forty-five minutes the retired postmaster repeatedly chanted, sprinkled the bench with water, and showered the replica of the guru's throne with flowers. Often he was prompted by the head *pandita* who read from a Sanskrit text, and at one point he merely repeated the *pandita*'s words. The audience of approximately thirty-five remained attentive. At noon all those learned in ritual began to chant. Fifteen minutes later the Brahman officiant (*pujārī*) entered and presented a new white cloth to each man who had assisted in the service.

Saccidananda Sarasvati Svami, the head ascetic of the monastery, then entered the room and marched to a leopard skin near the wooden bench and seated himself. Four *panditas* began the solemn rite of washing the Guru's feet. Others showered him with flowers. At the climax of the ceremony, everyone present approached the head ascetic, bowed before him, and touched his feet.

Shortly thereafter, Saccidananda, carrying his staff (*danda*), led a procession of his followers to the Lingaraja Mahaprabhu Temple where rice was offered before the *lingam*. Thirty minutes later the procession moved back to the monastery, where the rice was distributed among the disciples.

Those who attended the Guru Purnima were Oria Brahmans from the Old Town or from Puri. One of the four head ascetics present was from the Old Town; the others were visitors from Puri. Several of the laymen were *panditas* at local high schools. The head *pandita* claimed that throughout the day over three hundred people, including a few important government officials from the New Capital, would come to the monastery and pay their respects to Saccidananda Sarasvati Svami.

The Shankarananda Matha is the only endowed institution that attracts a large number of disciples. Saccidananda is learned in Sanskrit, a master of austere practices, and an able administrator. None of the other four head ascetics of endowed monasteries has more than a few disciples; two are efficient administrators, but they lack charismatic qualities.

Guru Purnima was also observed at a patronized monastery. According to Jagadananda, the head ascetic of the Arya Rishikula Bhuvaneshvari Ashrama, the worship of the guru at his monastery begins on the day of Dola Purnima, the full moon of the Hindu month of Phalguna (March). The 1964 observance of Guru Purnima began in the early afternoon. The residents of the monastery kindled a sacrificial fire (*homa*) in a pit. Those who came during the afternoon bowed before the fire and threw a spoonful of clarified butter (*ghī*) upon it.

Most of them paid their respects to Jagadananda Bhakti Shastri Tirtha and left, though a few stayed for the evening worship, which included a *kīrtana* led by Jagadananda.

The following evening, the monastery held a "religious meeting," and nearly sixty men, women, and children attended. None of the honoured guests (dignitaries from the New Capital) mentioned in a private invitation appeared, but Jagadananda claimed that one high government official had attended. The Deputy Secretary of the Community Development Department presided over the meeting, at which five men presented short speeches before the head ascetic gave a long, emotional sermon in Bengali, summarized in these words:

> I founded this institution for the purpose of serving humanity. Man should not be a hero of words; he should transfer his words into action. The first and foremost duty of an ideal man is to pay attention to each and everyone equally. As long as the duality of "you and I," "India and England," "Russia and the U.S.A." exists among the masses of mankind, humanity will suffer and suffer. We are all part of the One Supreme Spirit (*brahman*); although *brahman* is One, he has been known by different names as Christ, Buddha, Chaitanya, and Confucius. This problem is merely a matter of names. Regardless of the name, each incarnation of *brahman* has preached the same law (*dharma*). Yet today spiritualism is now shattered because of the influence of materialism. The blind man no longer cares for the lame man. Therefore, the true saint (*sādhu*) must be dedicated to the concept of international brotherhood; he must serve for the benefit of humanity as a whole.

This religious meeting at the Arya Rishikula Bhuvaneshvari Ashrama appealed to a different social level from that served by the Shankarananda Matha. Jagadananda presented his sermon to secularly educated residents of the Old Town and the New Capital, many of whom were government employees. The ascetics and the *paṇḍitas* who had attended the Guru Purnima at the Shankarananda Matha were not present, and the only ascetics who came were associated with the monastery itself and its branch near Calcutta. The majority of the audience were laymen, Brahmans and Kshatriyas. After Jagadananda had finished his sermon, he invited his guests to enjoy a banquet. The men ate in one area of the monastery and the women and children ate in another. The festival was concluded with the performance of the evening worship.

It is possible to draw some general conclusions from a comparison of the two Guru Purnima observances outlined above. At the Shankarananda Matha the worship of the guru centres around an elaborate formal ritual which is incomprehensible to most of the audience who have not had intensive training in Sanskrit. Even the *panditas*, who are learned in Sanskrit, frequently refer to the written text for instruction and phraseology. After the lengthy preliminaries, the guru makes a brief appearance. The audience reveres him as a symbol of sacredness and an embodiment of the divine.

The traditional conception of the guru as an austere and learned exemplar is being replaced by a more "modern" conception of the guru as an educational or moral leader. The worship of the guru at the Arya Rishikula Bhuvaneshvari Ashrama illustrates this changed conception. This is evinced at the evening worship where the head ascetic takes the leading role. His participation blurs the roles of ascetic and layman, and the atmosphere is informal. At the religious meeting the speeches avoid Sanskrit in favour of Bengali, and are morally informative and at times humorous. Jagadananda is not as much an object of worship as he is a preacher who seeks to instill in his audience moral values such as religious tolerance and humanitarian concerns.

A Special Purpose Ritual

One monastery in Bhubaneswar, the Harihari Satsangha Ashrama (1962), was founded for the performance of a specific ritual in response to a specific threat. The story of its founding for the single purpose of ritual performance makes a direct contrast to the histories of the other twenty-one monasteries, none of which is known to have been founded for ritual purposes alone.

In 1961 Indian astrologers predicted that an alignment of the planets on 3 February 1962, would bring about a disaster of unthinkable proportions. They asserted that the earth would be shattered by "quakes, floods, air crashes, revolutions, and wars."[3] In the terms of modern astronomy, the earth, moon, sun, and five nearest planets would be aligned in an unusually compact grouping, and on 4 February 1962 (Indian time), there would be an eclipse of the sun. However, according to Indian astrology, this configuration would be complicated by the presence of the mythical planet Ketu in the House of Capricorn and by the appearance of the demonic astral being Rahu, who would swallow the sun. Throughout India, therefore, Hindus sought the intercession of priests who by ritual performances could avert the threatened disasters.

In December, 1961, a committee of influential Oria residents of the Bhubaneswar area organized a sacrificial fire ceremony (*yajña*) "to combat the evil

---

3. *Time*, 19 January 1962, p. 56.

influence of the planets.'' The members of the Managing Committee were:

Chief Patron:	Saccidananda Sarasvati Svami, the Guru, the head of the Shankarananda Matha
President:	The Speaker of the Orissa Legislative Assembly
Co-Vice President:	The Editor of the *Samaj* (an Oria newspaper published in Cuttack)
Co-Vice President:	The Minister of Public Works for Orissa
Secretary–Treasurer:	A retired district judge

This committee requested Brahmananda Dharmatithi, a renowned sacrificial priest from Berhampur, Orissa, to officiate. Brahmananda established the Harihara Satsangha Ashrama, whose name indicates a union of Vishnu (Hari) and Shiva (Hara). Businessmen from Bhubaneswar, Cuttack, and Berhampur donated money and materials for the construction of two shelters, one for the chanting of the Bhagavad Gita and one for the sacrificial fire ritual. On 18 December Brahmananda, assisted by twenty-six Brahman priests, began a recitation of the Bhagavad Gita that was to continue for fourteen months and eighteen days. During the critical period, 3 and 4 February, Brahmananda kindled a sacrificial fire that consumed three truckloads of wood.

Although the alignment of the planets did not result in immediate disaster, in 1964 several residents of Bhubaneswar identified the Chinese invasion of October, 1962, with the evil influence that was predicted. The invasion, in turn, led to the twenty-four hour chanting of the *mahāmantra* at the Chintamanishvara Mandira which continues in order to remove the contamination caused by the 1962 invasion.

Later in 1962, differences arose between Brahmananda and members of the Managing Committee, and by the end of 1962 no one except Brahmananda expressed an interest in continuing the recitation of the Gita. Brahmananda kept no records of income and expenditures, a procedure that the Managing Committee found highly unsatisfactory; hence, the original Managing Committee dissolved itself after the initial crisis period was over and the predicted disasters had apparently failed to occur. In 1963 another Managing Committee was formed with Saccidananda Sarasvati of the Shankarananda Matha as the President.

From the time of its conception, Brahmananda had insisted that after the *yajña* was completed, the *āśrama* should become a home for the aged who had reached the *vānaprastha* stage of life, and Saccidananda, his close friend, agreed. In 1964 this was still Brahmananda's intention although only he, his wife, and his widowed sister were permanently in residence. He was shrewd enough to purchase for himself at a price of Rs. 2,100 the 36,000 sq. ft. piece of land on which the buildings were constructed. Thus a monastery established primarily to mitigate a crisis through ritual observances is now justifying its perpetuation by stressing a social service that in fact it hardly serves.

Private Internal Observances: Daily Worship

Daily worship (*pūjā*) is the one religious function performed at all monasteries, whatever their religious persuasions. The standard feature of daily worship is the waving-of-light ceremony (*ārati*, literally "pleasure" or "delight"). This is a widespread act of reverence in Hindu worship. It is not peculiar to monasteries, and it does not differ from the daily rituals performed before the household altars in pious Hindu homes or in temples. Full-fledged Shankara Dashanami Sannyasins may not perform the daily worship because they have renounced all worldly ties including the performance of household ritual. They either entrust this duty to a novice (*brahmacārin*) or hire a lay Brahman as an officiant (*pujārī*). The Brahman officiant (*pujārī*) at monastic daily worship is distinguished in Oria from the officiating priest at temple ceremonies (*pūjā paṇḍā*). Because no more convenient English term exists, "officiant" is used here to mean only the *pujārī* who serves in monasteries. In a monastery, daily worship must be maintained; cessation of worship provides grounds for censure from the laity. At Vairagin monasteries the daily worship is performed by an ascetic and is the focal point of monastic life. Some monasteries of the Madhva Gaudiya order, a tradition which stresses devotion (*bhakti*), attract the regular attendance of several clients at daily worship. Some of the old endowed monasteries attract no clients at all, but the ritual performances continue.

The Arati
Technically, the term *ārati* designates only the first step of the rite, the waving of a five-pronged lamp before the image of the deity. In general usage the term has come to mean the entire ceremony, which involves the waving of four other items before the image; an incense holder with three sticks of incense, a small conch shell filled with water, a cloth napkin, and a yak-tail fly whisk.

Ideally, the *ārati* is celebrated four times during the day. The first rite of the day, performed at sunrise, is known as Mangala Arati. Mangala means "welfare, bliss, or happiness." The Madhya (middle) Arati and the Sandhya (union of day and night) Arati are held at noon and at dusk, respectively. The last waving-of-light ceremony is the Saya (evening) Arati.

The ritual procedures are identical at each of the four daily waving-of-light ceremonies. As the officiant faces the altar, he holds the lamp (*dīpa*) in his right hand and vibrates it repeatedly, making a clockwise circle before the image. After the third complete circle, he pivots toward the audience, and, turning back to face the image, makes four more circles with his right arm. He repeats the same motions with the remaining four articles. Throughout the whole performance he rings a brass bell with his left hand.

The symbolic interpretations of the *ārati* vary. Two that are current in Bhubaneswar are cited here. Some say that the *ārati* is a delight to the deity because it symbolizes the five basic elements of the material universe: the flame of the lamp represents fire; the incense, air; the water, water; the cloth napkin, earth; and the sound of the bell, ether.

Several head ascetics hold the pietistic interpretation that the *ārati* represents the symbolic meal eaten by the deity. The flame of the lamp provides light for the deity, and the incense adds a pleasant aroma. The water and the cloth presented at the end of the meal enable the deity to wash and dry his right hand, an Indian custom upon finishing a meal. The fly whisk serves throughout the meal. After the deity has partaken of the offered food, it is transformed into sacred food, *prāsada*, meaning "grace," which the officiant distributes among those present.

The *ārati* is therefore a communion service in which an interchange takes place between man and the deity. The *ārati* is not only a delight to the deity, but an act of worship through which men enter into the sacred sphere and participate in the grace and the in-dwelling presence of the deity. A description of the Sandhya Arati illustrates this communion:

In the recitation room of the Chintamanishvara Mandira, a beggar who served as the sweeper was playing a drum (*khol*) and chanting the Great Verse (*mahāmantra*):

> Hari Krishna, Hari Krishna, Krishna, Krishna, Hari, Hari;
> Hari Rama, Hari Rama, Rama, Rama, Hari, Hari.

The head ascetic of a nearby monastery came in, sat down, and began to play the harmonium. One of the resident ascetics, Virendra Natha Sadhukhan, the Troubadour, entered and picked up the chant. A few minutes later three young laymen entered: the grandson of the head ascetic at another monastery, an assistant draftsman for the Orissa Planning Department, and the owner of a restaurant near the railroad station. The two ascetics began to intensify the emotional atmosphere by first increasing and then suddenly decreasing the tempo.

As the sun began to set, a Brahman officiant began to perform the Sandhya Arati in front of the Naga (snake) Lingam enshrined in the main temple. Everyone but the resident ascetic left the recitation hall and stood before the entrance to the temple. As the officiant rotated the ritual objects before the *liṅgam*, one of the laymen struck a gong with a steady monotonous beat, ending abruptly with the last sweep of the fly whisk. Everyone knelt facing the *liṅgam*, touched his forehead to the ground, and then moved to the Hanuman Temple, where the Brahman officiant performed a second *ārati*. The men re-entered the recitation hall, and once again the officiant began the *ārati*. The men danced about the altar circling clockwise and chanting the *mahāmantra*. As the dancing became ecstatic, more laymen joined the circle. All movement and sound ended with the last sweep of the fly whisk and everyone knelt. The officiant then distributed handfuls of *prāsada* among those present.

Throughout the celebration of the *ārati*, the atmosphere was emotionally intense. Those who had sung and danced about the altar were wet with perspiration. This exhausting experience conveyed their belief that Vishnu as Krishna or Rama had sung, danced, and eaten with them.

The monasteries' most important religious function is the performance of ritual. Hindu monastic establishments do not serve as storehouses of grace for the layman, who must work out his own salvation. The layman may, however, hope to gain a small measure of religious merit toward his next reincarnation by donating money or goods to support an ascetic or by attending annual or daily celebrations. The monastery may act as a representative of the deity by spreading moral precepts, although some missionary preaching is usually characteristic of individuals rather than of institutions. Probably the only institution that regards spreading moral precepts as its religious duty is the Ramakrishna Matha, which publishes leaflets and also holds religious meetings for the purpose of preaching. This missionary emphasis, however, is partly the result of Christian influence upon the nineteenth-century Hindu revivalists. The characteristically Hindu religious functions of monasteries have always been mainly ritual and will continue to remain so, even though the quality of the rituals is changing.

Table 16 indicates that no relationship is easily discernible between the monastic social structure and the kinds of public and private rituals performed. There is also no direct relation between teaching tradition and ritual functions, though of course a monastery's chosen deity determines the stress given to certain sectarian festivals.

With the exception of the five oldest monasteries that are required by the terms of their endowments to play certain roles on public occasions and the five

Table 16
Ritual Functions Compared with Social Structure

Ritual Category	Social Category of Monastery		
	ENDOWED CORPORATE	PATRONIZED CORPORATE	NON-CORPORATE
Public External Festivals	All associated with annual festivals connected with temple. Attendance in inverse proportion to the monastery's role	None	None
Internal Monastic Celebrations	None	Minor national holidays celebrated within the monastery. Sarasvati Puja. Janmashtami	None
Sectarian Festivals	None	Celebrated within the monastery. Audiences of about 12–25. Janmashtami	None
Guru Purnima	Guru Purnima at all monasteries. Attendance depends upon reputation of head ascetic	Guru Purnima. Audiences of 6–50	None
Special-Purpose Rituals	None	None	Fire sacrifice to avert planetary disaster. Chanting of *mahāmantra*
Private Internal Observances	Daily worship	Daily worship	Daily worship

or six patronized monasteries that attract sizable congregations on special days, annual festivals are of minor importance in an establishment's life. They do serve to remind the laity of a monastery's existence, but the inner life of the monastery still remains centred upon the daily rituals that are presented before the chosen deity.

Chapter 9

Social Functions: Their Range and Trends

The social functions of monastic establishments are less readily apparent than are religious functions such as the performance of ritual. Indeed, many monasteries serve no broadly social function at all. In the words of one honest and forthright solitary ascetic, "these are very unimportant *mathas* and do nothing for the welfare of the people of the Old Town or the New Capital." The ascetic's use of the word "unimportant" to indicate a lack of social function rather than a failure in ritual functions points to an interesting shift in values. This does not mean that there has yet been any large-scale shift toward performance of social welfare activities, though there are some indications of a trend in this direction.

The traditional economic and social functions of monastic institutions include: the administration of lands for the Lingaraja Mahaprabhu Temple; provision of lodging for pilgrims and wandering ascetics; treatment of mental and physical illnesses; and teaching of Sanskrit and ancient traditions. Monastic orders also provide escape hatches for individuals ill-adapted to roles required of them in a bureaucratically structured and closed society.

Laymen have traditionally sought out the holy man to cure illness through an appeal to his supernatural powers supplemented by treatment according to pharmaceutical knowledge based on the Ayur-vedic tradition (native medical tradition of India). Neither in India nor in the West can medical practices always clearly distinguish between spiritual (psychic) factors and physical ones. In fact, the distinction is possibly spurious.

A few ascetics still claim supernatural cures for mental and physical ailments. These cures, however, can be operative and appealed to in addition to treatment at the "modern" dispensaries operated by some institutions. For instance, a dispensary may be operated by a lay practitioner supported by the monastery "for the benefit of humanity," and, at the same time, an ascetic at the same monastery may still perform cures by spiritual means.

Ideally and traditionally Hindu education has been given in the schools founded by ascetics for the training of Brahman boys in Sanskrit, priestly ritual, and caste duties. In ancient times, the upper levels of these schools concentrated on Hindu philosophy. Many ascetics of those times came from the ranks of such Brahman pupils or *brahmacārins*, just as they do today. In the contemporary world this traditional education, with its implications of a religious and social elite, has been greatly modified. Even in Sanskrit schools modern subjects have been added to the original curriculum. Often, enough modern subjects are added to meet the state educational requirements, qualifying the school for financial aid from the government. Instead of teaching rituals and caste duties a monastery may try to promote literacy in Oria or Bengali "for the general welfare of the population" and as preparation for work in the modern world.

While missionary activities date from the nineteenth-century revivalists and reformers like Ramakrishna and Vivekananda, the appeal to outcaste groups also is characteristic of two recent non-sectarian establishments, the Chintamanishvara Mandira and the Trinatha Gosvami Matha. Their activities contrast directly with the exploitation of an outcaste group by an old feudal landholding institution.

The traditional and still predominant socio-religious function of the majority of monasteries is simply to house ascetics who represent centres of sacredness for the community. This is evident from the composite description provided later in this chapter of a typical day in the life of a monastery, which includes much ritual and a surprising amount of leisure time, but little or nothing in the way of welfare activities. Many laymen who never attend ritual performances and who do not expect welfare activities would be disturbed if all monasteries were to disappear, for in the Indian mind the *maṭha* provides a focus for sacredness.

The Monasteries as Feudal Landlords

The five monasteries endowed by rulers of Orissa in the medieval period were founded partly to administer agricultural lands to support the Lingaraja Mahaprabhu Temple, and to supply the Temple staff either with rice or with money from the sale of the surplus crops. Like some of the large Christian abbeys, these institutions were really feudal landowners. They exacted rents and labour services from lower-caste populations living on their lands. Today most tenants pay in crops or cash instead of labour. However, one monastery, the Sadavrata Pitha, still requires a lengthy list of unpaid labour services from the Bauris, a Scheduled Caste of day labourers who have built houses on some of the monastery's land.[1] The Bauris are a caste of "water carriers" who were assigned to the Sadavrata Pitha by the medieval patrons of the monastery. They perform various duties for the monasteries. Those performed for the Matha Sahi (monastery ward) are:

Water supply. Bauris daily supply water for all cattle owned by the monastery. In 1940 this amounted to sixty-five buckets daily, but in 1964 only twenty buckets were required since there were fewer cows. This and the next two were services performed by each family in rotation. In October 1965 the Bauris ceased to supply water in protest against the head ascetic's sale to an outsider of a plot of land that they used. The head ascetic sought police intervention to end the dispute.

Fuel supply. Bauris had to cut and haul wood daily from forests owned by the monastery. This service ended in 1965 when the monastery illegally sold the forests with which it had been endowed to a contractor for new construction.

Grass supply. During the rainy season families take turns supplying grass for the monastery's cattle.

House thatching. In 1940 the Bauris thatched two rooms for a cowshed. In return they were allowed to fish in three monastery tanks and were also given a feast. In 1964 all male Bauris were required to thatch without pay for two days a year although fishing privileges had been suspended.

Construction of temporary shades. Three times a year the Bauris must make shades to shield the images of the deity on public festival occasions.

Cleaning the granary. All Bauris, male and female, must spend two days preparing the storehouses to receive the new harvest.

Bundling the straw and storing the grain and rice. This requires another two days' labour.

1. The information about the labour services rendered by the Bauris is taken from: Manmohan Mahapatra, "Urbanization Processes in a Scheduled Caste: The Bauris of Oldtown Bhubaneswar," dated 23 August 1967 (a paper in the files of the Harvard–Bhubaneswar Project, Cambridge, Massachusetts).

Planting the rice crop. All females, including children, must spend one day planting the monastery's rice.

Transplanting the rice crop. All males, including children, must transplant rice in the monastery's paddy one day a year.

Ploughing. Those who cultivate the monastery's land as tenants must also plough the monastery's land.

Ritual duties connected with major public festivals. At Ashokashtami Yatra, the Bauris have the dangerous task of stopping the processional car at intervals by throwing chocks under the wheels. This duty is especially resented.

In addition to these services, which consume a maximum of fourteen days a year per man, Bauris are employed by the monastery for wage labour at two-thirds of the market rate. In return they receive rent-free houseplots. The Sadavrata Pitha collects fees from the Bauri ward and has control over wells and sanitary facilities. It also controls the routes that Bauri marriage and funeral processions must use.

Relations between landlord and tenants have been strained in recent years. Some of the Bauris have rumoured that the head ascetic has killed three of their number who refused to perform traditional services, but they have produced no evidence to substantiate their claim. They have also complained that they are forced to share drinking water with the monastery's cattle and that the monastery has sold their land and houses out from under them. In retaliation, they have ceased to honour several of the free services, demanding instead that they be paid fair wages. They have also petitioned the Commissioner for Scheduled Castes in New Delhi. Within a generation the free services will probably cease to exist altogether.

The Monastery as Guest-House

A second traditional function of the endowed institutions was to provide lodging for wandering ascetics and for lay pilgrims who had come to visit the temple-complex, much as Christian monasteries served as hostelries. Wandering ascetics were often given by the headquarters monastery of their order a kind of "pass card" that entitled them to stay overnight at other monasteries without charge and identified them as genuine ascetics rather than spurious mendicants. Lay pilgrims added to the monastery's revenue by paying in goods or money.

Several endowed monasteries still take in pilgrims, but their guest quarters are rarely full. One endowed monastery that is mostly in ruins (the Kapali Matha) has become a clubhouse for young ex-schoolboys who belong to the Mahabir Club. Founded in 1960, it has a dozen members, mostly Shudra temple servants. The boys organize performances of Sarasvati Puja and Ganesha Puja. Between these festivals, the building serves as a dormitory for the youths, who are permitted to live there rent-free. They may eat only vegetarian meals within the monastery building but are allowed to cook non-vegetarian dishes outside on the platform near the image of the goddess Kapali.

The ancient function of providing a hostelry has been largely taken over by the patronized institutions. Young civil servants who have come to work in the New Capital sometimes take advantage of the inexpensive lodging offered by the monasteries. Thus a monastery may have several permanent guests who are not at all concerned with the religious beliefs or practices of the institution, if, indeed, they are concerned with religion at all. A strict head ascetic may try to expel a tenant who eats meat or uses wine on the monastery grounds but otherwise no interest in the monastery's activities is expected or required.

Several of the patronized monasteries founded in the 1920s and 1930s with money from Bengal have lost their original patronage and now support themselves largely by acting as guest-houses. Eventually three or four of these may cease to function as monasteries altogether. Two former institutions had already ceased religious activities in 1964. One building was rented to a publisher and one was used by the Archaeological Survey of India. A third monastery (the Jagannatha Deva Mandira) was building a row of small shops to be rented out for profit, and a fourth (the Nimbarka Ashrama) was building houses on some of its land. Three others were in the process of converting their present buildings to secular purposes. The following are several sketches of monasteries in the process of becoming guest-houses.

Radhakrishna Sevashrama (1918)
In the 1930s the monastery compound and buildings of the Radhakrishna Sevashrama had been impressive, but by 1948 the head ascetic, then in his sixties, had lost the ability to manage his finances. He asked his brother, a photographer from East Pakistan, to assume these duties. The brother, who had lost most of his money in the partition of India and Pakistan, gladly accepted the invitation. Ever since his arrival, he has tried to assume legal control of the properties. In 1964 he was operating a photography studio in the main residential quarters and had rented out not only the former library, but also the renovated cattle stalls and three of the four single rooms. He had pushed the

head ascetic and his wife into the remaining one-room cell and had walled up
the gate between the ascetic's quarters and his own studio. He then white-
washed his side of the cupboard, leaving his brother's side dark. The tenants
of the rented-out parts of the compound were mainly clerks or government
employees who had come to the New Capital to work. The total rents came to
Rs. 160 a month, which was supplemented by profits from a larger photo-
graphic studio in the New Capital.

Sadguru Nivasa Ashrama (1940)
At the Sadguru Nivasa Ashrama the rental income from rooms amounts to
about Rs. 100 a month and suffices for the daily needs of the two resident
ascetics. The Calcutta headquarters has provided Rs. 15,000 to add a second
story to the residence for rental purposes. The head ascetic sees a bright future
for his monastery as its guest-house activities expand and thinks that the New
Capital, while unfortunately "increasing materialism and decreasing spiritual-
ism among the people," is bringing in new tenants for the owners or managers
of rental property like himself.

Kapali Matha (13th to 15th century)
The family of the head ascetic at the ruined Kapali Matha has plans for reconstructing the building. The head ascetic's brother and nephew are both medical
practitioners who treat villagers with home remedies, Ayur-vedic medicines,
and modern drugs. They plan to use their combined savings of Rs. 1,000 toward
reconstruction. Their architectural plans include several rooms that can be
rented. They know that they have a prime location on the main street of the
Old Town and are determined to capitalize on it, although Rs. 1,000 is not nearly
enough to build the structure they envision. When asked whether the aim in
reconstructing the building was for purposes of religion or for income, they at
first replied that it was for religion, but without conviction. Later they admitted
that "there is really no question of religion in our plans."

Institutions established more recently with the patronage of Orias or
Bengalis living in the Bhubaneswar or Cuttack areas are flourishing, though
they may also take advantage of the New Capital's housing shortage by renting
extra space.

In direct contrast to monasteries that are in the process of becoming secular
hotels stand several newer establishments that have become monasteries
although founded for other purposes. Thus there is no general trend toward
secularization of religious institutions. The reverse process, sacralizing, has
occurred at the Chintamanishvara Mandira, the Trinatha Gosvami Matha, and
the Harihara Satsangha Ashrama.

Dispensaries

Two patronized monasteries operate charitable dispensaries. The dispensary sponsored by the Ramakrishna Mission is the only one that treats a considerable number of patients. The smaller dispensary at the Arya Rishikula Bhuvaneshvari Ashrama is less modern in methods of treatment. Other monasteries influenced by reformist–revivalist movements maintain dispensaries at some of their branches outside Bhubaneswar.

Ramakrishna Mission Dispensary (1920)

Svami Brahmananda, the first president of the Ramakrishna Order, founded the monastery at Bhubaneswar in 1919. In 1920 he opened a charitable dispensary under the direction of an Indian doctor trained in modern medicine. In 1964 the dispensary was staffed by a Bengali who had received his medical degree from the University of Calcutta. He was assisted by two Oria pharmacists. The dispensary treated a great variety of illnesses. In 1962–63, the staff examined 23,459 patients, including 11,611 new cases.

The Ramakrishna Mission Dispensary is the only monastery sponsored dispensary to provide Western medical treatment. It receives about half its income from grants from the Orissa government welfare department. Without this government money it would be difficult to maintain welfare services, since the monastery, although the largest physical complex in the Old Town, is far from the wealthiest.

The Arya Rishikula Bhuvaneshvari Ashrama Dispensary (1962)

The Arya Rishikula Bhuvaneshvari Ashrama Dispensary uses homeopathic medicine, combining Ayur-vedic remedies, other herbal treatment, patent medicines, and whatever modern medicines the homeopathic practitioner can obtain. These sometimes include antibiotics and inoculations. The dispensary is run by a retired Bengali homeopathic medical practitioner who has a bachelor's degree in homeopathic medicine from a college in Burma. In 1964, he had no salaried assistants, although an employee at an Old Town Ayur-vedic store often aided him. The homeopath claims that he treats approximately thirty patients per day. The head ascetic claims to have performed several miraculous cures himself, especially of mental illnesses, but he neither visits the dispensary nor sees patients on a regular basis.

The head ascetics at two other monasteries are former Ayur-vedic practitioners who occasionally treat patients but refer all serious cases to the Old Town hospital. It is possible that more monasteries would operate modern dispensaries if they had the means to pay a physician. However, wealth and welfare activities do not seem to be directly related. The poverty of smaller establishments prevents them from engaging in welfare activities, but the wealthiest institutions, the old endowed monasteries, often lack interest in such activities.

Educational Institutions

Two monasteries operate schools. The Utkalmani Gurukula Brahmachary-ashrama is primarily a Sanskrit school of the type traditionally associated with monasteries. Its unique feature is that the head ascetic has never restricted it to Brahmans only, although there is no evidence that a low-caste pupil was ever admitted. In recent years this school has shifted its emphasis from traditional to modern learning, and the Orissa government has provided support. The second school, the Ramakrishna Mission School, was founded for purposes of increasing literacy rather than perpetuating traditional caste duties and has been modern in orientation since its founding.

The Utkalmani Gurukula Brahmacharyashrama (1939)
The Shankarananda Matha financially supports the Sanskrit school (*tol*) known as the Utkalmani Gurukula Brahmacharyashrama. The name of the school reflects the fact that the students at a traditional Sanskrit school were required to remain at the home (*kula*) of their teacher (*guru*) and to live a student's austere life (*brahmacaryāśrama*). The name Utkalmani honours Gopabandhu Das, the nationalist hero of Orissa, whom Orias call the Jewel of Utkal (*utkal-maṇi*).

In 1934 Saccidananda, the Guru and founder of the school, prefaced his proposals for a *gurukula brahmacaryāśrama* with the following words, which reflect provincialism as well as religious revivalism:

> Our motherland, Utkal [Orissa], should be re-oriented once more toward her former glory and richness. Spirituality and spiritual thinking should be instilled into the life of every village of Utkal, and the *varṇāśrama dharma* [the *dharma* or law of the classes and stages of life] should be professed and propagated once again in this country. . . . We have now left the basic practices and beliefs of our land far behind us and a barbarous, naked, un-disciplined civilization has overtaken us. Yet the intellectuals of our land are expressing their deep sense of resentment over this matter. Within different states of India efforts are being made to ameliorate this situation. Many *gurukula āśramas* and educational institutions have already been established

. . . but Orias have always adopted an apathetic attitude toward such a vital matter. . . . The principal aim in establishing a *gurukula āśrama* at Bhubaneswar is to focus the attention of Orias on the ancient civilization of their motherland.[2]

Saccidananda sent his proposals to influential residents of Orissa, thirty-three of whom responded enthusiastically. In December 1934 all interested parties, both ascetic and lay, met in Bhubaneswar and appointed a managing committee consisting of nine laymen plus Saccidananda as the head of the committee. The lay members began to solicit funds from the higher economic levels of Oria society, and Saccidananda undertook an extensive tour of Orissa in order to reach the villagers. During the period from December 1934 to December 1938 he visited approximately sixty-five villages, speaking at numerous community assemblies. By the end of 1939 sufficient funds had been raised and construction of the Sanskrit school was begun.

In a report issued to the patrons of the school, Saccidananda underlined the severity of *brahmacaryāśrama* by listing the rules that would govern the students of his school:

Boys ranging from eight to twelve years of age or older will be accepted in the school. The inmates will observe the vows of *brahmacarya* and eat only pure food and wear simple dress, as sanctioned by the eternal law (*sanātana dharma*). The inmates will be taught traditional yogic postures (*āsana*) and breath-control exercises (*prāṇāyāma*) for self-purity. The *brahmacārins* will adopt the daily habit of performing such duties as prayer and worship at sunrise and sunset, recitation of scripture, care of cows, and service to elderly people. The *brahmacārins* will remain at the school continuously for a period of twelve years. If any *brahmacārin* desires to go home or is requested to do so by his guardian, then the guardian must take all the precautions necessary to insure that the boy will eat and dress in the manner prescribed by the rules of the school.[3]

Saccidananda wanted a return to *varṇāśrama dharma*, but in theory, at least, he was willing to allow Shudras the right of admission to his Sanskrit school, though no evidence exists that a Shudra ever attended.

In 1940 four Brahman boys undertook vows of *brahmacarya* at the Sanskrit school. By 1945 the Utkalmani Gurukula Brahmacharyashrama had twelve students and two teachers, including Saccidananda. During the 1950s the

---

2. Saccidananda Sarasvati, *Report of the Utkalmani Gurukula Brahmacaryasrama of Bhubaneswar.*
3. Ibid., pp. 11–13.

managing committee was able to increase the endowment of the institution, and in 1955, with the financial aid of the Shankarananda Matha, a larger school was constructed upon the land opposite the monastery. Since 1955 Saccidananda has played a less direct role in the education of the students. In 1959 the managing committee appointed Jayadeva Brahmachari of the Arya Rishikula Vasishtha Yogashrama as Principal of the Sanskrit school. In 1964 the school had twenty-five students and three teachers. One man, who had had eight years of training at the Puri Sanskrit school, teaches courses in Sanskrit; two others, one of whom is a graduate of the University of Calcutta, teach English and such courses as geography, history, and mathematics.

In 1964 the Orissa State Government, at the request of the managing committee, paid the salaries of the two general education teachers and two-thirds of the salary of the Sanskrit instructor. Saccidananda is not alarmed at the possibility of increased government aid to and influence on the Sanskrit school. In fact, he has submitted a recommendation to the managing committee proposing that the state government be permitted to assume full responsibility for the management and curriculum. He is convinced that this is the only way in which his school can continue to grow.

The curriculum has changed greatly since the founding of the school. The students, with the exception of a few ascetics, cannot be distinguished from the students at a secular school. They no longer wear the distinctive white garments of a *brahmacārin*, nor are they required to adhere to the strict rules of studentship outlined by Saccidananda in 1940. By his acceptance of certain changes in policy and management, Saccidananda is not being inconsistent in his denunciation of Westernization and in his plea for a return to Hindu tradition. He insists that the government, although enlarging the present curriculum, must retain an emphasis upon Sanskrit grammar, literature, and philosophy. Furthermore, he considers changes in student dress of no importance in accomplishing his goal of providing young Orias with a traditional Sanskrit education. In Saccidananda's opinion, the Utkalmani Gurukula Brahmacharyashrama will remain the best Sanskrit school of its kind in Orissa.

The Shankarananda Matha pays the expenses of room and board, amounting to Rs. 30 per month, for ten of the more advanced students. The government issues scholarships of Rs. 15 per month to a few of the other students. About half the students are from the Bhubaneswar area; most of the others come from Puri.

At a Sanskrit school such as this, the program leading to the degree of preceptor (*ācārya*) is divided into three phrases. The first course (*prathama*) consists of two years' training in Sanskrit grammar in addition to instruction in

Oria literature, geography, history, mathematics, and hygiene. According to the Principal, the level of education that the students attain by completing the *prathama* is approximately the equivalent of grade seven at a public school.

The middle course (*madhyama*) consists of four years' instruction in Sanskrit literature, Oria literature, algebra, geometry, geography, and history. Completion of the *madhyama* is about equal to finishing high school.

The final course (*ācārya*) consists of four years' training in Sanskrit. Since Sanskrit is the only subject taught, the educational level is not directly comparable with college, although the number of years required to attain the degree of Acharya is about the same as required for a Bachelor of Arts degree.

The specialized degree of Acharya has been the traditional preparation for an ascetic life and possibly the headship of a monastery. Only three out of the forty-one ascetics in the Old Town hold that title. One of these is Saccidananda. Three other ascetics have completed between four and eight years of instruction in Sanskrit; two of these three are heads of monasteries. An individual with the degree of Acharya also has the choice of becoming a public high school instructor of Sanskrit as an alternative to entering monastic orders.

The Ramakrishna Mission School (1933)

The Ramakrishna Matha and Mission founded the Ramakrishna Mission School in order "to remove illiteracy among the poor boys and girls of the locality."[4] In contrast to the Sanskrit *ṭol* the Mission school provides a broad, general education for a portion of the children of the Old Town area.

In 1933 the managing committee of the Ramakrishna Mission established a lower primary school (grades one to three). Forty pupils enrolled, but the managing committee employed only one teacher. By 1945 the enrolment had increased to 75 boys and girls, and in 1949 the managing committee secured sufficient funds to create an upper primary school (grades four and five). The staff was increased to seven teachers, who taught 150 students. In 1963 the mission added a middle English school (grades six and seven) and increased the staff to ten teachers. In 1963, 179 boys and 72 girls attended the upper primary school. The Mission also has a library of 2,230 books on a variety of subjects, traditional and modern.[5]

In 1964 construction began on a new high school building. The head ascetic also arranged for the establishment of a Vivekananda Chair of Religious Studies at the Utkal State University in the New Capital.

4. The Ramakrishna Math and Mission, *Bhubaneswar Report, 1939–40*, p. 6.

5. The Ramakrishna Math and Mission, *The General Report of the Ramakrishna Math and Mission, April 1962 to March 1963*.

The Mission school follows the curriculum established by the state government, which pays the teachers' salaries. The managing committee adds another Rs. 200 annually to their salaries. The students in the lower and upper primary schools receive their education free; however, the students in the middle English school pay Rs. 2.50 per month. The majority of the students at the school are from the Old Town, although several come from nearby villages. The general opinion among the students and their parents is that the Mission school provides better instruction than do the public schools of the Old Town. It maintains better facilities and a better staff than do the public schools because it receives financial support from the Ramakrishna Mission in addition to its heavy state subsidy. The Ramakrishna Mission School, therefore, may provide an example for monastery-supported schools of the future and probably reflects a trend from traditionally oriented education of a highly specialized type to an education presumed to prepare students for contemporary life.

Religious Parks and Roadside Shrines

In contrast to the old endowed monastery that related to its Scheduled Caste tenants primarily as a feudal landlord, two non-corporate establishments founded since the establishment of the New Capital (Chintamanishvara Mandira and Trinatha Gosvami Matha) are providing the kind of rituals that appeal to low and Scheduled Castes. Both monasteries are non-sectarian and at both monasteries religious specialists have assumed control over a lay-initiated establishment.

The Chintamanishvara Mandira is situated at the site of a medieval temple to Shiva. The name of the institution means "Lord (*īśvara*) of the philosopher's stone (*chintāmaṇi*)," and thus refers to Shiva. The old temple houses a *nāga* (snake) *liṅgam* about ten inches in diameter, over which is poised a bronze king cobra with hood expanded, also a symbol of Shiva. Since the temple is only half a mile from the railway station, it is conveniently situated for pilgrims and for wandering ascetics, who are sometimes permitted to ride free in third class coaches. The neighbourhood immediately surrounding the railway station is one of the roughest in town; it includes the town's houses of prostitution and shanties along the tracks, built of refuse by beggars and transient contract labourers. The area immediately surrounding the Chintamanishvara Temple, however, is rice-paddy belonging to Lakshmisagara Village. It provides a peaceful contrast to the railway bazaar area and thus makes an excellent resting-place for those travellers who wish to stop and refresh themselves.

In view of the possibilities of this excellent location, a committee of prominent Orias decided in 1950 to refurbish the temple and to construct a "religious park" on the land surrounding it. This managing committee included the wealthiest businessman in town, an engineer for the Public Works Department, and the owner of a publishing company in Cuttack who had contributed to the reconstruction of other temples.

A pilgrim approaching the *mandira* in 1964 would follow the path outlined in figure 4. On entering the compound, he would first pay his respects to the sacred *tulasī* plant. Entering the Mahamantra recitation hall, he would reverence a shrine that included a picture of the resident ascetic's guru surrounded by coloured prints of major deities. After passing through another audience hall, he would prostrate himself before the Shiva *lingam* without entering the sanctum. As he left the major temple, he might deposit money in a collection box. He could then either visit the small temple to the monkey king Hanuman or proceed directly to an image of Durga built into the main temple's outside wall. Before leaving the compound, he might circumambulate the sacred banyan tree with fragments of ancient sculpture at its feet. A pilgrim arriving in the evening might take advantage of the institution's well-designed tank, which occupies about one-third of the compound. Separate dressing stalls are provided for men and women. Here the medicinal waters of Bhubaneswar's famed underground stream come to the surface. The water flows from the bathing tank into a smaller tank for washing clothes and then is used to irrigate the rice fields.

The Managing Committee had begun a recitation of the *mahāmantra* three months after the Chinese invasion of India in October, 1962, in order to purify India from the evil resulting from this invasion. Virendra Natha Sadhukhan, the Troubadour, is in charge of the recitation that is broadcast over a public address system which can be heard in both the nearby villages and the railway bazaar area. It continues day and night with ascetics alternating on four-hour shifts. Any wandering ascetics who happen to be there, as well as the one resident beggar, a low-caste sweeper, are expected to take their turns at the recitation. They are assisted by two Brahman priests from the nearby village of Lakshmisagara who are hereditarily assigned to the Shaiva temple. The priests also conduct worship at the shrine of the Troubadour's guru, since, as a Shudra, he is not permitted to perform daily worship (*pūjā*).

Although initial patronage from the managing committee was substantial, funds had run out in 1964, and the institution had become dependent upon daily contributions from its numerous pilgrims and regular clients from nearby areas. The latter range from a few wealthy individuals down to the Scheduled

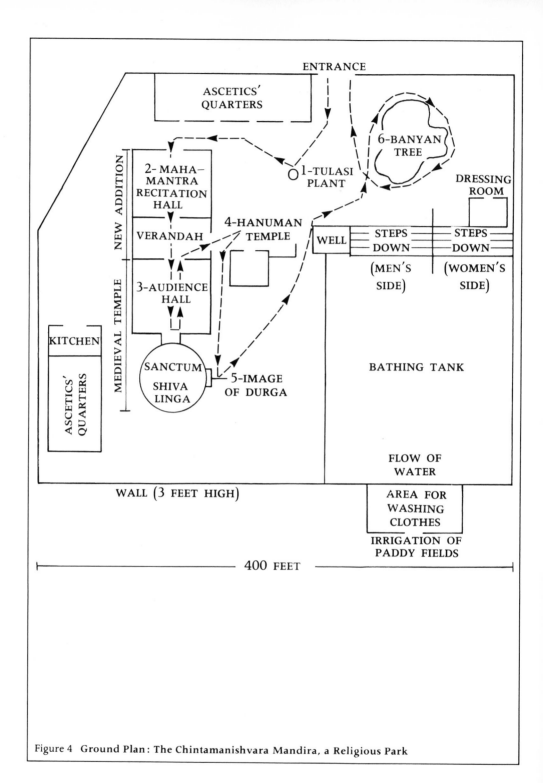

ENTRANCE

ASCETICS'
QUARTERS

6-BANYAN
TREE

DRESSING
ROOM

2- MAHA—
MANTRA
RECITATION
HALL

NEW ADDITION

○ 1-TULASI
PLANT

VERANDAH

4-HANUMAN
TEMPLE

WELL

STEPS
DOWN

STEPS
DOWN

MEDIEVAL TEMPLE

3-AUDIENCE
HALL

(MEN'S
SIDE)

(WOMEN'S
SIDE)

KITCHEN

BATHING TANK

ASCETICS'
QUARTERS

SANCTUM

SHIVA
LINGA

5-IMAGE
OF DURGA

FLOW OF
WATER

WALL (3 FEET HIGH)

AREA FOR
WASHING
CLOTHES

IRRIGATION OF
PADDY FIELDS

———— 400 FEET ————

Figure 4 Ground Plan: The Chintamanishvara Mandira, a Religious Park

Caste members of the nearby Depressed League School. In 1964 the establishment seemed to be doing quite well financially and always had sufficient food for wandering ascetics. Its future looks secure, since it appeals to a wide range of social and economic groups and encourages lay participation in its ceremonies.

The monastery's proximity to the government-financed Depressed League School for Scheduled Castes partly accounts for frequent attendance by lower-caste groups. Unlike most sectarian traditional institutions, the Chintamanishvara Mandira does not discriminate on a caste basis.

The Trinatha Gosvami Matha (1954). The name Trinatha (meaning three lords) is often applied to the numerous small roadside shrines that house coloured prints of Brahma, Vishnu, and Shiva. The Trinatha cult emphasizes both material gain and the ultimate equality of all castes, thereby attracting the lower and Scheduled Castes.[6] Twenty-five of the sixty-three adherents in the area are Bauris, the Scheduled Caste of labourers mentioned earlier. A few members are of the higher castes who are having financial troubles and wish for gain also attend; this group includes twelve Brahmans. The cult of Trinatha in Bhubaneswar has at least nine different shrines.

The Trinatha Gosvami Matha is the only such shrine administered by an ascetic, Trinatha Gosvami, an Oria Kshatriya. According to Trinatha Gosvami's account, in 1954 an elderly hermit gave him the sacred black stone of Trinatha. He thereupon took the name of the deity as his own and installed the stone image in a mud hut built for him by villagers near the Ramakrishna Matha. In 1964, Trinatha Gosvami's earnings amounted to Rs. 100 a month, considerably more than any other solitary ascetic. He listed only three regular low-caste disciples. Two were artists earning Rs. 150 a month, and one was a carter earning Rs. 60 a month. Thus Trinatha Gosvami's income almost equalled that of his clients.

The weekly meetings appeal to popular taste by their simplicity and festive atmosphere. They strongly resemble the average village *kīrtana*. The leader reads the myth of Trinatha, which offers reassurance to those who are ill, in economic troubles, or depressed by their low social position. The myth also stresses the importance of performing the duties associated with one's station in life. Betel, *gañjā* and some food are offered to Trinatha. The whole group then begins a series of songs that may include both devotional hymns and popular film theme songs, with the accompaniment of drums and harmonium.

6. The material about the Trinatha cult is taken from: Richard Shweder, "A Report on Trinatha and Trinatha Shrines in Old Town, Bhubaneswar."

During the meeting, which lasts for several hours, the leader passes the *gañjā* pipe and betel-nut preparation (*pān*), as is done at the *kīrtanas* held in villages nearby. Trinatha Gosvami believes that the age of destruction (*kali yuga*) began in 1954, when Jagannatha–Vishnu incarnated himself as Lord Trinatha and came to him in a vision asking him to be his messenger on earth. He has been proselytizing ever since. Equality is his major social message. As he said to the interviewer, "Even a leper is welcome; even *you*."

The kind of institution represented by the Chintamanishvara Mandira and the Trinatha Gosvami Matha will probably flourish in the future because of the emphasis on reducing caste distinctions, on non-sectarianism, and on non-intellectual devotions of the kind that people newly arrived in the Old Town and the New Capital have previously enjoyed in their home villages.

The removal of caste distinctions exists only *within* religious meetings; there is no attempt to reform the social order as a whole. In each case it is laymen, rather than ascetics, who have been the moving force in opening the establishment to lower castes. The Ramakrishna Matha is the only large institution that formally claims to conduct missionary activities among Scheduled Castes, but the intellectual nature of its theological discussions appeals mainly to the educated upper castes. A few Bauris claim that the Ramakrishna Mission is "doing good work," referring to its welfare activities, but they do not attend religious meetings there.

Centres of Sacredness

Lay expectations influence the responses of the more prominent ascetics. The one service that *every* ascetic is expected to perform for both patrons or clients is the giving of personal advice on many matters, including religion, philosophy, private donations, management of money, choice of career, or marital life. If an ascetic has wealthy and influential patrons, he may be asked for his opinions on political or social issues. In other words, every ascetic is expected to give pastoral counseling about all sorts of personal problems that are often purely secular in nature. In addition, certain highly respected ascetics such as the Guru and the Preacher are consulted, sometimes indirectly through an official's secretary, by men in high government positions who want to keep in close touch with religious and social currents in the Old Town. These government officials also wish to be assured of the ascetics' followers' support in elections. This relationship resembles the contact between some political leaders of North American immigrant groups and their parish priests.

On a more personal level, Jagadananda, the Preacher, for instance, helped with the career decision of a young man from Calcutta, who came to Bhubaneswar with some training in radio repair, but could not find employment. The youth spent a month in the monastery, until Jagadananda had built up the young man's courage to such an extent that he was willing to venture setting up his own radio repair shop in a room that Jagadananda found for him. The monastery provided funds and the labour of several *brahmacārins* to establish the young man in business.

Although some clients request their guru's advice in secular affairs, the majority come to the monastery either to worship or to seek their guru's help in their private devotions. For instance, a retired sub-inspector of police visits one monastery daily to perform his devotions and usually stays until evening talking with the head ascetic about the life and teachings of Chaitanya. Many monasteries have clients of this kind, who regard the monastery as a centre of sacredness and a place where one can learn religious lore and devotional practices with expert help.

The primary social function of every monastery is to house ascetics, who provide a centre of sacredness in the eyes of the lay community. Daily life revolves around the performance of worship (*pūjā*) and affords much leisure time for reading, meditation, and chatting with friends.

The day-to-day activities at a monastery are highly routinized, though no formal orders are given and no formal assemblies are required. The performances of morning, noon, and evening rituals before the chosen deity determine the order of the day, but the different residents of the monastery interact rather casually with each other, and their activities vary only slightly from day to day. Daily social conversation is unmarked by hierarchical distinctions between head ascetic, ascetics-in-training (*brahmacārins*), paid performers of ritual (*pujārīs*), and other employees. Each resident or employee knows his duties and follows his own individual schedule without being ordered to do so by the head ascetic. An employee or a *brahmacārin* can approach the head ascetic at will without having to make an appointment or to go through a formal procedure. Life in a Hindu monastery is casual and informal in comparison to life in either European Christian monasteries or Chinese Buddhist monasteries. The day affords a good deal of leisure to all residents, especially the head ascetic, unless he is a rare individual given to practising traditional austerities. If it appears that ascetics have little else to do but to spend the day in gossip, this is the case also for many lay residents of the Old Town, where life moves slowly.

Each of twenty-two head ascetics provided us with a list of his usual daily activities. These are roughly similar, though some tend to say "high philosophical reading" when they actually mean reading the daily newspaper, or "meditation" when they are really gossiping with friends. The daily schedule of Saccidananda, the Guru and the leader of the Oria religious community, is typical.

Daily Routine of a Head Ascetic

4:00 A.M.	Leaves bed.
4:30 to 5:00 A.M.	Finishes his toilet and takes his posture (*āsana*) for meditation.
5:00 to 6:00 A.M.	Bathes.
6:00 to 8:00 A.M.	Worships Shiva and Parvati (privately). Reads the Bhagavad Gita and the Upanishads. He does this as an example for the other residents of the monastery.
8:00 A.M.	Takes a cold drink, normally water or milk.
8:00 to 11:00 A.M.	Reads newspapers, writes letters, takes care of the garden, worships cows, and serves guests.
11:00 to 12:00 noon	Takes noon bath, worships his deity, and eats a meal of rice and curries. He does not eat spicy food. He has never eaten excessive food; he follows the rule to "keep one-quarter of the stomach empty."
12:00 to 2:00 P.M.	Rests.
2:00 to 5:00 P.M.	Discusses philosophy and reads Sanskrit texts.
5:00 to 6:00 P.M.	Takes evening bath and worships his deity.
6:00 to 7:00 P.M.	Meditates.
7:00 to 9:00 P.M.	Answers the questions of visitors. Reads the Puranas. Eats ripe fruit and drinks milk.
9:00 to 10:00 P.M.	Rests.
10:00 to 12:00 P.M.	Thinks about his deity and pays homage to other deities.
12:00 P.M. to 4:00 A.M.	Sleeps.

The only major differences between this and the other calendars are that Saccidananda arises at an early hour to practise meditation and that he actually reads philosophy in Sanskrit. Few other ascetics have his degree of traditional learning.

Although details of daily schedules vary somewhat, life in most monasteries follows a certain daily pattern.

Daily Routine of a Monastery
4:00 to 6:00 A.M. All residents of the Old Town get up at about 5:00 A.M. Those ascetics who place a greater emphasis upon meditating arise earlier (with the help of alarm clocks) to meditate. The person who officiates at early morning devotions also arises earlier to bathe.

The Mangala Arati (waving-of-light ceremony) is conducted at sunrise by a resident ascetic or a Brahman officiant in front of the monastery's chosen deity.

6:00 to 6:30 A.M. All the residents of the monastery perform their morning toilet. The residents then take a bath in a nearby tank or douse themselves with buckets of water drawn from the monastery well. For the Hindu, bathing has both a religious and a hygienic significance.

6:30 to 7:00 A.M. At 6:30 the celebrant offers the first food (*bala bhoga*) before the image of the chosen deity. The food normally consists of sliced cucumbers and bananas. The general belief is that the chosen deity symbolically "eats" the offered food, transforming it into sacred food (*prasāda*, meaning "grace"). After the completion of the ritual, each resident eats a portion of the food, thereby participating in the grace and in-dwelling presence of the deity. The residents then drink several cups of tea and perhaps smoke cigarettes.

7:00 A.M. *to 12:00 noon.* The head ascetic begins the morning in a leisurely fashion by reading a newspaper in Oria or Bengali. The cook bicycles or walks to the market to buy whatever food is needed for the day. One or more *brahmacārins* cycle to the homes of their patrons, some of whom may live in the New Capital, to ask for a donation in cash.

After glancing through the newspaper, the head ascetic takes care of such business matters as writing letters and inspecting the monastery. He then returns to his room or office and awaits any visitors who may come to him with a problem, or he may simply gossip and smoke cigarettes. Sometimes he leaves the monastery and visits another ascetic or perhaps makes a deposit in the monastery's postal account, which is registered in the name of the deity. In general, few demands are made upon the head ascetic's time, and he organizes his morning as best suits his interests.

12:00 noon to 3:00 P.M. At noon the celebrant returns to the *pūjā* room to perform the Madhya Arati. The food offered before the image of the chosen deity is the rice that the residents of the monastery will eat for their noon meal. After the end of the ceremony, the cook places a plantain leaf with a mound of rice and four to six curries before each client or patron. Guests always eat first. The head ascetic eats in his room, the *brahmacārins* or other male residents in the assembly hall, and the women eat last in another room. A nap follows the noon meal. Almost all activity in the Old Town halts or slows down from 1:00 to 3:00 P.M.

3:00 to 6:00 P.M. At 3:00 P.M. the residents of the monastery serve themselves tea and possibly a light snack or "tiffin." They talk and joke with each other about the day's events. The head ascetic returns to his room or office and once again receives visitors. Some head ascetics, notably at the Ramakrishna Matha, use this time to lecture to small groups of clients who gather in the assembly room of the monastery or at the home of one of the disciples. Some solitary ascetics invite their friends in to smoke *gañjā*. The ascetics are free to structure their afternoons as they please. Some claim that they read Sanskrit texts or Oria or Bengali translations of the Bhagavad Gita, the Ramayana, and the Upanishads, but the most common reading materials are newspapers and magazines. One ascetic even has a collection of Bengali movie magazines.

6:00 to 9:00 P.M. At 6:00 P.M. all the residents come together for the Sandhya Arati. A few clients who are employed in the New Capital but who live in the Old Town may remain afterwards for a discussion with the head ascetic. At the Chintamanishvara Mandira the Sandhya Arati always attracts a large audience. The ascetics broadcast on loudspeakers the recitation of the *mahāmantra*.

Afterwards the residents engage in the talk of the day. Normally the evening meal is lighter than the noon meal and consists of *puris* (fried rounds of unleavened bread) and curries.

The celebrant performs the Saya Arati, the last *pūjā* of the day, sometime between 7:00 and 9:00 P.M. At a few monasteries, such as the Arya Rishikula Bhuvaneshvari Ashrama where the head ascetic is a gifted singer, a *kīrtana* lasting about an hour follows.

9:00 to 12:00 midnight. Six monasteries are fully electrified, and three more are partially electrified; the rest have pressure kerosene lamps that make reading possible. The head ascetics of the larger monasteries use part of this time to go over daily income and expenditures or to consult with their subordinates. Some engage in personal devotions or meditations. Others, especially the younger ascetics, leave the monastery and wander about the marketplace. However, it is beneath the dignity of an ascetic to attend the local movie theatre. Sometime before midnight the ascetics go to bed.

Conclusion

An

Evaluation

When compared with Christian or Buddhist monasticism, the most striking features of Hindu monasticism in Bhubaneswar as viewed in 1963–64 are the diversity and the flexibility it allows individual ascetics. The largest institution studied (the Ramakrishna Matha) contained five ascetics, and even in that institution there were only minimal internal rules or forms of etiquette concerned with status or hierarchy. Often two disciple-brothers of the same guru, instead of living in one monastery, would each found his own institution and would jealously guard his independence and his own way of doing things. A *sādhu*, especially if he is a solitary ascetic, has his choice of deity, sets his own daily schedule, and regulates his own morals. Thus the life of an ascetic appeals to many strong personalities with different eccentricities and different styles of life.

The Westerner who accepts the Hindu's own statement often pictures a Hindu ascetic as a follower of the philosophical tradition: a spiritual, intellectual man, learned in Hindu philosophy, who gives ethical and religious advice, practises meditation and fasting, and who has mystical qualities and perhaps supernatural powers. The other picture in Western minds, often based on the folk tradition, is of an individual smeared with ashes begging by the roadside. Actuality may include both extremes but the subjects of this study do not conform to either stereotype.

The diversity of ascetic practices as variously viewed in Hindu life permits a flexibility that can be rationalized by appeals to an equally diverse philosophical and religious tradition. Hindu philosophers have long had at least three major conceptions of appropriate roles for sincere ascetics: those who withdraw from the world to meditate, those who practise devotions, and those who actively work for humanity. The earliest conception of an ascetic as a withdrawn, austere "holy man" whose primary concern is other-worldly and individualized has been repeatedly revised. Ascetics like Ramananda in the fourteenth century and Chaitanya in the sixteenth century adopted a concept of the ascetic as one who not only practises devotions by reciting the name of the deity, but who also actively helps humanity rather than centring his activities around himself. Their emphasis on concern for the sufferings of mankind was strongly reinforced in the nineteenth century by reformers and revivalists such as Ramakrishna and Vivekananda. Thus three major conceptions about Hindu ascetic life exist side by side: austere withdrawal and meditation, direct experience of the deity through intense devotional practices, and the selfless service of mankind. These may be mixed with each other in varying degree and may involve varying amounts of the folk tradition which, at its lowest level, concerns itself primarily with such externals as distinctive dress. In the 1960s, the better-educated laymen and some members of the lower castes seemed to expect a humanitarian emphasis from contemporary ascetics which they more or less aptly rationalized by appeals to the philosophical tradition.

At Bhubaneswar most ascetics representative of the tradition of austerity and meditation, such as the Guru and the Preacher, have died or are now elderly, and the younger men who will succeed to headship are more likely to emphasize good financial management, welfare activities, and possibly missions to the lower castes. The flexibility of Hindu monasticism, both in terms of the individual's freedom within the formal structure and of the variety of paths available in striving for religious fulfilment, suggests that change and adaptation have always been a part of Indian asceticism and are inevitable in the present and in the future. The impact of the modern world is particularly difficult to assess; the existence of the New Capital as an immediate neighbour of the Old Town has so far had surprisingly little external influence on the monasteries and ascetics of Bhubaneswar, aside from providing a new source of patronage and rental income.

Predictions for the future must be rather speculative. However, even though the observations of this book are based on the experiences of a limited stay in just one Indian city, we feel that enough trends made themselves apparent to enable us to attempt some predictions about the future directions of Hindu monasticism.

A trend in preferred deities is discernible. The earliest chosen deities were Shaiva or Shakta. From the late medieval period until the present, Vaishnava deities have predominated. Five of the seven monasteries originating from reformist–revivalist movements have selected their founding gurus as their chosen deities. An alternative to the worship of gurus found with increasing frequency is the choice of a non-sectarian Hindu deity corresponding to a non-sectarian teaching tradition.

An important factor that may account in part for the changes noted above has been the lack of lay support for some of the old Shankara monasteries, except where the head ascetic possesses rare leadership qualities. The lack of lay support, in turn, may be attributable to the austerity and the chosen deities associated with the Kapalika and Shankara movements, in which the sacred is wholly other-worldly and requires severe discipline to attain. The less austere, more devotionally oriented Vaishnava movements attract lay support because the concept of an incarnation of Vishnu, in the form of Rama or Krishna or Chaitanya, brings the sacred into this world. Under the leadership of a Vaishnava ascetic, even the average layman can reach the sacred sphere by simply chanting the names of Vishnu. The inclusion of the laity culminates in the worship of the guru, who becomes for the layman the very centre of sacredness. The guru may be a renowned ascetic at a large institution or he may be a former itinerant ascetic dwelling as a solitary ascetic in a small hut. Nevertheless, he represents the in-dwelling of the deity's power within this world and satisfies the layman's desire for the visible presence of the divine.

The recent emphasis on non-sectarian groups will probably continue to develop, particularly at the level of folk religion, although the primary functions of the monasteries will remain ritual in nature. Some monasteries currently belonging to sectarian orders may shift toward non-sectarian syncretistic Hindu deities, such as Trinatha (Brahma, Vishnu, and Shiva) or perhaps the five Hindu deities (Vishnu, Shiva, Shakti, Ganesha, and Surya). More monasteries may make verbal claims to preach a religion or philosophy applicable to "all mankind," but this will probably be definitely Hindu in character. Meanwhile the non-sectarian groups will in all probability widen their appeal to the lower castes. For centuries, Hinduism has elevated its human heroes to deities and taken *darśana* of the living. The popularity of guru-worship is part of this tradition. Heroes continue to be assimilated to the supernatural. Just as the historical Shankara in the ninth century was assimilated to Shiva, and Chaitanya in the sixteenth century was assimilated to Vishnu, so in the twentieth century the heroes of nationalism and international understanding—Gandhi, Nehru, and Kennedy—already find their places in popular lithographs beside Shiva and Parvati.

Apparently the monastic endowments founded in the Middle Ages had many elaborate public ceremonial functions. Records do not now exist of more casual and personalized monastic institutions in the past. Whether they predominated numerically, as they do today, cannot be ascertained. However, in the contemporary scene, the smaller, more personalized, internal or sectarian ceremonies held in newer institutions seem to hold more hope for future growth than those public observances in which the monasteries play a major role and which exclude lay participation.

Laymen will probably assume more of the administrative and ceremonial roles traditionally assigned to ascetics. In patronized monasteries in Bhubaneswar, the laity already serve on boards of trustees or managing committees, help to decide matters of finance or policy, and attend the annual conferences held by the order. The laity also actively participate in devotional forms of worship, such as the *kīrtana*. In some non-sectarian groups, such as the Trinatha cult, a layman, rather than an ascetic, may be the leader. At the Chintamanishvara Mandira, laymen had begun the chanting of the *mahāmantra* two months before an ascetic arrived to take charge. Probably the leadership role of the laity will continue to increase.

A proletarization of the monasteries is thus more likely to occur than is secularization. Proletarization will mean more lay participation, greater syncretism, and in some cases, the vulgarization of traditional Hinduism. The laity will want to play a part in monastic rituals, either by giving speeches or by community singing. They will also expect the ascetic of their choice to be available for advice or personal help, either in his office or in the tea-stall. An ascetic who is not accessible may lose both rapport and respect. Syncretism has been a steady stream central to Hinduism but lower caste participation has, and probably will, increase syncretic tendencies. The syncretistic monasteries in Bhubaneswar are more open to the folk than are monasteries of the more rigid and ancient sectarian traditions. This may be an old phenomenon in modern dress; no doubt, wandering magician–ascetics have always sought to strengthen their base of appeal by claiming non-sectarian status. The evidence points to a broadening of the base of recruitment of ascetics.

In 1964 the thirty-two ascetics who were interviewed included twenty Brahmans, eight Kshatriyas, three Vaishyas, only one Shudra, and no Scheduled Caste members. This uneven distribution reflects the ancient but still-powerful rule that asceticism should be permitted only to the three upper or "twice-born" groups. Ascetics are still recruited almost entirely from these three socio-religious groups for the following reasons: traditional prohibitions against initiating Shudras bar them from many monastic orders; asceticism has relatively little appeal for cultivators, many of whom are Shudras, and attracts more merchants, students, or civil servants, who tend to be upper-caste; and partly as a result of its upper-caste traditions, asceticism does not appeal to Shudras, except in non-corporate establishments, where the Shudra is not forced to compete in matters of religious practice or etiquette with ascetics higher on the socio-religious scale. In the last ten years, however, a greater number of Kshatriyas or Vaishyas have entered orders although Brahmans still predominate in numbers. The old endowed monasteries are open only to Brahmans. Non-sectarian groups and those orders arising from the Ramananda and Chaitanya movements are open to non-Brahmans, though such entrants are predominantly Kshatriyas and Vaishyas. A Shudra still finds it difficult to be anything but a wandering or solitary ascetic, and, indeed, Professor Du Bois's study of values shows that lower-caste groups would prefer government service rather than the ascetic life as a means of dedicating their lives to noble causes. The only monasteries that appeal to laymen of the Shudra and even outcaste groups are non-sectarian. Since more non-sectarian monasteries are likely to appear in the future, it would seem as though more monastic institutions will be accessible to the lower castes.

Since Independence, the lower castes have been affected by social and political reforms. They have become better organized, relatively speaking, than the traditional elites in respect to socio-political influence. In the religious sphere this means that more of the philosophical tradition is now available to the lower castes through increased opportunities for education. Although folk cults such as the Trinatha cult have probably always existed on a transient basis, the increased interest of the lower castes in the philosophical tradition may mean that similar folk cults will proliferate. This has been a world-wide phenomenon among both tribal and peasant peoples exposed to Western expansion.

Church and state have never been separated in the history of India and are not likely to be separated in the next generation or two in Orissa. The British became reluctantly involved in the financial affairs of temples and monasteries through a series of religious endowment acts beginning in the nineteenth century. Although the Republic of India declared itself a secular state in its constitution, it has not been able to divest itself of religious involvements. The state will continue to play a role in the upkeep of the older, endowed monasteries. Some temples, largely abandoned as places of worship, have become state or national trusts. Tourists are replacing pilgrims. Some of the great endowed monastic centres may have a similar fate. The Archaeological Survey of India already maintains over twenty structures in Bhubaneswar. Such buildings are more likely to be preserved by a "secular" state than they were in the medieval period when they were allowed by uninterested dynasties to sink back into the forest. But even though worship may cease, the symbol of the Hindu tradition remains. Temples and monasteries are perceived by tourists as sacred places of Hinduism even though they may come under the jurisdiction of state or national bureaucracies. The deities, no longer served by a hierarchy of temple priests or ascetics, are still revered by an increasingly mobile population.

This does not imply a loss of religious dedication in India. If, in the next generation, there should be a diminution of financial support and interest, this would in no way predict a decline in household devotions that remain at the centre of Hindu practice. Loss of interest in monastic institutions would not be equivalent to secularization. The Government of Orissa, which controls land allocations in the New Capital, has provided building plots only for the Christian Church, the Muslim Mosque, and the Buddhist Temple. Yet the New Capital, established in 1947, has seen a proliferation of small Hindu shrines which appear to be keeping pace with the expanding population. The Old Town, however, is still perceived as the sacred centre.

Hindus in Bhubaneswar will probably be able to reconcile to their satisfaction the scientific–secular stream of thought represented by the administrative elite with the religiosity and ceremonial tradition of the Old Town. Hinduism has repeatedly managed either to syncretize or to allow parallel existence to disparate world views. At present, the institutions originating from nineteenth-century revivalist–reform movements still claim that their founders, such as Vivekananda and Vijaykrishna, were "scientific thinkers" and that the greatest Western scientists, like Einstein, were "religious men." This syncretic thinking attracts both lay patrons from technological or scientific fields as well as those who are interested in India's spiritual heritage.

National pride and religious reverence are not incompatible in contemporary India. The present generation of Western-educated and influential residents of Bhubaneswar, men and women who in 1964 were in their forties and fifties, will continue to support the patronized institutions in the Old Town, in spite of their own somewhat ambivalent feelings about traditional practices and practitioners.

On a more practical level large endowments of land remain. Although the government may assume supervisory control of a mismanaged endowment, there are legal provisions for continued appointment of a head ascetic if a suit-able candidate can be found. For the patronized monasteries, financial backing will continue to be forthcoming from this generation of well-to-do citizens in spite of their own ambivalent feelings about religion. The patronized type of monastery, however, may be ultimately less viable than the medieval endowed monasteries. Land is more secure than dependence on continued cash dona-donations, whatever the condition of religious life in a monastery. Thus the present tendency toward an interest in social welfare may be temporary and not durable. The Arya Rishikula Bhuvaneshvari Ashrama is a typical example of a patronized monastery whose head ascetic inclined toward humanitarian interests. The monastery was having financial difficulties and had accomplished little in the way of welfare work. It will probably be survived by all five of the endowed monasteries even if they continue to decline in their religious prestige.

The solitary ascetics will continue to come and go as they have in the past, supported by their handfuls of clients. They have been and promise to be like the gnats in the Chhandogya Upanishad who are "born only to die and be reborn again."

Only the future and further research will determine whether or not our "educated guesses" are correct. We will be well rewarded if our efforts stimu-late other inquiries into Hindu monastic life, not as it is described in the sacred texts, but as it is lived in a changing world.

Table 17
Survey of Biographical Data on Ascetics

Monastery	SOCIAL STRUCTURE	RELIGIOUS NAME	TEACHING ORDER	SOCIO-RELIGIOUS GROUP	LEVEL OF EDUCATION	PRIOR OCCUPATION	MARITAL STATUS	MOTHER TONGUE	BIRTH-PLACE: URBAN OR RURAL	BIRTH DATE	AGE AT EN-TRANCE	YEAR ARRIVED BHUBANESWAR
Arya Rishikula Bhuvaneshvari Ashrama	Patronized	Jagadananda Bhakti Shastri Tirtha Maharaja	Dashanami Tirtha Sannyasin	Brahman	Sanskrit school 10 yrs.	Sanskrit teacher	Bachelor	Bengali	Urban	1901	27	1945
		Ramasvarupa Brahmacharin	Dashanami Tirtha Brahmacharin	Kshatriya	Class 10	Student, public school	Bachelor	Bengali	Rural	1925	19	1953
		Somash Chandra Dasgupta	Vanaprastha	Brahman	Bachelor of homeo. med., Burma	Homeopathic medical practitioner	Abandoned family	Bengali	Rural	1904	58	1962
Arya Rishikula Vasishta Yogashrama	Patronized	Jayadeva Brahmacharin	Dashanami Tirtha Brahmacharin	Brahman	Sanskrit school 10 yrs.	Student, Sanskrit school	Bachelor	Bengali (English)	Urban	1936	12	1948
		Satyavrata Dasa	Dashanami Tirtha Brahmacharin	Vaishya	Class 11	Student, public school	Bachelor	Bengali	Rural	1939	24	1963
		Jagannatha Dasa	Ramananda Vairagin	Brahman	Sanskrit school 6 yrs.	Student, Sanskrit school	Bachelor	Oria	Rural	1936	12	1958
Bhavani Shankara Matha	Non-corporate	Bhavani Shankara Babaji	Shankara Brahmacharin	Kshatriya	Class 11	Cloth merchant	Abandoned family	Bengali (English)	Rural	1920	39	1959

Institution	Type	Head	Order	Varna	Education	Occupation	Marital status	Language	Rural/Urban	Birth year	Age	Year
Chinta-manishvara Mandira	Non-corporate	Virendra Natha Sadhukhan	Ramananda Vairagin	Shudra	Class 8	Grocery store attendant	Bachelor	Bengali	Rural	1940	22	1963
		Mauna Babaji	Shankara Brahmacharin	Brahman	Class 7	Cloth merchant	Refused marriage	Gujarati (English)	Urban	1924	27	1957
Gopala Tirtha Matha	Endowed	Jagadguru 1108 Shri Gopala Tirtha Svami	Dashanami Tirtha Sannyasin	Brahman	Sanskrit school 4 yrs.	Student, Sanskrit school	Bachelor	Oria	Rural	1929	22	1951
Harihara Satsangha Ashrama	Non-corporate	Brahmananda Dharmatithi	Vanaprastha (non-sectarian)	Brahman	Class 7	*hotr* priest	Married	Oria	Rural	1888	73	1961
Jagannatha Deva Mandira	Patronized	Vrindavana Brahmacharin	Madhva Gaudiya Vairagin	Vaishya	Class 10	Mechanical draftsman	Refused marriage	Bengali	Urban	1902	24	1940
Kapali Matha	Endowed	Vanamali Natha	Tantric Yogi Sannyasin	Brahman	Class 3	Tenant farmer	Bachelor	Oria	Rural	1924	10	1934
Nigamananda Ashrama	Patronized	Prajnananda Sarasvati Svami	Dashanami Sarasvati Sannyasin	Brahman	B.A. Calcutta University	Orissa administrative officer	Abandoned family	Bengali (English)	Urban	1884	48	1963
		Samuttha Chaitanya Brahmacharin	Dashanami Sarasvati Brahmacharin	Brahman	Class 8	Ayur-vedic medical practitioner	Bachelor	Bengali	Rural	1910	50	1960
Nimbarka Ashrama	Patronized	Vasudeva Dasa	Nimbarka Vairagin	Kshatriya	Class 7	Tenant farmer	Bachelor	Bengali	Rural	1922	18	1960
		Jatananda Dasa	Nimbarka Vairagin	Brahman	Class 3	Tenant farmer	Bachelor	Nepali	Rural	1939	17	1963
Pashupatinatha Gita Ashrama	Non-corporate	Madhava Chandra Dasa	Ramananda Vairagin	Kshatriya	Class 3	Betel shop owner	Bachelor	Oria	Rural	1929	29	1957

Table 17 (continued)

Monastery	Social Structure	Religious Name	Teaching Order	Socio-Religious Group	Level of Education	Prior Occupation	Marital Status	Mother Tongue	Birthplace: Urban or Rural	Birth Date	Age at Entrance	Year Arrived Bhubaneswar
Radhakrishna Sevashrama	Patronized	Kripananda Sarasvati Svami	Dashanami Sarasvati Sannyasin	Brahman	Sanskrit school 8 yrs.	Student, Sanskrit school	Married	Bengali (English)	Rural	1884	15	1918
Sadavrata Pitha	Endowed	Taponidhi Sudarshana Bharati Gosvami	Dashanami Bharati Sannyasin	Brahman	Class 7	Land-owning farmer	Bachelor	Oria	Rural	1901	35	1936
Sadguru Nivasa Ashrama	Patronized	Vimala Sadhu	Madhva Gaudiya Vairagin	Brahman	B.A. Calcutta University	Customs inspector	Bachelor	Bengali (English)	Urban	1935	25	1960
		Sudhir Adhikari	Madhva Gaudiya Vairagin	Brahman	Class 7	Cloth merchant	Abandoned family	Bengali	Rural	1916	35	1964
Shadbhuja Chaitanya Mandira	Patronized	Nibaran Mukharji	Madhva Gaudiya Grihastha	Brahman	Class 11	Cloth merchant (head clerk)	Married	Bengali (English)	Urban	1894	47	1940
		Gaura Dasa Mukharji	Madhva Gaudiya Grihastha	Brahman	Class 11	Cloth merchant	Married	Bengali	Urban	1926	32	1958
Shankarananda Matha	Endowed	Jagadguru 1108 Dandi Saccidananda Sarasvati Svami	Dashanami Sarasvati Sannyasin	Brahman	Sanskrit school 10 yrs.	Student, Sanskrit school	Bachelor	Oria	Rural	1904	20	1924

Matha	Endowment	Abbot	Order	Caste	Education	Occupation	Marital status	Language	Location	Year of birth	Age	Date became ascetic
Shiva Tirtha Matha	Endowed	Jagadguru 1108 Shri Vishveshvarananda Tirtha Svami	Dashanami Tirtha Sannyasin	Brahman	Class 10	Ayur-vedic medical practitioner	Abandoned family	Oria	Rural	1894	52	1962
Someshvara Mahadeva Pitha	Non-corporate	Shivananda Brahmacharin	Shankara Brahmacharin	Brahman	Class 3	Ayur-vedic medical practitioner	Abandoned family	Oria	Rural	1879	32	Since birth (Became ascetic, 1911)*
Tridandi Gaudiya Matha	Patronized	Bhaktisarana Madhusudana Maharaja	Madhva Gaudiya Vairagin	Kshatriya	Class 11	Sub-inspector of police	Abandoned family	Oria (English)	Rural	1895	55	1950
		Kanai Dasa Brahmacharin	Madhva Gaudiya Vairagin	Kshatriya	Class 11	Student, public school	Bachelor	Bengali (English)	Urban	1942	16	1963
		Krishna Karuna Brahmacharin	Madhva Gaudiya Vairagin	Kshatriya	Class 8	Sculptor, religious images	Bachelor	Bengali	Rural	1908	54	1964
Trinatha Gosvami Matha	Non-corporate	Divyasingha Dasa Trinatha Gosvami	Madhva Gaudiya Vairagin	Kshatriya	Class 7	Land tax collector	Bachelor	Oria	Rural	1914	25	1954
Vishrama Ghatta Matha	Non-corporate	Lakshmi Charana Dasa	Ramananda Vairagin	Vaishya	Class 3	Goldsmith	Bachelor	Oria	Rural	1922	30	Since birth (Became ascetic, 1952)*

* Date used in computation.

Table 18
Survey of Monastic Establishments at Bhubaneswar

Name (listed alphabetically)	DATE OF FOUNDING	TEACHING TRADITION	CHOSEN DEITY	RESIDENT ASCETICS	SOCIAL STRUCTURE	ORGANIZA- TIONAL STRUCTURE	FINANCIAL STRUCTURE	SUCCESSION TO HEAD- SHIP	PRINCIPAL RELIGIOUS FUNCTIONS BESIDES DAILY WORSHIP	SOCIAL FUNCTIONS	LINGUISTIC COMMUNITY	FUTURE POSSIBILITIES
Arya Rishikula Bhuvaneshvari Ashrama	1945	Shankara Dashanami Tirtha	Worship of gurus	1 *sanyāsin* 2 *sanyāsinis* 2 *brahmacārins* 1 *vānaprastha*	Patronized corporate (head-quarters)	Managing committee	Continually patronized	Appointive	Guru Purnima (private)	Homeopathic dispensary	Bengali with Oria patronage	Possible expansion: completion of religio-cultural hall
Arya Rishikula Vasishtha Yogashrama	1955	Shankara Dashanami Tirtha	Worship of gurus	2 *brahmacārins* 1 *vairāgin*	Patronized corporate (branch)	Board of trustees	Continually patronized	Appointive	Guru Purnima (private)	Guest house	Bengali and Oria	Possible expansion: construction of temple
Bhavani Shankara Matha	1959	Shankara	Durga	1 Shankara *brahmacārin*	Non-corporate	Head ascetic	Client-supported	None	None		Bengali	Non-continuous
Chinta- manishvara Mandira	1950	Non-sectarian	Shiva Linga, Hanuman, gurus	1 Ramananda *vairāgin* 1 Shankara *brahmacārin*	Non-corporate	Managing committee	Initially patronized, now client-supported	None	Chanting of *mahāmantra* 24 hrs. a day (public)	Appeals to all castes	Bengali and Oria	Flourishing: religious park for pilgrims and wandering ascetics
Gopala Tirtha Matha	1000–1500	Shankara Dashanami Tirtha	Radha–Krishna	1 *sanyāsin*	Endowed corporate (branch)	OHREC	Endowed with land	Appointive possibly by OHREC management	Festivals connected with the Temple (public)	Administration of temple land	Oria	Decline: complete control by OHREC
Harihara Satsangha Ashrama	1962	Non-sectarian	Jagannatha	1 *vānaprastha* and wife	Non-corporate	Managing committee	Initially patronized, later client-supported	Hereditary or by managing committee	Ritual fire sacrifice and reading of Gita to avert disaster (special)		Oria	Possibly non-continuous: retirement home for *vānaprasthas*

Name	Date	Affiliation	Worship	Residents	Corporate status	Management	Economic basis	Succession	Festivals	Facilities/Activities	Language	Trend
Jagannatha Deva Mandira	1938	Madhva Gaudiya Vairagin	Jagannatha	1 *vairāgin*	Patronized corporate (branch)	Board of trustees	Continually patronized	Appointive	Vaishnava festivals (private)	Guest house	Bengali	Possible decline: buildings rented out for secular purposes
Kapali Matha	700–1500	Tantric Yogi	Kapali	1 Non-resident Tantric Yogi	Endowed	Head ascetic	Initially endowed, now without any income	Hereditary	Festivals connected with the Temple (public)		Oria	Decline: possible reconstruction of monastery
Nigamananda Ashrama	1964	Shankara Dashanami Sarasvati	Worship of gurus	1 *saṁnyāsin* 1 *brahmacārin*	Patronized corporate (headquarters)	Board of trustees	Continually patronized	Appointive	Guru Purnima (private)		Bengali with Oria patronage	Possible expansion: construction of library and school
Nimbarka Ashrama	1934	Nimbarka Vairagin	Radha–Krishna	2 *vairāgins*	Patronized corporate (branch)	Board of trustees	Continually patronized	Appointive	Vaishnava festivals (private)	Guest house	Bengali	Decline: building rented out for secular purposes
Pashupatinatha Gita Ashrama	1958	Ramananda Vairagin	Sita–Rama	1 *vairāgin*	Non-corporate	Head ascetic	Client-supported	None	Vaishnava festivals (private)		Oria	Non-continuous
Radhakrishna Sevashrama	1918	Shankara Dashanami Sarasvati	Radha–Krishna	1 *saṁnyāsin* influenced by Tantras	Patronized corporate	Board of trustees	Initially patronized	Hereditary	None	Guest house	Bengali	Decline: building used entirely for secular purposes
Ramakrishna Matha	1919	Non-sectarian	Worship of gurus	4 *saṁnyāsins* 1 *brahmacārin*	Patronized corporate (branch)	Board of trustees	Continually patronized	Appointive	Guru Purnima: Ramakrishna's birthday, Vivekananda's birthday	Primary and middle grammar schools, modern medical dispensary; appeals to all castes	Bengali	Flourishing: expansion of all welfare activities
Sadavrata Pitha	600s	Shankara Dashanami Bharati	Kamakhya	1 *saṁnyāsin*	Endowed corporate (headquarters)	OHREC and head ascetic	Endowed with land	Hereditary	Festivals connected with the Temple (public)	Administration of Temple lands, collection of state taxes from Bauri ward	Oria	Decline: partial control by OHREC
Sadguru Nivasa Ashrama	1940	Madhva Gaudiya Vairagin	Worship of gurus	2 *vairāgins*	Patronized corporate (branch)	Board of trustees	Initially endowed, now patronized	Appointive	Sarasvati Puja, Guru Purnima	Guest house	Bengali	Possible expansion: rental of building for income

Table 18 (continued)

Name (listed alphabetically)	Date of Founding	Teaching Tradition	Chosen Deity	Resident Ascetics	Social Structure	Organizational Structure	Financial Structure	Succession to Headship	Principal Religious Functions Besides Daily Worship	Social Functions	Linguistic Community	Future Possibilities
Shadbhuja Chaitanya Mandira	1941	Madhva Gaudiya Vairagin	Shadbhuja Chaitanya	2 grhasthas and their families	Patronized corporate	Managing committee	Continually patronized	Hereditary	Vaishnava festivals (private)	Appeals to all castes	Bengali	Possibly flourishing; possibly non-continuous
Shankarananda Matha	1400s	Shankara Dashanami Sarasvati	Lakshmi-Narayana	1 sannyāsin	Endowed corporate (headquarters)	Head ascetic	Endowed with land	Appointive	Guru Purnima (private), festivals connected with the Temple (public)	Sanskrit school, administration of Temple lands	Oria	Expansion under present head ascetic, but possible control by OHREC
Shiva Tirtha Matha	1000–1500	Shankara Dashanami Tirtha	Shiva Linga	1 sannyāsin	Endowed corporate (headquarters)	Head ascetic, formerly OHREC	Endowed with land	Appointive	Festivals connected with the Temple (public)	Administration of Temple land	Oria	Expansion under present head ascetic, but control by OHREC
Someshvara Mahadeva Pitha	1921	Shankara	Shiva Linga	1 Shankara brahmacārin	Non-corporate	Head ascetic	Client-supported	None	None		Oria	Non-continuous
Tridandi Gaudiya Matha	1933	Madhva Gaudiya Vairagin	Chaitanya and Radha-Krishna	3 vairāgins	Patronized corporate (branch)	Board of trustees	Continually patronized	Appointive	Vaishnava festivals (private)		Oria and Bengali	Possible expansion: establishment of welfare activities
Trinatha Gosvami Matha	1954	Non-sectarian	Trinatha	2 vairāgins	Non-corporate	Head ascetic	Client-supported	None	Weekly kirtanas	Appeals to lower castes	Oria	Non-continuous: associated with lay cult
Vishrama Ghatta Matha	1938	Ramananda Vairagin	Jagannatha	1 vairāgin	Non-corporate	Head ascetic	Client-supported	None	None		Oria	Non-continuous

Glossary

ācārya	a title indicating Vedic scholarship and teaching competence
Advaita Vedanta	non-dualism or absolute monism; Upanishadic thought (Vedanta) systematized by Shankara in the ninth century
ārati	pleasure or delight; the waving of light in the ceremony of daily worship (in households, temples, and monasteries) performed four times daily: various objects, including a lighted lamp, are waved before the deity, accompanied by prayers, chants, etc.
Ashokashtami Yatra	the "car" festival at Bhubaneswar; images of the four deities of the Lingaraja Mahaprabhu Temple are placed in a forty-foot vehicle which is pulled through the streets
āśrama	"forest retreat"; a monastery, or a solitary place where meditation is performed; also, one of the four stages of a Hindu's life
āsana	one of the postures taken during meditation; that upon which an ascetic sits, i.e., an animal skin; the seat or resting place of the image of a deity
Ayur-vedic medicine	a system of herbal medical treatment based on ancient medical knowledge found in the Ayur-vedas
bābājī	"grizzled old man"; a term used, particularly by unsophisticated people, to refer to an ascetic
bhajana	a religious song or litany
bhakta	a devotee, particularly one involved in an intensely personal and emotional relationship with his chosen deity
bhakti yoga	the path of devotion as a way to salvation; the cultivation of religious fervour

brahmacārin	a religious student; a monastic novice and celibate
brahmacarya	the disciplined life of a student of sacred knowledge; the first stage (*āśrama*) of Hindu life
Brahman	a member of the highest of the four socio-religious groups
brahman	the Absolute, supreme, indefinable spirit
Chaitanya	the sixteenth-century founder of the Gaudiya (Bengali) sub-order of the Madhva teaching order (see Madhva); Chaitanya was famous for devotional songs and dances (*kīrtanas*)
cāndrāyaṇa vrata	a vow to fast in accordance with the waning and waxing of the moon
daṇḍa	the staff carried by some ascetics
darśana	seeing, view; the blessing received from being in the presence of a person, deity, shrine, vision, etc.; also the Sanskrit term for a philosophical system as an intuitive insight into the nature of ultimate reality
Dashanami Sannyasin	the monastic order founded by Shankara about A.D. 820; also a member of that order
dharma	virtue, righteousness, daily observation of religious duties
dīkṣā	the initiation of a disciple by his guru, who gives him a sacred text (see *mantra*)
Dola Purnima Yatra	a festival in which the images of Krishna and Radha are rocked in a swing; women and children also ride on swings during this festival
Dvaita Vedanta	dualism; Upanishadic thought (Vedanta) as systematized by Madhva in the thirteenth century
Dvaita–Advaita Vedanta	dualistic non-dualism; Upanishadic thought (Vedanta) as systematized by Nimbarka in the twelfth century
Ganapatya	a devotee of Ganesha, the elephant-headed son of Shiva
Ganesha Puja	a festival in honour of Ganesha, usually celebrated by students preceding their examinations
gañjā	a form of marijuana

Gaudapada	the first philosopher of Advaita Vedanta (absolute monism), whose writings greatly influenced Shankara
ghī	clarified butter
Govinda	an epithet of Krishna
gṛhastha	a householder, the head of a family; the second of the four stages (*āśramas*) of Hindu life
guru	a religious teacher and mentor
guruparamparā	a list of gurus tracing the history of a monastery or monastic order
Harihara	a god uniting the attributes of Vishnu (Hari) and Shiva (Hara)
Holi	a religious festival sacred to Krishna, during which coloured powders and liquids are thrown by friends at each other
homa	a sacrificial ceremony in which a burnt offering is made
iṣṭadevatā	the favourite deity chosen by an individual, holy man, or monastery for particular worship
Ishvara	a name for the Supreme God, to whom all other deities are subordinated; usually, Shiva or Vishnu or one of their manifestations.
Jagannatha	"Lord of the Universe"; the name of Vishnu–Krishna at the temple at Puri in Orissa
Janmashtami	the festival celebrating the birth of Krishna
jñāna yoga	the way to salvation through the attainment of mystical knowledge of the Absolute
Kamakhya	a goddess who symbolizes the vulva of Parvati
karma	the totality of human action, including the burden of deeds from previous existences
karma yoga	the way to salvation through disciplined religious action
kīrtana	devotional singing, often including dancing
Kshatriya	the second highest socio-religious group
kuṇḍalinī yoga	the way to salvation through union with the divine power within, as taught by the Tantras

liṅgam	a phallic symbol representing Shiva, normally carved from stone (*see also* yoni)
Madhva	the thirteenth-century founder of a Vaishnava–Vairagin monastic order stressing devotional practices
Madhva Gaudiya	the Bengal branch of the Madhva order of Vairagin ascetics, established by Chaitanya
mahāmantra	"great verse"; a popular chant which celebrates the names of Hari (Vishnu), Krishna, and Rama; any oft-repeated sacred verse
maṅdira	the word commonly used to refer to a temple
mantra	a sacred mystical verse or incantation
maṭha	one of the most common terms used for a monastery
mokṣa	spiritual emancipation or salvation; the state of release from bondage to the chain of birth, death, and rebirth
Narayana	the god Vishnu as cosmic, archetypal man
Nimbarka	the twelfth-century founder of a Vaishnava–Vairagin monastic order
pān	a folded betel leaf containing areca nut, lime paste, and flavourings, which is chewed for its pleasant effect
prabhu	lord; master; powerful one
prasāda	"gift" or "grace"; food, blessed by having been offered before a deity, which is distributed after worship among those present
Prathamashtami Yatra	a minor public festival in which the deities are taken in procession about the streets of Bhubaneswar
pūjā	worship; performance of rituals and prayers; daily worship in household, temple, or monastery
pūjā paṇḍā	the temple priest in charge of a major festival
pujārī	the priest who performs *pūjā*, often an employee of a monastery
pūrṇimā	the day of the full moon; a favourite time for Hindu religious observances and festivals

Ramakrishna	the nineteenth-century Hindu reformer and revivalist
Ramananda	the fourteenth-century innovator of the Vaishnava–Vairagin monastic order founded by Ramanuja
Ramanuja	the eleventh-century founder of a Vaishnava–Vairagin monastic order
rudrākṣa	a plant having large seeds which are strung to make the rosary of a Dashanami Sannyasin
sādhu	an ascetic, monk, or holy man
samādhi	"absorption"; a state of contemplation so deep that one's entire being becomes one with the Absolute; also the name for the tomb of a dead *guru*
The Samāj	an influential Oria newspaper published in Cuttack; the word means "organization," "union," "community," etc.
sampradāya	a teaching tradition, begun by the founder of a philosophical school; hence, the monastic order begun by that founder
samsāra	the continuing cycle of life, death, and rebirth
sannyāsin	a final renouncer of all worldly ties; the last of the four stages of Hindu life; often the title of a member of Shankara's monastic order
sannyāsinī	a female ascetic
Sarasvati Puja	a festival held in honour of Sarasvati, the goddess of learning
Shaiva	pertaining to the worship of Shiva
Shakta	a worshipper of Shakti, the wife of Shiva
Shakti	the wife of Shiva; the goddess who personifies divine power, energy
Shakti Tantra	the philosophical system found in the Tantras that emphasizes the dynamic powers of creation (Shakti) as opposed to the static ground of being (Shiva); also called *tantra yoga* or Tantric Yoga
Shankara	the ninth-century founder of the Dashanami Sannyasin monastic order

Shivaratri	a festival in honour of Shiva
Shri	a term of respect and honour; also a name for the wife of Vishnu
Shudra	a member of the lowest of the four socio-religious groups
Svami	"master"; a title of respect often used for the head ascetic of a monastery
tantra yoga	see Shakti Tantra
Tantric Yoga	see Shakti Tantra
tulasī	the sacred basil plant, worshipped in the courtyards of homes and temples; it also supplies the beads worn by Vairagin monks
vairāgin	a member of one of the main divisions of Hindu ascetics, who were originally devotees of Vishnu
Vaishnava	pertaining to Vishnu
Vaishya	a member of the third socio-religious group
vānaprastha	a forest hermit; the third stage (*āśrama*) of Hindu life
Vedanta	"end of the Vedas"; the philosophical thought found in the Upanishads
Vishishthadvaita Vedanta	theistic monism; Upanishadic thought systematized by Ramanuja in the eleventh century
yajña	a sacrificial ceremony
Yama	the god who rules over the abode of the dead
Yamadvitiya Yatra	a minor public festival in which the deities are taken in procession about the streets of Bhubaneswar
yātrā	a journey, hence a car festival in which the deities of a temple make a journey
yoga	"act of yoking"; a set of disciplines leading to salvation, or release from the cycle of rebirth
yogī	a person who practices *yoga*; often, an ascetic who performs meditational practices
yoni	"source" or "womb"; the base upon which the *lingam* is placed, representing the female principle

Selected Bibliography

Hindu Asceticism

Aiyar, C. N. K. and Tattvabush, P. S. *Sri Samkaracharya*. Madras: G. A. Natesan and Co., 1902.

Barua, Benimadhab. *Brahmacari Kuladananda*, Vol. I. Puri: The Thakurbadi Committee, 1938.

Bhaktisastri, Sambidnanda Das. *Sri Chaitanya Mahaprabhu*. Madras: Sree Gaudiya Math, 1958.

Bhandarkar, R. G. "Vaisnavism, Saivism and Minor Religious Systems." *Collected Works of Sir R. G. Bhandarkar*. Edited by Narayan Bapuji Utgikar. Vol. 4. Poona: Bhandarkar Oriental Research Institute, 1929.

Bharati, Swami Agehananda. *The Ochre Robe*. Seattle: University of Washington Press, 1962.

Bharati, Swami Agehananda. "The Hindu Renaissance and its Apologetic Patterns." *Journal of Asian Studies*, Vol. 29/2, 267–88, 1970.

Bhardwaj, Surinder Mohan. *Hindu Places of Pilgrimage in India: A Study in Cultural Geography*. Berkeley: University of California Press, 1973.

Brunton, Paul. *A Search in Secret India*. New York: Dutton, 1935.

Caycedo, Alfonso. *India of Yogis*. Delhi: National Publishing House, 1966.

Das, Bishnu Charan. *Life of Vijaykrishna*. Calcutta: Sree Saraswaty Press, 1940.

De, Sushil Kumar. *Early History of the Vaishnava Faith and Movement in Bengal*. Calcutta: Firma K. L. Mukhopadhyay, 1961.

Demaitre, Edmond. *The Yogis of India*. London: G. Bles, 1937.

Farquhar, J. N. *Modern Religious Movements in India*. The MacMillan Company, 1915.

Gambhirananda, Swami. *History of the Ramakrishna Math and Mission*. Calcutta: Advaita Ashrama, 1957.

Gambhirananda, Swami (ed). *The Apostles of Sri Ramakrishna*. Calcutta: Advaita Ashrama, 1967.

Ghurye, G. S. *Indian Sadhus*. Bombay: Popular Praksham, 1964.

Gupta, Mahendranath. *The Gospel of Sri Ramakrishna.* Translated by Swami Nikhilananda, Mylapore: Sri Ramakrishna Math, 1964.

Isherwood, Christopher. *Ramakrishna and His Disciples.* New York: Simon and Schuster, 1965.

Koestler, Arthur. *Lotus and the Robot.* London: Hutchinson, 1960.

Mahadevan, T. M. P. (ed). *A Seminar on Saints.* Madras: Ganesh and Co., 1960.

Mahadevan, T. M. P. *Ten Saints of India.* Bombay: Bharatiya Vidya Bhavan, 1961.

Monier Williams, Monier. *Brahmanism and Hinduism.* London: J. Murray, 1891.

Monier Williams, Monier. *Religious Thought and Life in India.* London: J. Murray, 1885.

Muktananda Paramahamsa, Swami. *Guru: Chitshaktivilas: The Play of Consciousness.* New York: Harper and Row, 1971.

Oman, John Campbell. *The Mystics, Ascetics and Saints of India: a Study of Sadhuism.* London: T. F. Unwin, 1903.

Osborne, Arthur. *Ramana Maharshi and the Path of Self-Knowledge.* London: Rider, 1954.

Purani, A. B. *Life of Sri Aurobindo.* Pondicherry: Ashram Press, 1958.

Ramakrishnanda, Swami. *Life of Sri Ramanuja.* Madras: Sri Ramakrishna Math, 1959.

Rutledge, Denys. *In Search of a Yogi: Himalayan Pilgrimage.* London: Routledge, 1962.

Schulman, Arnold. *Baba.* New York: The Viking Press, 1971.

Sen, Pankaj K. *A Short Sketch of the Life of Prabhupad Bijoy Krishna Goswami.* Calcutta: J. N. Dutta Roy, 1957.

Singer, Milton. *When a Great Tradition Modernizes.* New York, Praeger, 1972.

Singh, Pritam. *Saints and Sages of India.* New Delhi: New Book Society of India, 1948.

Sivananda, Swami. *Lives of Saints.* Calcutta: S. P. League, 1944.

White, Charles S. J. "Sāi Bābā Movement: Approaches to the Study of Indian Saints," *Journal of Asian Studies,* 31 (1972): 863–78.

White, Charles S. J. "Swami Muktananda and the Enlightenment through Sakti Pat," *History of Religions,* May 1974, 306–22.

Wilson, H. H. *Religious Sects of the Hindus*. Ed. Ernst R. Rost. 2nd ed. Calcutta: Susil Gupta Privite Ltd., 1958.

Yogananda, Paramahamsa. *Autobiography of a Yogi*. Los Angeles: Self-Realization Fellowship, 1956.

Orissa and Bhubaneswar

Acharya, Iyotish C. "The Interstitial Area in a Double Town: Bhubaneswar." Ph.D. Thesis. Utkal University, 1966.

Banerji, R. D. *History of Orissa*, Vols. 1 and 2. Calcutta: R. Chatterjee, 1930.

Bose, N. K., Patnaik, N. and Ray, A. K. "Organization of Services in the Temple of Lingaraj in Bhubaneswar." *Journal of the Asiatic Society Letters*, no. 2, 24 (1958).

Census of India, 1901. Vols. 6, 6A, and 6B, *The Lower Provinces of Bengal and their Feudatories*. Calcutta: Bengal Secretariat Press, 1902.

Census of India, 1911. Vol. 5, *Bengal, Bihar and Orissa*. Calcutta: The Bengal Secretariat Book Depot, 1913.

Census of India, 1921. Vol. 7, *Bihar and Orissa*. Patna: Superintendent, Government Printing, 1923.

Census of India, 1931. Vol. 7, *Bihar and Orissa*. Patna: Superintendent, Government Printing, 1932–33.

Census of India, 1941. Vol. 11, *Orissa*. Simla: Government of India Press, 1942.

Census of India, 1951. Vol. 11, *Orissa*. Cuttack: Superintendent, Orissa Government Press, 1953.

Census of India, 1961. Vol. 7, *Orissa*. Delhi: Manager of Publications, 1963–65.

Donaldson, Thomas E. "Sculptural Decoration on Hindu Temples of Orissa." Ph.D. Thesis. Case Western Reserve University, 1973.

Du Bois, Cora. "Paths to Modernization: Temple and Government," 1966. In the files of The Harvard Bhubaneswar Project.

Freeman, James M. "Occupational Changes Among Hindu Temple Servants." *Indian Anthropologists*, no. 1, 1 (1971): 1–13.

Freeman, James M. "Power and Leadership in a Changing Temple Village of India." Ph.D. Thesis. Harvard University, 1968.

Grenell, Peter. "Planning for Invisible People: Some Consequences of Bureaucratic Values and Practices," pp. 95–121. In *Freedom To Build: Dweller Control of the Housing Process.* Ed. John F. C. Turner, and Robert Fichter. New York: Macmillan Co., 1972.

Guruparampara of the Samkarananda Math, Puri And Bhubaneswar. Translated by J. K. M. Rayguru and J. M. S. Tirtha. Puri: A. C. Chakarverty, 1926.

Mahapatra, Manamohan. "Lingaraj Temple: Its Structure and Change." Ph.D. Thesis, Utkal University, 1971.

Mahapatra, Manamohan. "Organization of Caste Among the Bauris of Bhubaneswar." Adibasi-Cuttack: Government of Orissa Press. No. 3, 8 (1966–67): 46–53.

Misra, Srinibas. *The Orissa Hindu Religious Endowments Act 1951.* Cuttack: Cuttack Law Times, 1957.

Mitra, Debala. *Bhubaneswar.* New Delhi: Department of Archaeology, 1958.

Mitra, Rajendra Lala. *The Antiquities of Orissa,* vols. 1 and 2. Calcutta: P. K. Maitra, 1963.

Mukherjee, Prabhat. *The History of the Gajapati Kings of Orissa.* Calcutta: General Trading Company, 1953.

O'Malley, L. S. S. *Bengal District Gazetteers, Puri.* Calcutta: The Bengal Secretariat Book Depot, 1908.

Orissa Hindu Religious Endowments Commission, 1963–64, files for Gopala Tirtha Matha, Sadavrata Pitha, and Shiva Tirtha Matha.

Panigrahi, K. C. *Archaeological Remains at Bhubaneswar.* Bombay: Orient Longmans, 1961.

Parija, P. and Mukherjee P. (eds). *Orissa Past and Present.* Cuttack: Utkal University, 1962.

The Ramakrishna Math and Mission: Bhubaneswar Reports 1939–1963. Belur: The Ramakrishna Math.

Ramakrishna Math and Mission. *The General Report of the Ramakrishna Math and Mission, April, 1962 to March 1963.* Belur: The Ramakrishna Math, 1964.

Sarasvati, Saccidananda. *Report of the Utkalmani Gurukula Brahmacaryasrama.* Bhubaneswar: Shankarananda Matha. November, 1941.

Sarasvati, Svami Nigamananda. *Trust Deed of Assam Bengal Sarasvati Matha.* Sagar (Assam): Sarasvati Matha, 1930.

Shweder, Richard. "A Report on Trinatha and Trinatha Shrines in Old Town Bhubaneswar," 1968. In the files of the Harvard-Bhubaneswar Project.

Taub, Richard P. *Bureaucrats Under Stress.* Berkeley: University of California Press, 1969.

Index

References to ascetics included in field study are indicated by an asterisk (*); those to Bhubaneswar monasteries studied by a dagger (†).

control of, 40, 94, 151–52; financial control by, 138, 139, 145–46, 147, 162, 206–8; history of, 145–46; organizational control by, 139, 145, 146–47, 206–8; records, 11, 124–25; succession arranged by, 153

Old Town: attitudes of laity in, 93–97; festivals in, 157–70; history of, 7–9; relationship to New Town, 9–11, 21, 196; religious leaders of, 21, 39–40, 93, 110, 131; as sacred centre, 15–16, 200. *See also* History; New Town

Opposition to monasticism, 93–94

Orias, 7, 10, 15–16; ascetics as, 22, 77, 206–8; relations with Bengalis, 15–16; religious leader of, 21, 39–40, 110. *See also* Bengali-Oria relations

Orissa, 7–10, 24–25, 199–200

Orissa Hindu Religious Endowments Commission. *See* OHREC

Pagalananda Thakur, Mada Brahmarishi, 130–31

Parvati, 56, 90, 120, 121, 132, 158, 159–60, 161, 192, 198

†Pashupatinatha Gita Ashrama, xviii, 13, 134, 144, 203, 207

Paths to salvation, 2, 17, 30, 33, 34–35, 41, 43, 71, 129, 131, 136, 195–96

Patronized monasteries, 102, 202–8; background of residents, 76–77; chosen deities of, 154; defined, 138; future of, 200–201; guest-house in, 179; lay participation in administration, 41, 198–99; organizational structure of, 148–50, 150–51, 206–8; sectarian celebrations at, 155, 163–65, 173, 174. *See also* Financial structure; Patrons

Patrons: attendance at public ceremonies, 94–95; attitude toward other ascetics, 94; attitude toward religion, 95–96, 105, 200; Bengali and Oria, 39–40; defined, 95, 137–38; donations requested, 193; influential, 21, 39–40, 135, 170, 187; living in New Capital, 11, 196; living in West Bengal, 141; officials (government) as, 11, 39–40, 137–38, 141. *See also* Clients; Patronized monasteries.

Pilgrimages, 22, 44–45, 56, 69, 83, 145

Pilgrims, 178–79, 186–90, 199, 206

Political advice, 39–40, 190

*Prajnananda Sarasvati Svami, 84, 203

Prathamashtami Yatra: festival, 156, 157, 166

The "Preacher." *See* Jagadananda Bhakti Shastri Tirtha Maharaja

Preaching: by ascetic, 29–30, 31–33, 38–39, 40; as function of ascetic, 173; as part of festival, 168–69

Prestige: of ascetics, 62, 74, 93, 103, 105–6; of a monastery, 201. *See also* Respect of laity

Property rights, of ascetics, 50, 76, 152

Public rituals, 155–62, 169–71, 206–8; attendance by patrons and clients, 94–95

pūjā. See Daily worship

pujārī. See Officiant

Radha, 5, 12–13, 14, 83, 120, 132, 133, 142, 159, 206–8

†Radhakrishna Sevashrama, xviii, 12, 144, 152, 179–80, 204

Rama, 5, 13, 48, 114, 133, 134, 158, 173, 197

†Ramakrishna Matha, xviii, 12, 16, 71, 94, 96, 102, 103 n. 10, 109, 123, 135, 136, 142, 158, 165, 166, 173, 181, 185–86, 190, 194, 195, 207

Ramakrishna Mission School, 142, 182, 185–86, 207

Ramakrishna movement, 34, 41, 100, 136. *See also* Non-sectarianism; Ramakrishna Paramahansa; Social welfare action

Ramakrishna Paramahansa, 30, 33, 34, 71, 90, 100, 135–36, 166, 176, 196

Ramananda, 6, 30, 196

Ramananda Vairagin (sub-order), 5–6, 12–13, 144, 202–5. *See also* Vairagin orders

Ramanuja, 1, 4–6, 27, 34. *See also* Vairagin orders; Vishishtadvaita Vedanta

*Ramasvarupa Brahmacharin, 202

Reality and ideal, ascetics' confusion of, 30, 51–54, 63, 69–72, 75–76

Recitation of name of deity, 3, 48–49, 103, 196. *See also kīrtanas; mahāmantra; mantra*

Religious experiences, 22–23, 30–31, 37–38, 47–48, 53, 88–92. *See also* Conversion experience; *darśana;* Visions

Religious leaders, head ascetics as, 21, 39–40, 43, 110, 131. *See also* Old Town, religious leaders of

Religious park, 43, 51, 135, 150, 186–89, 206. *See also* Chintamanishvara Mandira

Religious seeking: as goal of ascetic, 2, 88–89, 92; as satisfaction of monastic life, 89–92

Religious tradition: decline of, 95–97, 103, 200; diversity of, 195–96

Renewal of Hindu tradition, 23–25, 30, 32–34, 39. *See also* Synecretism; Tradition; Trends

Rental income, 10, 138, 141, 165, 178–80, 196. *See also* Guest-houses

Renunciation of world, 2, 48, 98–99, 102–3, 196; consequences for ritual, 171; final stage of life, 3. *See also* Austerities; Final renouncer; Vows

Resident ascetic: description, 2; role with management committee, 151. *See also* Ascetics,

ATE